MOTHERS OF INVENTION

THE FEMINIST ROOTS OF CONTEMPORARY ART

Eleanor Heartney is Contributing Editor to *Art in America* and *Artpress*. Recent publications include *Doomsday Dreams: the Apocalyptic Imagination in Contemporary Art* (2019).

Helaine Posner is Chief Curator Emerita at the Neuberger Museum of Art, SUNY, Purchase College, Purchase, NY. She is the author of monographs on the artists *Kiki Smith*, *Louise Fishman*, and, most recently, *Donna Dennis: A Poet in Three Dimensions* (2023).

Nancy Princenthal is a writer whose most recent book *Unspeakable Acts: Women, Art, and Sexual Violence in the 1970s* (2019) was named one of the best art books of the year by the *New York Times.* She is also the author of *Agnes Martin: Her Life and Art* (2015), which won a PEN America award for biography.

Sue Scott is an independent curator and writer. She was Adjunct Curator of Contemporary Art at the Orlando Museum of Art from 1989 to 2008 and founder and director of Sue Scott Gallery in New York City.

All four writers are co-authors of the award-winning book *After the Revolution: Women Who Transformed Contemporary Art* (2007) and of *The Reckoning: Women Artists of the New Millennium* (2013).

MOTHERS OF INVENTION

THE FEMINIST ROOTS OF CONTEMPORARY ART

Eleanor Heartney, Helaine Posner,
Nancy Princenthal and Sue Scott

LUND HUMPHRIES

First published in 2024 by Lund Humphries

Lund Humphries
Huckletree Shoreditch
Alphabeta Building
18 Finsbury Square
London EC2A 1AH
UK
www.lundhumphries.com

ISBN: 978-1-84822-540-4

A Cataloguing-in-Publication record for this book is available from the British Library

Copy edited by Ellen Hurst
Designed and Project Managed by Crow Books
Set in Arnhem Pro and Geograph
Printed in Bosnia and Herzegovina

Front cover: Ann Hamilton, *The Event of a Thread*, 2012, Park Avenue Armory, NY, dimensions variable

This book is printed on sustainably sourced FSC paper.

MIX
Paper | Supporting responsible forestry
FSC
www.fsc.org
FSC® C118234

CONTENTS

BREAKING THE RULES, REWRITING THE SCRIPT

FEMINIST INFLUENCES ON CONTEMPORARY ART

Roundtable Conversation with Eleanor Heartney, Helaine Posner, Nancy Princenthal and Sue Scott

EH: We four have been collaborating on books about women artists for almost 20 years now. We've published two. The first, in 2007, was *After the Revolution: Women Who Transformed Contemporary Art.* It offered a sampling of groundbreaking contemporary women artists of several generations working in various media. By focusing on the rich complexity of women's art at the turn of the 21st century, we wanted to suggest how far we had advanced since Linda Nochlin provocatively asked in 1971, 'Why have there been no great women artists?' Our second book, *The Reckoning: Women Artists in the New Millennium* (2013), took up questions about the impact of feminism on contemporary art by looking at a group of younger women artists. In our new collaboration, we are going back to the origins of feminist art in the '60s and '70s in order to explore, as our subtitle suggests, the feminist roots of contemporary art. When we were casting about for a title, Nancy, you had the inspiration to call it *Mothers of Invention*. Can you explain what you meant to convey by that?

NP: Well, with all due respect to Frank Zappa, I thought it was apt because we wanted to clarify the contributions that women have made to key movements in the past 25 years or more that have either not been acknowledged or have been attributed to men. As one of the authors who will be referred to said, 'It's time for women to call in their debts'. So we're doing that.

SS: The key word is *invention*. Women often don't get credited with being at the forefront of or inventing new ways of making art. For this book, I am writing about abstraction, which isn't always identified with feminism. I'm interested in the way that abstraction is invention.

HP: I think it's also important to say that we're going back to the rise of the feminist movement of the '60s and '70s. That is also where we began with the first book. And again, we are tracing that history forward. It's a history of almost 50 years. This time, instead of a set of artists, we each explore a theme from the early days of feminist art to the present. Each of us spends time looking at the '70s, not only in terms of what that moment was but also how some of the activities, events and ideas that circulated then continue to resonate today. In my chapter on performance, for instance, I show that women in the 1970s really were at the forefront in a way that wasn't acknowledged at the time. This is partly because they were women and partly because performance itself was marginalized. And it's interesting to note that performance is something that went from the margins to the mainstream. Now you see performance art at major museums like MoMA and the Tate, and at international biennials in Venice, Sao Paulo, Havana, and Performa in New York. So it's particularly important to bring women into the story because it is their story and it is also the story of performance art being incorporated into mainstream thought.

SS: Right. They started it, it was on the edge, it was minimized as an art form, and then it was taken over and brought into the mainstream by men.

EH: For my chapter on ecofeminism I realized that what I'm doing is writing an alternative narrative. The emergence of ecological art in the 1970s is often tied to the earth artists – mostly men like Michael Heitzer, Robert Smithson and Walter de Maria – who left the gallery to create monumental projects on the land. But I want to present a different origin story that stresses women's contributions to a cooperative and mutualistic conception of the relationship between humans and nature. It's a narrative that relegates those male land artists to the sidelines and actually presents them as part of an older concept of art that these women were leaving behind.

In *Mothers of Invention*, we are all presenting alternative narratives, often by excavating narratives that have been buried. That's certainly the case for your chapter on abstraction, Sue, where the story that has long been told really marginalized women. Recently that seems to have changed, and we are seeing lots of exhibitions focusing on abstraction, both group shows and shows of individuals, that acknowledge the importance of women artists, from the early abstract expressionist days. It's time to redo these stories we tell about the evolution of contemporary art.

SS: I actually start with a discussion of Hilma af Klint because her marginalization was so egregious, yet the public rediscovery of her place in the development of abstraction was so glorious.

NP: I'm focusing on craft. And what you say is certainly true of what's been called 'craft adjacent' or 'craft related artwork', which is so much in ascendance now. I confess that I went back significantly earlier than the '70s in trying to figure out when women began making a virtue of necessity about being relegated to crafty kinds of things. I found it fascinating that Walter Gropius, for instance, actually prohibited women from participating in any Bauhaus workshops other than textiles, ceramics and bookbinding. Once he realized that there were an awful lot of very qualified women who were populating the Bauhaus, where architecture had the most prestige, it was 'nope, actually, I think what women best do are the things they've always done.' A critical change came in the '60s and '70s with the advent of women saying, 'you know, we can do something really exciting and challenging' with textiles and ceramics.

EH: An interesting thing about my section on ecofeminism is that the narrative is not really about women being marginalized by men working in that arena. In fact, ecofeminism and, I would argue, ecological art generally, really did pretty much start with women. It was the outcome of the convergence of environmentalism and feminism as a way to challenge the very similar patriarchal domination of women and nature. Ecofeminism was woman-oriented from the beginning. This stems in part from the long-held identification of women with nature. But as we come toward the present, the ecofeminist ideas I've been exploring are very widespread and are not gender-specific, which is why I also discuss several male artists.

SS: Women were the ones that created or instigated the ecofeminist movement. But when it comes to abstract painting, this was very much a male realm. You see it especially in the '60s and '70s with minimalism coming to the fore and Judd and Morris, for instance, writing the rules. He who creates the rules can then criticize or negate people like Anne Truitt or Mary Heilmann who don't live by the rules. And yet there was a purposeful kind of humor with these women who were coming in and breaking the rules. I said once to Mary Heilmann that I was playing with the idea that women artists like her were purposely challenging these rules, purposely defiling the purity of abstraction. And she smiled and said, 'Absolutely!'

HP: The phrase that keeps running in my head that is almost a cliché now is 'the personal is political'. In performance women's experience, subjectivity and, particularly, their bodies were really front and center. Women used their nude bodies to make a statement. 'Look at me. The world isn't defined by a male perspective only. There's a female perspective and I'm going to embody that perspective and show it to you.' It was very provocative, and it was meant to be.

NP: That points to something that we have discovered as we have been working on our separate areas. We've come to see how all these things overlap. There was a lot of performative stuff going on in craft in the 1920s and '30s, and that continues to the present. Such demonstrations of craft processes, and also the long-standing use of craft's therapeutic and pedagogical value, are being talked about now as a kind of proto-performance work.

SS: You see it in abstraction as well. The way Helen Frankenthaler painted *Mountains and Sea* has a real performative aspect to it. She mixed and thinned the paint with turpentine in coffee cans and then spilled it onto the raw cotton duck, sometimes using wide brushes to spread the color around but really letting it soak in. She created it in a single day! Lynda Benglis, in her poured-latex pieces of the '70s, was combining performance with the tactility of material to create these fantastic abstract floor sculptures that both acknowledged Frankenthaler and was a repudiation of Carl Andre's floor sculptures. And I think about Pat Steir, too, and how much of her work is performative. She said one time, 'I had a hot hand in the '80s', and you can just see it in the fluidity and gesture of those waterfall paintings from that time. She relies on process to make her waterfall paintings and of course on chance, just how the paint will splatter and fall. She threw or poured paint on the canvas, often standing on a ladder. She said, surely a tongue-in-cheek reference to Pollock, that dripping wasn't macho enough for her.

EH: One of the things that really surprised me when I started researching ecofeminism was how many of the originators started with performance or included performance as an important part of their early practice. I think it goes back to what Helaine was saying, about the centrality of the body. For a lot of these women, there was this identification of nature with the body. Some of them went from the body to nature, while others went from nature to the body, and many went on to create environmental works involving remediation and restoration. But it's fascinating that so many of them felt the need to express their ideas originally through performance.

SS: This relates as well to ideas of the personal and notions of memory. Anne Truitt was making these very abstract works, but they were very evocative for her of a small town on the eastern shore of Maryland, of the place where she grew up, or her memories about the light in Washington, DC.

NP: It's the same in craft's emphasis on tactility. The slippery boundaries between functional work and fine arts have to do with things that are not just handmade but which invite being handled, whether or not they have practical uses. Which in turn brings in touch and the body. And that's even before you have works like Faith Wilding's *Womb Room*, which is a crocheted environment. It's a sticky space, created not only by Wilding but also Lenore Tawney and others. Or Magdalena Abakanowicz, with these great big textile hangings that make space more physical, almost proto-installations. The body is implicated in so much of fiber arts and ceramics. There's also a slippery boundary between craft and abstraction. Some early 20th-century modernists were both abstract painters and decorative artists, like Sophie Taeuber-Arp, whose recent show at MoMA featured her wonderful beaded bags. Anni Albers is now celebrated as an abstractionist, along with being an exceptionally inventive weaver.

SS: Do you think Taeuber-Arp, for instance, felt freer to jump to complete abstraction with these beaded bags because it was in the realm of craft?

NP: That's such a good question! Makes sense to me. Craft was a place that was much less policed than painting, a really open place for women.

EH: Perhaps now would be a good time to talk about how each of us chose our area.

SS: I've had a long interest in abstraction, both in the formal qualities and the way abstraction conveys the unknown, or more to the point the unseen. As one artist said to me, representation may answer questions, but abstraction raises the question why? We didn't include abstraction in our first two books because it didn't seem to have a place in a feminist discussion. But it turns out it does. For this book I wanted to discuss abstraction as a form of feminism that has to do with innovation, and the idea grew from there. I always thought that women abstractionists were really ignored in those early feminist shows. But then I went back and checked it out and it wasn't 100 percent true. If they weren't featured, there was always some abstraction early on. Feminist art was still being defined at that point.

EH: And Nancy, why craft?

NP: You know, I've been finding recently that I learn what I'm interested in by looking at what I've written about. Early on I didn't really identify myself as a feminist, and then I looked at what I'd been writing about and realized I've written a lot, maybe mostly, about women. It's the same with the kinds of work by women that I was interested in. I've always written a lot about sculpture, especially sculpture that is very organic and where the hand is involved. I thought, 'Yeah, I love this work'. And I wanted to know how women came to own it and what the backstory is.

HP: I always knew I was a feminist from early on, but performance was something that I hadn't realized I was interested in. But like Nancy, I realized when I look back that I've worked with performance artists from time to time. Tania Bruguera is probably the best example. And of course, Nancy and I cocurated a show called *The Deconstructive Impulse* that was not about performance per se but included a lot of performative work. We showed the Guerrilla Girls, Cindy Sherman, Martha Rosler, Adrian Piper and others. I realized that it had long been a current in my thinking. But in order to create my chapter, I needed to go back and construct a history of performance in my head. And I have found a very interesting progression, starting with the body, subjectivity and personal experience, and then moving on to specific feminist actions. Then there was a move away from essentialist feminism. When I came into the field in the '80s and '90s, we were already talking about social constructivism and that was my bible. Some great women like Mary Kelly and Dara Birnbaum came out of that, but I've come to question the scorn I once felt for essentialism. Performance has always been political in one way or another, whether it's overtly political through the body or whether in the '90s and the 2000s issues became less individually personal and more related to society as a whole. So I'm trying to create that history for myself and for the reader in a way that I think will be useful.

EH: My interest in ecofeminism goes back to things I have been writing for a long time. Since the beginning of my career in the early 1980s I've been exploring eco-art, though not specifically ecofeminist art. That comes out of my overall interest in art and politics. Eco-art has always been very interesting to me because it seems to be one area where art really can have concrete effects in the world. I've been following many of the artists I write about here for years. My interest in ecofeminism takes us back to what you were saying, Helaine, about a renewed respect for approaches that used to be dismissed as essentialist. And I don't think I'm alone in this. I also entered the art world during that deconstructive moment when we looked down on notions of women as nature. But now we realize the denial of that connection can be very limiting. Ecofeminism presents a much richer way of thinking about women and nature, especially in a world where climate change is threatening human survival.

HP: There was too much of an either/or in that critique: nature or culture, essentialism or deconstruction. One thing we're trying to do in this book is to get away from those binaries. We want to embrace the idea of feminism as an evolving concept. We're trying to broaden the definition of feminism and go beyond early perceptions that it was a white, middle-class and rather exclusive club. We want it to be more intersectional and to include people of color, people of different classes and men as well as women.

NP: And we're thinking about politics differently than we were in the '80s. There was really important work to be done then around challenging the power of the institution, starting with the institutions in the art world. But looking back, it was an insular kind of investigation, partly about things like: how does commercial imagery express patriarchy? But also, how do museums exercise their power? I think all of us are thinking about the political aspects of our subject matter in ways that are more inclusive. So much in craft comes from traditions that are borrowed from indigenous or non-western cultures that were not acknowledged throughout the history of modernism. I'm also thinking about labor, which is a big issue in craft-related art. Whose labor counts? What is it to buy something that's handmade? Whose hand is being acknowledged? And from the other end, what does it mean when we're buying something that's really inexpensive and mass-produced? Is that really made without labor, or is it just made with unacknowledged labor? *Craftivism* is the term that describes using craft for political activism. It suggests ways to rethink how to be a creative person and how to be an artist. A political perspective can really shake up calcified notions about what it is to make a living as an artist or to fail to do so.

HP: While we don't talk too much in the book about the economics of the art world, I've been thinking about how that shapes this discussion too. I mean, the growth of feminist art in the early part of this period was very US-based. It's where the money was. Then you have the fall of communism. The rise of global capital. And then the internet. Everything starts circulating much more widely. Artists from areas that were considered marginal now become more part of mainstream culture because there's money to support that. Now there is a way to share this information. In most of our essays, we begin with a focus on the US, which is where the feminist movement really exploded, and move to looking at a more global or interconnected world.

EH: Exactly. As I started working on my chapter, I began to realize almost all of ecofeminism's foundational artists were American. Today, of course, eco-art is extremely international. But in the 1960s and '70s something special was going on in the US. That's when second-wave feminism took root. Even though things were much more progressive, politically, in Europe, in terms of environmental consciousness, ecofeminist art was originally mostly American. In America feminism and environmental consciousness got entwined. The combination of an explosion of interest in feminism, the resistance to patriarchal culture and a burgeoning environmentalism led to powerful expressions in art.

SS: The same with abstraction. It was very much centered in New York post–World War II. But I'd like to get back to ideas about feminism and economics. Labeling is a great way to put somebody down. It's saying, 'Oh, Helen Frankenthaler is a second-generation abstract expressionist.' But in fact, for her first show the term was 'the New Generation'. New as opposed to second. Think of the implications of those words. It was a title that she liked so much that she had the postcard from the show on her studio wall till she died. But I'm also thinking about someone like Alma Thomas, who was always considered marginally a Washington Color School painter, or second or third generation. She was born in 1891 and was 21 years older than Morris Louis, the oldest of the Washington Color Field painters. It's just that she couldn't afford to be a full-time artist. She had to teach art in high school to support herself. But when she finished teaching, she began creating this work that is uniquely her own. It doesn't make her less of a painter and less of an innovator that she came to it a little bit later in life. Her work was built on 30 years of experience in teaching and taking classes and being aware of what was going on in the art world.

EH: This goes back to our first book, where we talked about Linda Nochlin's question 'Why have there been no great women artists?' And her answer had to do with the constraints women artists experienced that men did not.

SS: Thomas had the racial bias on top of the gender bias and the socioeconomic bias. Yet she still emerged out of it as this incredible innovator.

HP: Linda Nochlin was talking about the constraints in place centuries ago. These constraints were still in force during the period that is our starting point. The politics of oppression inspired the feminist resistance. That oppression relented earlier here in the US, where people were fighting against it, than in other places I am writing about. It took women artists from Israel, Cuba and South Africa longer to find their voices because they didn't have the access.

NP: And they didn't have the recognition. When we're talking about artists who were working without a market, we're also talking about artists who were doing things that had a different market, especially with respect to craft. Joyce Scott, for instance, was succeeding in a field that she, more or less, invented, making beaded sculptural jewelry that is amazingly expressive and profoundly narrative and tells very complicated stories. She gained a place in the art world more slowly. Or there are the artists of Gee's Bend, Alabama, who are finally now being celebrated for their quilts as art. They have an art market now. But some of these things are less clear than they might appear at first blush and have to do as much with status as with the actual dollars and cents of market value. Artists who were working with glass or textiles were so often dead set on having a place in the art world even if they were successful within the craft world. It was feminism that helped make it seem ridiculous to have to defend these distinctions. Agnes Martin was horrified at the idea of being identified with textiles, with weaving, despite her close connection to the textile artist Lenore Tawney. Now it's possible to see how intimate those connections were, including Martin's connections to Navajo blankets, which really can't be denied.

HP: That's one of those binaries that is really harmful. I was just thinking of Marina Abramović as you were talking because she's one of the best examples from my chapter of an early purveyor of performance who uses the body to make statements of incredible strength and endurance. Forty years later, she was the first feminist performance artist to have a retrospective at the Museum of Modern Art. That show was not only a tribute to Marina Abramović but also put performance on the map. I believe it was one of the most visited shows that they ever had. People who didn't know anything about performance saw a woman artist who has called herself the grandmother or the godmother of performance art.

NP: She gets called a prima donna, but in the *Seven Easy Pieces* roundup she did at the Guggenheim in 2005, in which she re-performed her own performances and also work by her peers, she really credited other artists.

HP: She re-performed their works maybe a decade before the show at MoMA. She has really contributed to an understanding of performance.

SS: Right, because it cemented these as enduring works of art, not just something that happened one time.

HP: It had the imprimatur of the museum. On one hand, it's a very strong statement. On the other hand, it's the hand of the patriarchy saying, 'good girl'.

EH: There's always that tension. In terms of constraints, my chapter begins with Mierle Laderman Ukeles. The way that she dealt with the constraints of her life, of being a mother and a wife, was to simply say, 'Okay, I do that and that's my art'. It was really a brilliant idea. She called it Maintenance Art and then moved from maintenance of her family out into the world, eventually helping to create this field of ecological art. But for her, it started actually from the constraints.

SS: Historically for women the constraints included not being able to take classes and not being able to work in a certain media and craft, and not be included in exhibitions or collected by museums.

NP: For some women who got involved in craft, it began as vocational therapy. Beginning in World War I, there was this idea that women could help men recover from shell shock by sitting down and having them learn how to be potters or some other productive craft. That carried over into a nurturing, pedagogical role that's been part of crafts ever since. It's a complicated history.

EH: Another commonality that we have discovered in our chapters is that we all write about a sense of collectivity. Many ecofeminists work in groups and regard the world as their community. And Nancy, your craft discussion begins with associations like the British-based Arts and Crafts movement and the Austrian Wiener Werkstätte. Performance can be a group activity and always involves interaction with an audience. Perhaps collectivity is somewhat less apparent in abstraction, but still, Sue, one of your starting points is Hilma af Klint, whose work comes out of her involvement with a collective. Another thing that we share is recourse to ideas of impurity, instability and hybridity. And then of course, there is the importance of body knowledge. We've all talked about that. Finally, I'm struck by how we deal with going beyond the human. Ecofeminist art is about connecting the human to the non-human world, while in abstraction there is often the desire to go beyond the corporeal to the spirit, especially in the case of someone like Hilma af Klint. In craft it means going beyond the human to embrace the intelligence of materials. As for performance, it may be a bit less clear.

HP: Actually, I am starting to deal with the notion of a cyborg. This is something that occurred to me when I went to the Venice Biennale which had a section called 'The Seduction of the Cyborg'. I wouldn't say it's a major emphasis in my chapter, which is very much about body performance and performativity. But in terms of the notion of breaking down binaries, one could cite Donna Haraway's *A Cyborg Manifesto* in which she describes how the boundaries between the human, the animal and the machine have been blurred. Women are always on the losing end of binaries, for example, male / female, culture / nature, reason / emotion. Why don't we just dispense with the dichotomies? This is theoretical, of course, but regarding the relationship of the human body to technology and the machine, perhaps we can liberate ourselves from a notion of humanity that has been very dualistic. Certain artists who have moved in that direction: Laurie Anderson is probably the best example, in early performances where she uses a vocal modulator to create a male voice. She has electronic instruments that become parts of herself and take her beyond the human into a whole other realm. That's also the case with some of Rebecca Horn's work. And there's Lynn Hershman Leeson, who really astounded me. Her early work was about taking on various personae, specifically that of Roberta Breitmore, but it evolved over time. Technology is very much a part of her work. She had a piece in Venice where she took on the notion that the cyborg was now 60 years old. The idea of a cybernetic organism was first defined around 1960 by two scientists. Hershman Leeson asks: What does it mean to bring humanity and technology together? She created a performative video in which a female cyborg speaks with her human avatar to find ways to negotiate her human and technological selves. It was beautifully done, and it really touched a chord in me. I think for so many years I've been so attached to the gender binary. It was really stimulating to think of discarding all of those old definitions and accepting the idea that we live in a highly technological world. What does it mean that Hershman Leeson created this cyborg who was figuring out what it means to be both machine and human?

NP: That makes me think of Louise Bourgeois and her very late cloth sculptures with prosthetic limbs. I'm glad we've touched on the idea of transcending the human and blurring the distinction between the human and the technological. This is something that comes into discussions of craft from the beginning. David Pye famously pointed out that if we're talking about things that are handmade, the only things that are actually made without a tool are probably coil-made pots. Almost everything we make by hand, so called, involves some kind of tool. That's something that goes clear through to contemporary craft-related art. Some women have made that a subject of their work. Rosemarie Trockel has made machine-knitted, computer-programmed paintings that look as if they were done with knitting needles. But they're not, and they wind up seeming to be a kind of minimalism.

SS: When we talk about breaking those constraints you get to the place where artists like Amy Sillman or Suzanne McClelland find there are no longer rules in place. When they came on the scene, it was more accepted that women could be making paintings and be in the art world. And yet they did experience chauvinism and misogyny. Then there came a time when they just created their own rules. They had an uneasy relationship with abstraction and didn't want to be put in that box. They were saying, 'You're not going to call me an abstractionist and you're not going to call me a realist. I'm going to do both and I'm going to do them when I want to do them and I'm going to mix them up.' That was another source of innovation. But with reference to constraints, these have changed for younger artists. As younger women have come along, some have been lauded and celebrated in each of these fields. Where does that fit into our discussion?

EH: We dealt with that in our second book when we discussed younger artists. For them the question of what was possible for them was different than for the pioneering generation.

SS: For me it's also a question of who made use of these tools and innovations. In the case of abstraction, I talk about male artists like Franklin Evans or Mark Bradford who brought abstraction into explorations of personal memories and used materials that had very much to do with their private or studio lives, like painter's tape or end papers used to give permanents in hair salons.

EH: What I want to get at in bringing up things like collectivity, impurity and hybridity is the question of how we are defining feminism. We want to go beyond narrow definitions that reduce it to fitting women into the patriarchy. I think we are trying to see it more philosophically, as a way of approaching the world and understanding reality. That's part of ending binaries, breaching boundaries and going beyond the human. But what exactly do we mean by feminism here?

NP: I think we're talking about seeing women's experience in work that acknowledges something that's quite personal but also shared by others. And that includes the broader community that identifies as women. In the 21st century we know that we can't limit our definition of women to people who are identified as female at birth. Nonnormative gender identity comes up in my discussion of craft and probably in every chapter. In craft there is the contribution of the LGBTQ community, for example, with the AIDS quilt, which was such an important model for using textiles politically. Or in Pattern and Decoration: one of the things that mattered about that movement is that women led but men, and especially gay men, were really important. And then there are artists like Harmony Hammond, whose work is acknowledged by Julia Bryan-Wilson as a kind of queer activism. Hammond put her work on the floor as a kind of anti–Carl Andre gesture. It was not meant to be walked on, as Andre's floor pieces were, but at the same time it created a feminine space, a subversive space, a kind of exhibition space that really hadn't existed before. It was about using sexuality and gender identity for its subversive capabilities.

EH: Sue, you in particular have had to wrestle with this question, because you are dealing with how abstraction can be feminist. Especially in the formalist Greenberg era, abstraction was shorn of any of that kind of emotion or meaning or personal statement.

SS: Innovation is, in its own way, a feminist statement. It's about taking power back and creating something new. And when the artist says, I am going to make it personal, put my own ideas into it, make it a hybrid or break the rules. That's where power comes from. And speaking of Harmony Hammond, she felt that wanting art to be political in order to be feminist was just continuing notions of the patriarchy. That it was in the making of the work – the mark, the language, the repetition – that women claimed the art for themselves.

EH: I've also struggled with this. What makes ecofeminism feminist? For me it has to do with a notion of interconnectivity. In my chapter I talk a lot about Gaia theory, which is the idea of the Earth as a kind of living thing or at least a living system in which everything is interconnected. Again, part of what makes this feminist is getting rid of binaries. Nature isn't something outside of us that we can either manipulate or attempt to salvage. We are all part of the same entity. And of course when you start thinking this way, you start discarding certain notions of individualism and control that are at the heart of our current economic system.

SS: Feminism is also about where inspiration comes from. Especially when I was writing about Hilma af Klint and about some of the early definitions of feminist art, I realized it was about garnering inspiration from something bigger than yourself and connecting to the universe by way of some sort of universal spirit or astral guide. Or through nature, channeling intangible ideas through repetition and asserting who has the right to authorship.

HP: What comes to my mind is a fundamental definition of performance as breaking down the boundaries between life and art. That's really where all discussions start. It's what you mean when you're talking about interactions with the audience. When I started my chapter, I was thinking about artists making individual statements, saying 'this is what it means to be a woman'. But it has become broader, more sophisticated. I find that feminist performance art is speaking for larger communities and their issues, including marginalized or oppressed communities, and being a voice for those cultures and communities. That's where politics keeps coming in. And I like the idea of feminism as the philosophical underpinning. It's not, 'I'm the leader and I'm telling everyone what to do'. I'm speaking with or for others or representing something broader than just myself.

SS: I have a very simple definition. Feminism is equal opportunity for women to do the things that men can do. Hilma af Klint, who we reference repeatedly, mostly because she is the 'nevertheless she persisted' woman of the ages, was part of the second generation of women allowed to study at Stockholm's Royal Academy of Art, where she excelled. (Women had to pay tuition while men attended for free.) And yet throughout her career she had to listen to the likes of Carl Larsson, one of Sweden's leading artists, railing against what he saw as the ineptitude of women artists.

HP: I am more and more interested in the title of Eleanor's chapter. The rejection of dominionism is very important in ecofeminism. But when I think further, I realize the philosophical underpinnings of feminist performance art are also opposed to dominionism. They are about connectivity, interaction, interrelation.

NP: We've gotten to some of the things that really unite us. One of the exciting things about doing this book is finding all of these connections. And another thing is finding a way to avoid the darkness that sometimes surfaces in discussions of feminism. I think we are focusing on the positive things that women can achieve. I mean, even if it does go into some very difficult areas, ecofeminism is amazingly foresightful, effective and aims to change the world we live in. Similarly, performance blew open a way of being an artist in the world; it opened a box that can never be closed again. And everything you've said about abstraction is the same. Abstraction is not only what Donald Judd said it was.

SS: Yes, he set up the rules and then said that Anne Truitt didn't work within the rules.

NP: What we are talking about is opening things up rather than shutting things down.

HP: Take the things that were said about Carolee Schneemann when she was pulling the scroll out of her vagina. It was like, 'She's too messy. She's too emotional, and we can't take her seriously'. She was dismissed, dismissed.

EH: And now she's one of the Mothers of Invention.

NP: Yeah. Or take women like Patty Mucha, Oldenburg's first wife. He couldn't have made soft sculptures without her, and look how long it took for that to be acknowledged.

HP: Nancy, the term you have used in the past is that this is not special pleading. These are really serious, substantial contributions and points of view. And that's what we're about and why it's positive. This book is about shining a light on all that's been accomplished.

SS: In spite of all the constraints!

HP: There are different perspectives. It's not just one oppressive, white, male, patriarchal culture. It's a much broader culture, and it always has been. Our question has been how do we acknowledge that and how do we document it?

EH: And how do we show how much these ideas have penetrated into the mainstream art world so completely that the feminist influence sometimes seems almost invisible?

SS: Feminists gave all artists the freedom to do things.

EH: Feminism broke things open. I think that's what we're trying to get at.

SS: But even if these feminist ideas seem ubiquitous today, it doesn't mean they are no longer relevant. When we look at statistics, they are daunting. Women still get just 25 percent of the pie. And politically, *Roe v. Wade* was overturned in the United States, taking away women's decision-making over their own bodies. There is still important work to be done.

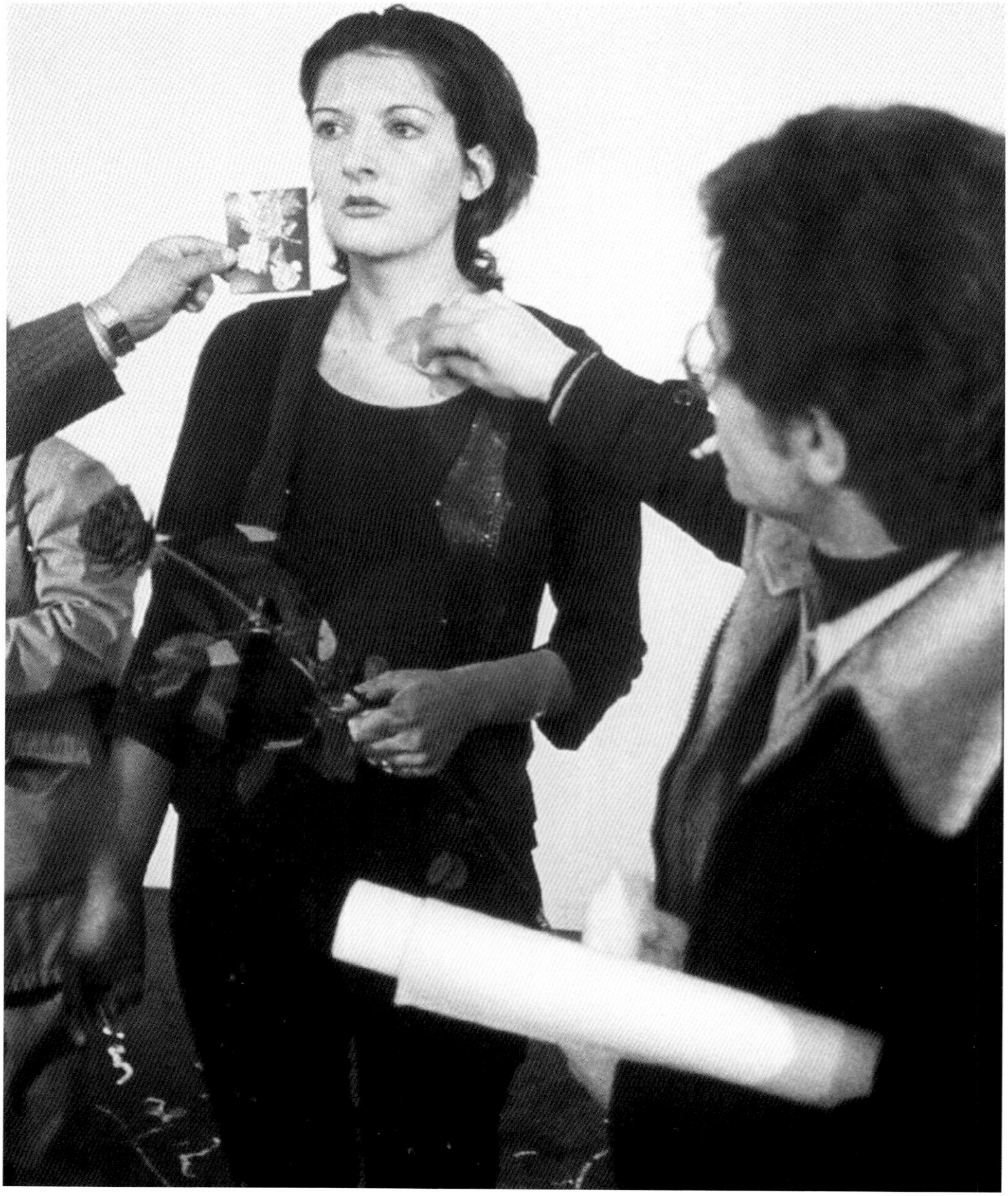

PERFORMANCE ART AND ACTION

Helaine Posner

[Performance is] the most immediate art form, which aspires to the immediacy of political action itself. Ideally, performance means getting down to the bare bones of aesthetic communication – artist/self confronting audience/society.[1]

—Lucy R. Lippard

The late 1960s to the early 1970s was a period of great political, social, and cultural upheaval across the United States and Europe. Around this time growing challenges to the dominant straight, white, male power structure by individuals and groups advocating *for* civil rights, women's rights and gay and lesbian rights, and *against* the Vietnam War, exploded. The time had come for a radical break from the established order as patriarchy was being called into question by those long excluded from its privileges. It was a fertile moment for the pioneers of performance art, including many women, who channeled their creative impulses into this provocative, often visceral, newly energized medium. Performance openly embraced the unruly, countercultural spirit of the era in works that expressed an urgent need for social change. Defying the boundaries between public and private, between art and daily life, female performance artists often relied on their naked bodies to portray women's embodied experience and to return personal meaning to art. The contemporary feminist rallying cry 'the personal is political' echoed throughout their work.

Fig.1 Marina Abramović, *Rhythm 0*, 1974, performance lasting six hours, Studio Morra, Naples

These bold acts of self-exposure did more than simply subvert existing social taboos. Feminist performance work collapsed the distance between art and daily life, the artist and the artwork, and the artist and the audience. By putting the details of their sexual and racial identities on display – along with other distinct features made visible via their nude bodies – and by stimulating desire, feminists effectively exploded the modernist myths of the male as the universal, unitary artistic standard and of formal analysis as the primary, objective measure of artistic value.[2] Their work exposed 'the hidden logic of exclusionism underlying modernist art history and criticism', revealing the unexamined assumptions and biases of the field.[3] By putting female subjectivity on display in all its sexual and gendered forms, they effectively announced the end of modernism and embodied the shift to the more complex, contradictory, experiential approaches of postmodernism. Basically, feminist performance art is the essence of the postmodern. In fact, performance, with its emphasis on knowledge through the body, plays a significant role in much postmodern practice including photography, video, craft and, notably, ecofeminism.

The term *performance art*, which gained currency in the early 1970s, describes an evolving genre that eludes easy definition even today. It includes live performance that may or may not take place before an audience and/or its documentation through photography, film, video or text. And while early works typically featured the artist's physical body in a specific space, by the late 1970s much performance was staged for the video or still camera. Further confounding expectations, performance artists are *not* actors playing scripted roles (as in traditional theater or in film), nor are they individuals simply living their life in public; instead, they occupy a 'middle position that has always been unstable', for the artist as well as the audience.[4] Performance art, by its nature, resists fixed meanings. Open-ended, noncommercial and disruptive, lacking the historical baggage of established disciplines such as painting and sculpture, performance provided an outlet for women seeking to redefine their art and their lives in light of the major changes spurred by second-wave feminism.

Feminist performance took a variety of forms during the 1970s. Works featuring encounters between the artist and the audience, as well as those focused on the artist's embodied experience, emerged in New York and several European capitals. On the West Coast, a number of feminists combined art and activism to address the issue of sexual violence against women, heighten public awareness thereof and, thereby, promote social change. Later in the decade, conceptually based performance works examining the cultural construction of identity and femininity within a patriarchal society arose in London and New York. Other artists created fictional characters or personae to explore issues of gender, race and class as well as the impact of those issues on women's lives.

Origins

The origins of performance art may be traced to early 20th-century avant-garde movements in Europe. In Italy, Futurist performance artists staged deliberately disruptive *serati*, or evenings, that celebrated speed, the machine, violence and the vitality of modern life, wholly rejecting the weight of their country's cultural past. Dada shared Futurism's rebellious, anarchic spirit. Formed in Zurich by artists seeking refuge from the horrors of World War I, Dada art, poetry and performance was notably antiwar, antibourgeois, irreverent and highly absurd. Performances at the Café Voltaire, a satirical nightclub founded by writer Hugo Ball and cabaret artist Emmy Hennings, were raucous events featuring spoken word, music and dance, deliberately designed to shock and agitate the audience. Later on in the United States, performance art flourished at Black Mountain College, an experimental, interdisciplinary school founded in North Carolina in 1933. The faculty included Josef Albers (1888–1976), who fled Germany after the Nazis closed the Bauhaus, as well as a veritable who's who of America's most advanced artists, including painters Willem de Kooning (1904–97) and Robert Rauschenberg (1925–2008), choreographer Merce Cunningham (1919–2009), and composer John Cage (1912–92), who presented his first musical happening at Black Mountain in 1952.

Cage's work at Black Mountain College, along with the Beat poetry movement and the rise of Pop art, fed the improvisational, antiformal theatrical events known as *happenings* that emerged in New York in the late 1950s and early 1960s. Happenings performer and theorist Allan Kaprow (1927–2006), who coined the term *happening* in 1959, credited the drip paintings of Jackson Pollock (1912–56) with helping transform the status of a work of art from a fixed object into a performative, process-oriented experience, as seen in Hans Namuth's photographs of the artist as action painter and performer.[5] Performance artists further advanced this radical notion by fully eliminating the object and becoming the work of art itself.

Embodiment

In 1975 multimedia artist Carolee Schneemann (1939–2019) performed her iconic work of feminist body art, *Interior Scroll* (fig.2), for the exhibition *Women Here and Now* at a gallery in East Hampton, New York. She began by entering the performance space wrapped in a white sheet, undressing and then ritualistically painting the contours of her body and face with mud. She proceeded to read excerpts from her book, *Cezanne, She Was a Great Painter*, quoting misogynistic slurs a female artist might expect to hear over the course of her career. She put down the book and slowly began to pull a thin, typewritten scroll from her vagina, reading the lines aloud. The text, a tongue-in-cheek response to a contemporary film critic's accusation that she made messy, women's work, read, in part, 'You are charming/but don't ask us/to look at your films/we cannot . . ./the personal clutter/the persistence of feeling/the hand-touch sensibility/the diaristic indulgence/the painterly mess/the dense gestalt/the primitive techniques.'[6] In her deliberately raw, transgressive performance, Schneemann unabashedly asserted her naked body, affirming the vagina as the source not only of procreation and pleasure but as the site of creativity, language and 'sacred knowledge'.[7] Her provocative piece was largely ignored by the mainstream press and, when discussed, most often was dismissed or disparaged.

During this period, feminist performance artists regularly appeared in the nude, using their bodies to create works that openly politicized personal experience. A few years before Schneemann first performed *Interior Scroll*, Japanese artist Yayoi Kusama (b.1929) exposed her naked, polka-dotted, doubly marginalized Asian female body in public performances staged across New York in protest of sexism, racism and the Vietnam War, and in support of the women's movement and the sexual revolution. Hannah Wilke (1940–93) captured the spirit of women's

Fig.2 Carolee Schneemann, *Interior Scroll*, 1975, performance, *Women Here and Now*, East Hampton, NY

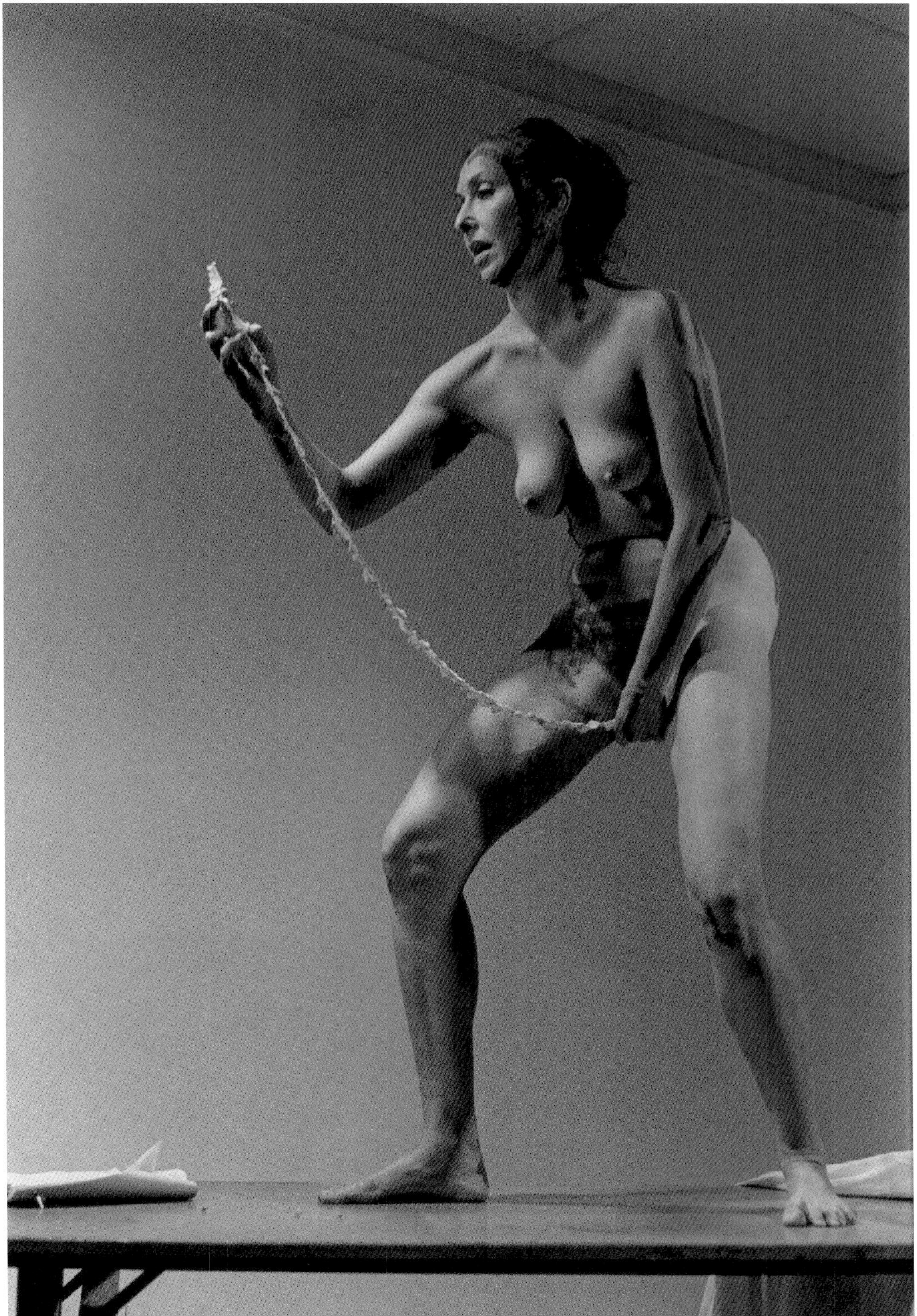

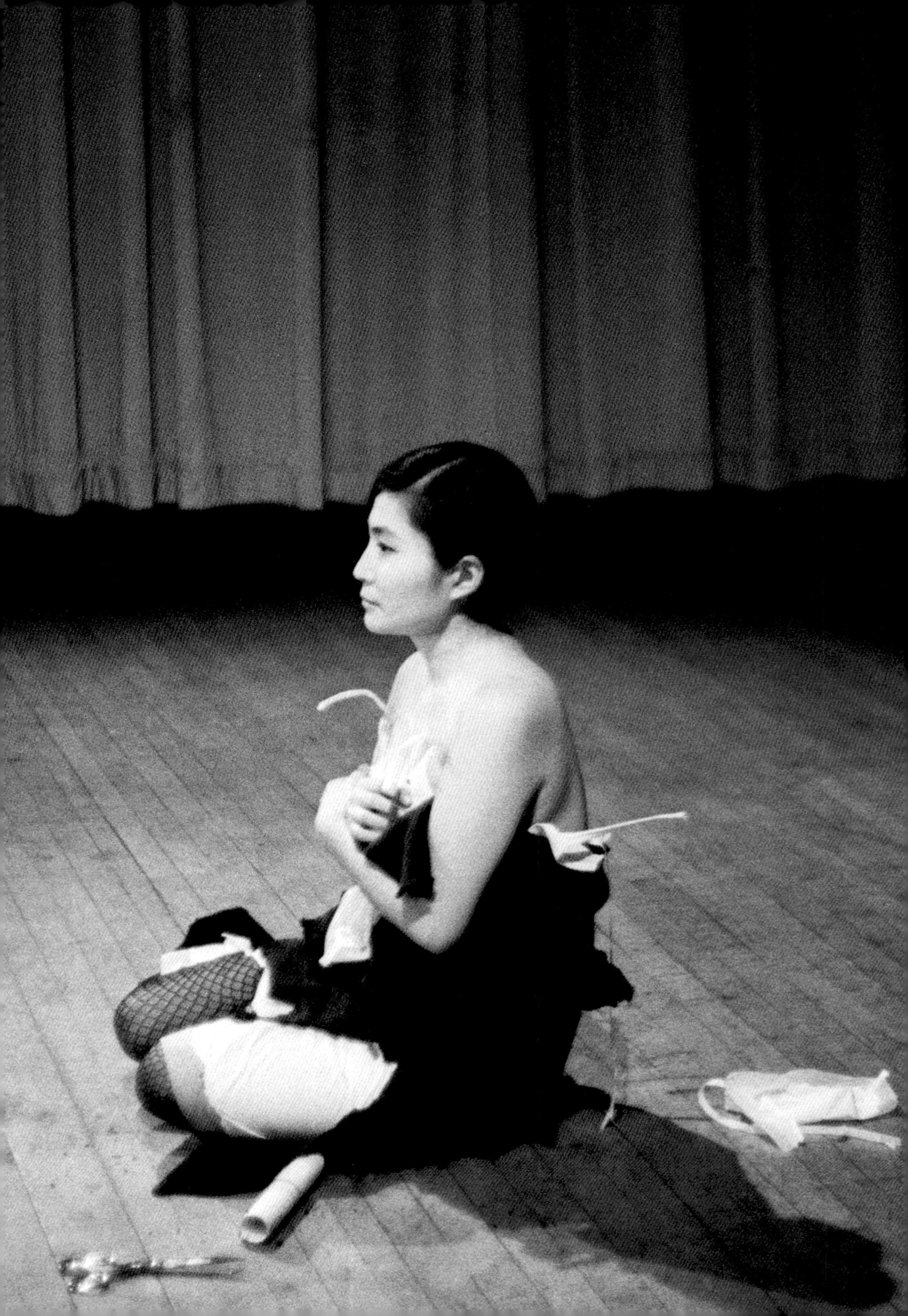

liberation, female empowerment and the pursuit of pleasure in a series of provocative performance-based photographs featuring her nude body posed seductively and, at times, confrontationally for the camera. Her *S.O.S., Starification Object Series: An Adult Game of Mastication* (1974–5), a group of twenty-eight self-portraits, featured the artist striking a range of fashion-model poses. She stands topless, her face, chest and fingernails decorated with bits of chewing gum, sporting a range of accessories including an Arab headdress, a cowboy hat, toy guns, a tie, sunglasses and hair curlers. Criticized for being an exhibitionist and a 'narcissistic flirt',[8] she was, in fact, presenting the artist as both subject and object, using her body and her beauty to engage the viewer while challenging conventional notions of femininity through acts of radical self-expression.

Engagement

Fluxus, a movement that arose in the early 1960s as a loose network of international artists with roots in Dada, promoted an antiart, non-commercial, absurdist sensibility. Fluxus artists often invited audience members to participate in their events, democratizing the roles of artist and audience, and encouraging a more intimate level of engagement. Yoko Ono (b.1933) was one of the pioneers of this early form of participatory performance art. In her landmark *Cut Piece* (fig.3), begun in 1964, Ono sat on a stage floor, dressed in her best suit, with a pair of scissors placed before her. Audience members were instructed to take turns approaching her and using the scissors to cut off pieces of her clothing. Some people approached cautiously, snipping off bits of her jacket or skirt, while others aggressively cut away the front of her blouse and bra straps, as Ono covered her breasts with her hands. She remained silent and motionless throughout, her face impassive, later stating, 'I get into a trance, and so I don't feel too frightened'.[9] Nevertheless, *Cut Piece* was an exercise in physical exposure and vulnerability, with the audience placed in the uneasy role of victimizer and/or voyeur as allusions to female subordination, sexual aggression and violence against women remained palpable. Even today it is hard to escape the chilling sense of violation that was depicted in *Cut Piece* nearly sixty years ago.

Fig.3 Yoko Ono, *Cut Piece*, 1965, Yoko Ono performing at Carnegie Recital Hall, New York

Marina Abramović (b.1946), a leading and influential performance artist, originally from the former Yugoslavia, also addressed issues of submission and aggression in ritualistic works that tested her physical and mental limits through a series of demanding trials. For *Rhythm 5* (1974), she lay down inside the frame of a five-pointed wooden star that had been set on fire. When her oxygen supply was depleted by the fire, she lost consciousness and had to be rescued by concerned onlookers. In *Rhythm 0* (also 1974; fig.1), Abramović offered her body as an object of experimentation, as Ono had done, in an attempt to see just how far the public would go. She set the following terms:

> Instructions. There are 72 objects on the table that one can use on me as desired.
> Performance. I am the object. During this period I take full responsibility.
> Duration: 6 hours (8 pm–2 am)

Throughout *Rhythm 0*, the artist remained passive and expressionless as audience members used objects designed for pleasure or for pain – a rose, a feather, honey, a whip, a scalpel, a gun and bullet – on her as they pleased. Benign acts, like offering a rose or a kiss, gradually escalated into violence as the spectators became increasingly emboldened: her clothes were cut with razor blades, her throat was cut and blood sucked and a loaded gun was pointed at her head. As Abramović concluded, 'What I learned was that . . . if you leave it up to the audience, they can kill you . . . I felt really violated'.[10] Yet when the performance ended and the artist stood up and approached the members of the audience, they fled, unwilling to face the consequences of their actions.

Abramović's performance works are extreme, intense and exceptionally bold. She repeatedly endures pain, exhaustion and risk in pursuit of a higher state of consciousness. As she proclaimed in her manifesto, 'From suffering comes the best work, / Suffering brings transformation, / Through suffering an artist transcends their spirit'. And although she repeatedly lays herself bare, physically and emotionally, she endures. As Nancy Princenthal has observed, 'Far from conveying an experience of vulnerability through submission to viewers, as did . . . Ono, Abramović aims to express her triumph over danger and pain . . . And while other artists of the period undertook physical and emotional hazards, none courted them as assiduously as Abramović, nor with greater confidence in overcoming them'.[11]

Of course, women were not the only practitioners of body art in the 1970s. The defining traits of performance, including testing the physical and psychological limits of the body/self, challenging the relationship between artist and audience and exploring ritual and risk, endurance and exposure, also animated the work of male artists. Like Abramović, artist Chris Burden (1946–2015) notoriously submitted his body to danger, taking dramatic yet, in his case, calculated risks. For example, he had a friend shoot him in the arm at point blank range in *Shoot* (1971) and ordered others to nail his palms to the hood of a Volkswagen in *Trans-Fixed* (1974). He was the artist as martyr subjected to masochistic acts of violence that triggered feelings of fear and anxiety in artist and audience alike. Male subjectivity was put on display in all its fragmented, complex and contradictory forms as Burden examined the power of the artist to control his own fate and found that very sense of control to be an illusion. And while Burden's work is quite daring, it also reveals a deep sense of masculine vulnerability. By comparison, and perhaps paradoxically, Abramović's art of endurance, with all its attendant risks, ultimately is an expression of strength.

Vito Acconci (1940–2017) enacted his ambivalent masculinity in several consciously transgressive performances of this period. In *Seedbed* (1972), his best-known work, he laid beneath a custom-made ramp installed at Sonnabend Gallery in New York and responded to visitors' footsteps by ostensibly masturbating while sharing his fantasies and moans of pleasure with them via a loudspeaker. Acconci considered *Seedbed* to be a reciprocal exchange between artist and viewer; however, the work violated the boundaries between public and private and ignored any notion of consent. The artist remained hidden, his position both vulnerable and predatory. In contrast, the naked, erotic body performed by Carolee Schneemann in *Interior Scroll*, was a candid celebration of female sexuality, sensuality and empowerment, not a furtive activity concealed beneath the floorboards.

Feminist Action

A new form of feminist art and activism emerged in Los Angeles in the 1970s as female artists addressed the issue of sexual violence as a fact of women's lives in a city reputed to be the rape capital of the country. The artists drew on painful personal experience to create installations and performances designed to shed light on a long-hidden history of oppression and abuse, and potentially to effect social change. They often worked collectively, using consciousness-raising sessions as a means of generating artistic content that was visceral, confessional and emotionally honest. In 1971 the Feminist Art Program, founded by Judy Chicago (b.1939) and Miriam Shapiro (1923–2015) at the California Institute of the Arts, produced *Womanhouse* (1972), a groundbreaking project in which the artists and over 20 of their students transformed a dilapidated mansion into a space for artworks and performances that confronted the banality and tedium of domestic life. This influential effort inspired other significant works including a collaboration between Chicago and artists Suzanne Lacy (b.1945), Sandra Orgel (b.1951) and Aviva Rahmani (b.1945) titled *Ablutions* (1972) in which they pointedly addressed the subject of rape. Lacy described the collaboration's opening moments: 'A loud audiotrack would begin, as woman after woman told her story, confronting the audience with the reality of sexual violence not yet found in the public consciousness.'[12] Their testimony played as nude performers bathed in tubs containing raw eggs, beef blood and liquid clay in a space littered with broken eggshells, piles of rope, chains and entrails in an altogether frightening scene. The performance was a deeply emotional and cathartic experience for artists and audience alike.

In 1977 Lacy and collaborator Leslie Labowitz (b.1946) took activist art to the streets in a dramatic performance staged on the steps of Los Angeles City Hall. They produced *In Mourning and in Rage* (fig.4), a public response to the 'Hillside Strangler' murders in which ten women were found raped and killed, their bodies dumped along hillsides. The artists were deeply distressed by these horrific acts and by press reports that sensationalized the sexual nature of the deaths, fueling a growing climate of fear among women. *In Mourning and in Rage* unfolded as a sequence of events. It began when a hearse transporting ten women, nine veiled in black and one in red, arrived at City Hall, followed by

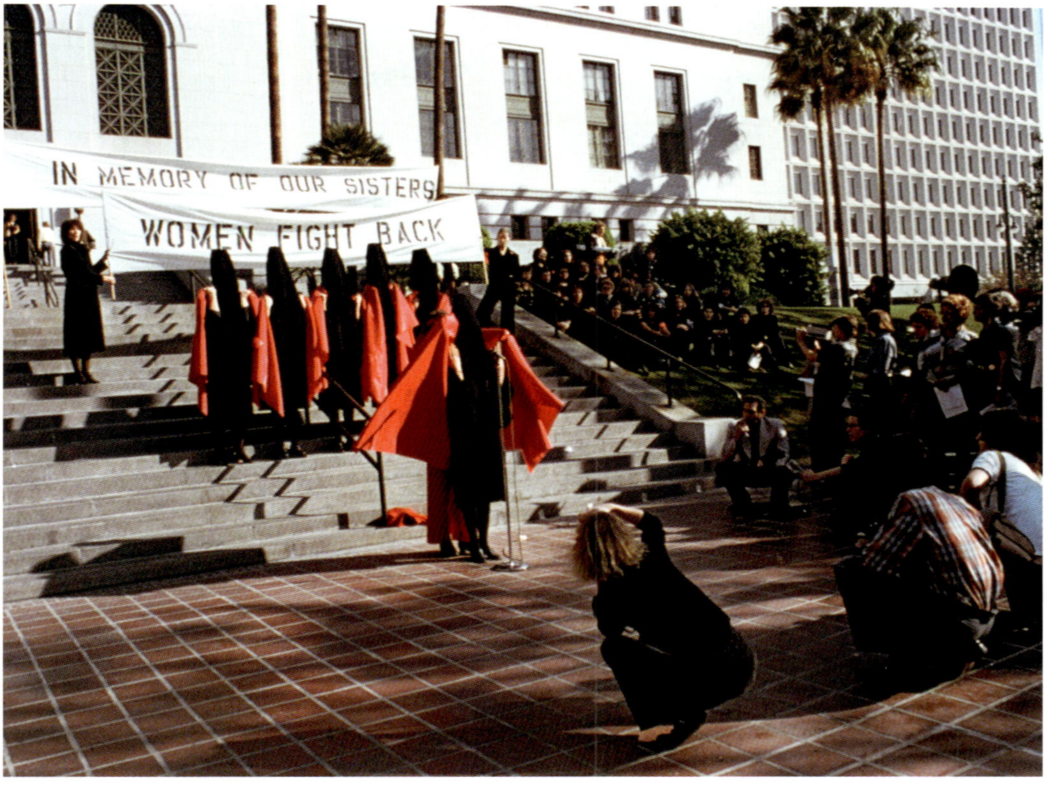

Fig.4 Suzanne Lacy and Leslie Labowitz, *In Mourning and in Rage*, 1977, public performance at Los Angeles City Hall, www.againstviolence.art

a motorcade of 22 cars filled with 60 black-draped women. The ten mourning figures assembled on the steps and, one by one, voiced their solidarity with the strangled women and with the countless female victims of beatings, rapes and murders committed by strangers or by domestic partners. Each of their declarations was followed by a Greek-style chorus chanting, 'In memory of our sisters, women fight back!' All told, the performance was a powerful expression of collective grief and rage, and a solemn memorial to all women who have experienced violence at the hands of a patriarchal society.

Lacy and Labowitz's work offered a feminist perspective on violence against women in stark visual and narrative terms. They amplified their efforts by working in conjunction with local government officials, community organizers and representatives of the media to establish a broad base of support and reach the widest possible audience. They were successful on all fronts. In addition to receiving extensive media coverage on local and statewide news, the tangible results of their performance included increased support from members of the Los Angeles City Council and a commitment from the Rape Hotline Alliance to provide self-defense classes for women. Their combination of art and activism proved to be invigorating to both.

The Absent Body

While West coast performance art was generally confessional and essentialist in nature, more conceptually based practices, wary of the embodied subject, began to emerge in New York and London. Some feminist artists considered essentialism, the theory that women have innate, universal qualities or a fixed biological essence, to be overly reductive, even reactionary. They argued that the nude body was far too vulnerable to exploitation and objectification by the male gaze and that performance centered on the body had to be resisted. In fact, a backlash arose against the essentialist approach by deconstructivist-oriented feminists who adopted a more critical view of femininity as socially and culturally constructed, turning their attention to the exploration of female identity or difference as it is defined within patriarchy.

In 1979 Mary Kelly (b.1941) completed a groundbreaking work of feminist art and identity, recording the mother-child relationship as it unfolded over a six-year period. She tracked the growth of her son as he learned to speak, draw and write through diagrams, texts and found objects as she examined her 'lived experience as a mother' and her 'analysis as a feminist of that experience'.[13] *Post-Partum Document* is a conceptual and psychoanalytical investigation of early motherhood comprised of 135 components arranged in six sequential sections. The work is at once highly methodical and deeply personal as Kelly details the role of artist as mother through the presentation of ordinary items and in the performance of mundane rituals. The artist deliberately avoids direct representation of herself and her son, empirically evoking their presence and thereby eluding the oppressive gaze. *Post-Partum Document* is, in fact, a systematic study of female subjectivity.

Kelly continued her examination of women's lived experience in *Corpus* (1984–5), consisting of thirty panels that pair first-person, hand-written texts expressing women's anxieties about entering middle age with photographic images of accessories or articles of clothing such as purses, shoes, leather jackets and black nightgowns that are twisted or folded. These narratives explore a growing sense of powerlessness and invisibility in relation to patriarchy as seen through the lens of fashion, medicine, romantic fiction, the family and the media, as related to women's consumption of those things as they mature. In substituting clothes for the female body and in shifting focus from the act of looking to that of listening to women's stories, the artist prevents her subjects from becoming the fetishized object of male desire. And by radically absenting the body while simultaneously asserting its presence through images and texts that women may identify with and take pleasure in, Kelly offers an alternative to the customary representation and performance of femininity that is openly directed to the female spectator.

In Ana Mendieta's (1948–85) performance works and their documentation, the perpetual interplay between the presence of the body and its absence, signified by a trace left on the landscape, has the aura of a private ritual. Rooted in nature and the body, her earth-body works, or *Silueta Series* (1973–80), explore personal identity and femininity along with a desire for cultural connection from the perspective of a Cuban cast into exile in the United States. As the series progressed, her seemingly reciprocal relationship with the land became more ambiguous as her body vanished and only her silhouette, or shadow, remained. These ethereal works consist of nothing more than grass sprouting in a field, foam forming on the shore or a bit of gauzy white fabric placed on a piece of driftwood, suggesting a sense of loss and longing for her homeland and for mother earth or the maternal source. Like Kelly, Mendieta employs surrogates for the body/self as a means of exploring women's experience and the societal forces that shape it, forming a visceral collection of ephemeral works.

Personae

While autobiography played a significant role in feminist performance art of the 1970s, several women artists took a different tack. They challenged the notion of a stable or fixed identity by creating, constructing

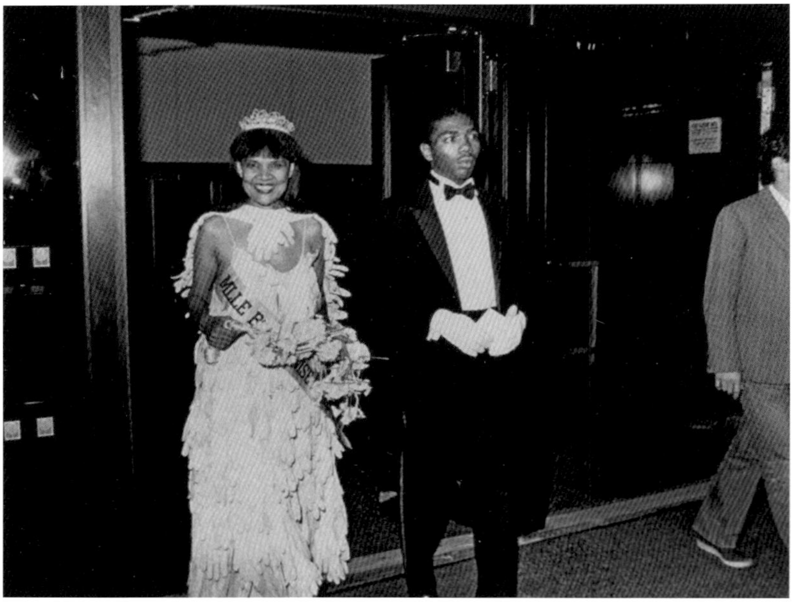

Fig.5 Lorraine O'Grady, *Untitled (Mlle Bourgeoise Noire and her Master of Ceremonies enter the New Museum)*, 1980–83/2009, silver gelatin print, 18.4 × 23.8 cm (7 ¼ × 9 ⅜ in)

and inhabiting fictional characters or personae that explore society's gender-, race- and class-based restrictions and assumptions. Perhaps the most complex and nuanced of these was a character created by artist Lynn Hershman Leeson (b.1941) named Roberta Breitmore. Leeson transformed herself into Roberta physically – through makeup, clothing and wigs – and psychologically, inventing a separate personality or alter ego that grew through experience. Roberta had a driver's license, credit cards and a bank account, kept a diary and saw a psychiatrist, all as part of an extended public performance lasting five years (1974–8). It was a demanding and extreme exploration of identity and authenticity that, at times, was met with negative, gendered responses. (She posted a newspaper ad for a roommate that was answered by a man who tried to lure her into prostitution.) The project concluded with an exorcism performed within the tomb of Lucrezia Borgia in Ferrara, Italy, during which Roberta was expelled from Leeson's body.

In an even more radical act of self-transformation, artist Adrian Piper (b.1948) merged a male alter ego with aspects of her personal history to create *The Mythic Being* (1973–5), a persona characterized as the embodiment of 'everything you most hate and fear'.[14] She masked her identity as a light-skinned female philosophy student by wearing a large Afro, dark sunglasses, a large moustache and an aggressive male swagger, essentially recasting herself as a working-class black man. She / he walked the streets of New York City, rode the subway, and attended cultural events like gallery openings and the opera, as the artist would, but in male guise. These highly public performances were intended to challenge viewers' perceptions and long-standing biases and cause them to reflect on their own stereotypes. *The Mythic Being*, a caricature of the macho black male as portrayed by a woman artist, was conceived to spark a conversation regarding the fraught intersection of gender, race and class in America.

Lorraine O'Grady (b.1934) addressed a similar set of issues in the form of *Mlle Bourgeoise Noire* (1980–83; fig.5), or Miss Black Middle Class, a character known for staging guerrilla-style actions at New York City art openings. Posing as a 1950s beauty-pageant winner from French Guiana, wearing a rhinestone tiara, ceremonial sash and evening gown and cape made of 180 pairs of white dinner gloves purchased at second-hand stores, O'Grady disrupted the proceedings by shouting poems of protest against racism and sexism in the art world and whipping herself with a cat-o'-nine-tails. The contrast between her genteel facade and her aggressive behavior 'spoke to the complicated position of African-Americans who, she felt, simultaneously resisted the hegemony of white power while being complicit in their own victimization'.[15] With subversive wit, *Mlle. Bourgeoise Noire* urged Black artists to fight conformity and assert themselves, while forcefully confronting the mainstream art world's exclusionary practices.

Deconstruction

The theory of femininity as a social and cultural construction that first emerged in the 1970s became central to feminist practice in the 1980s as the often-objectified female body retreated further from view. Around this time, women artists became increasingly media savvy, recognizing that advertising, television, newspapers, magazines and the movies play a major role in shaping the visual arts. They understood that gender identity and its representation is complex, and they began to employ the language of the mass media to deconstruct its codes and reveal embedded gender, sexual and racial inequities. Postmodern practice was no longer defined in terms of personal identity, subjectivity and embodiment but in relation to conceptual strategies such as appropriation, allegory and pastiche, employed as tools for uncovering the operations of cultural power from a feminist perspective.

Popular culture, disseminated through the media, was the source of much of the imagery subject to the deconstructive impulse. In fact, the artists who came of age in postwar America were members of the first generation to be raised in a mass-media-saturated world. They soon became alert to the manipulative and coercive effects of advertising, TV and the movies in fostering a culture of capital and consumption and reinforcing gendered power relations. Women artists were among the leaders of this theoretically based art, which typically took the form of performative photographic work and deconstuctivist video, as well as live performance. They explored a wide range of issues including femininity as masquerade, stereotypes and the mass media and critique of cultural institutions and the culture wars that erupted during the boom years of Reagan Republicanism (1981–9).

Masquerade

In his essay 'The Discourse of Others: Feminists and Postmodernism' (1983), art critic Craig Owens astutely observed that discussions of postmodernism to date had been 'scandalously indifferent' to the issue of sexual difference. He stated, 'In being represented by [men], women have been rendered an absence within the dominant culture', noting that 'in order to speak, to represent herself, a woman assumes a masculine position; perhaps this is why femininity is frequently associated with masquerade'.[16] This theory, first advanced by British psychoanalyst Joan Riviere (1883–1962) in her essay 'Womanliness as Masquerade', held that womanliness 'could be assumed and worn as a mask, both to hide the possession of masculinity and to avert the reprisals expected if she was found to possess it'.[17] Later, French psychoanalyst Jacques Lacan (1901–81), building on Riviere's theory, posited that 'masquerade is a

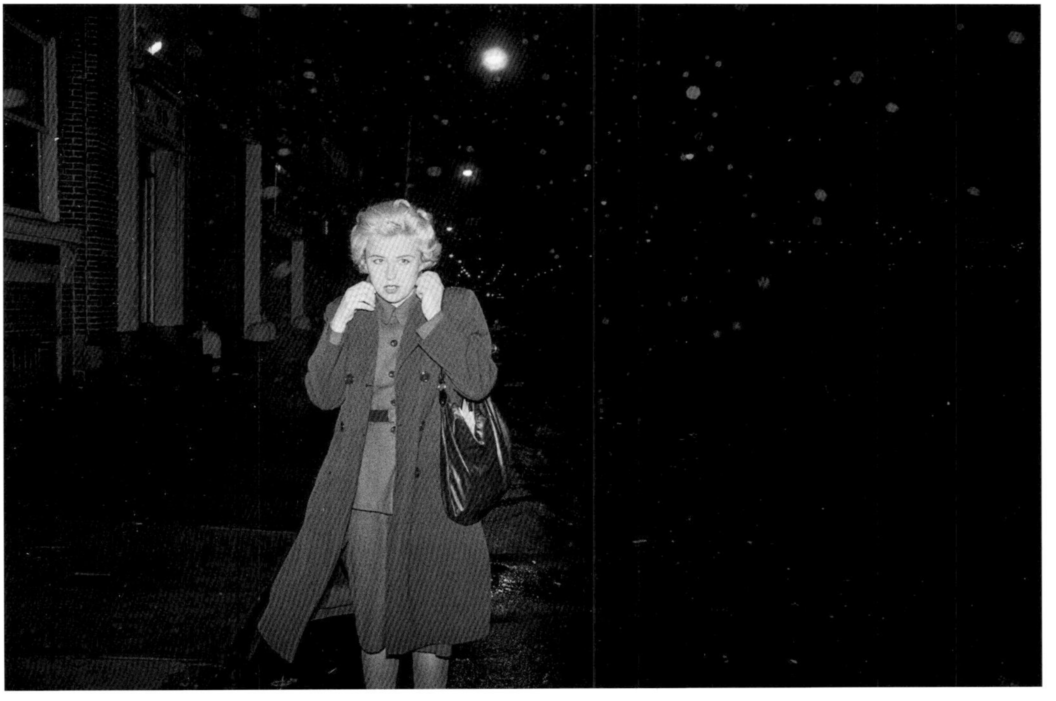

Fig.6 Cindy Sherman, *Untitled Film Still #54*, 1980, gelatin silver print, 20.3 × 25.4 cm (8 × 10 in)

representation of femininity but then femininity is representation, the representation of the woman'.[18] Masquerade served as one of the key strategies used by women associated with deconstruction to explore femininity as a guise or a gender performance and to understand the ways in which social and cultural pressure shapes one's identity.

With carefully selected clothing, makeup and hairstyles, and equally stylized expressions, poses and settings, Cindy Sherman (b.1954) created a cast of fictional personae easily recognizable to anyone familiar with popular culture. In literally hundreds of photographic portraits, beginning with the black-and-white *Untitled Film Stills* (1977–81; fig.6) depicting standard female types from B movies of the 1950s and 1960s, she created a seemingly infinite series of dramatic characters with Sherman herself as the protagonist. The seductive appeal of the melodramatic narratives she invokes is embedded in their artifice. The 'Untitled Film Stills' focused attention on the way Hollywood's portrayal of women reflected male desire, highlighting the notion of femininity as a pose or a masquerade. She continued to mine this concept in the centerfold series before veering into the grotesque in the fashion, disasters and sex pictures. Sherman's photographs both personify and deconstruct media representations of women as social types in images that are highly specific yet strangely elusive.

Instead of creating multiple personae to construct fictional narratives focused on female characters, Carrie Mae Weems (b.1953) initially represented just one. Her domestic drama features the artist as protagonist in a story of relationships, love and loss. She tells her tale around the kitchen table in an unfolding sequence of twenty vignettes comprised of staged black-and-white photographs and related texts. In *Untitled* (1990) from the *Kitchen Table Series*, Weems tells a story of a strong yet vulnerable Black woman who enters into a deepening relationship with a man and then seeks support from family and friends as it fails. She depicts her main character in her role as mother and lover and, finally, as a woman alone, in a finely tuned performance that seems to draw on personal experience. Like Sherman, Weems functions as an actor in and director of a narrative designed to stir the viewer's emotions. In focusing on the trials of a single female protagonist who directly confronts our gaze across a kitchen table, Weems challenges us to acknowledge the personal toll exacted when one inherits a social position shaped, in part, by sexual and racial difference.

Mass Media

Some women artists associated with deconstruction saw the imagery produced by the news and entertainment industries as a form of control that could be challenged through techniques such as appropriation and recontextualization. By adopting the verbal and visual tools of network television and advertising, they uncovered their hidden biases and inequities, delivering a shrewd critique of gendered stereotypes with considerable wit. Dara Birnbaum (b.1946) reedited video footage taped from the most popular television programs of the day, including the action, game-show and soap-opera genres, using the postmodern strategies of quotation, repetition and fragmentation to decipher their messages. In her best-known work, *Technology/Transformation: Wonder Woman* (1978–9), she exposed the inherent absurdity of main character Diana Prince's spinning transformation from drab secretary into dazzling superheroine adorned in a patriotic yet revealing costume of red, white and blue. As Birnbaum explains, 'By dislocating the visuals and altering the syntax, these images were cut from the narrative flow and countered with musical texts, plunging the viewer headlong into the very experience of TV – unveiling TV's stereotypical gestures of power and submission, of self-preservation and concealment, of male and female egos'.[19]

Martha Rosler (b.1943) deconstructs images of romance, glamour, allure and the promise of 'having it all' as she 'reads' *Vogue* magazine in a videotaped performance from 1982, breathlessly narrating a fantasy of luxury and beauty likely beyond the reach of much of the magazine's predominantly female readership. She goes on to use statistics to compare the salaries of highly paid *Vogue* models with the sweatshop earnings of third-world women on whose labor the fashion industry relies. Rosler's video pulls back the curtain on a business that sells unattainable dreams, one that objectifies the female subject as it exploits her needs and aspirations across class lines. A few years earlier, in a performance-based video titled *Semiotics of the Kitchen* (1975), Rosler created a deadpan parody of television cooking shows in which she aggressively wielded knives, a rolling pin and other kitchen utensils in an expression of frustration and anger over the oppressiveness of women's domestic role. Like Rosler, Barbara Kruger (b.1945) and Sarah Charlesworth (1947–2013) made use of photographs from fashion magazines and other sources (including pornography), to observe how they both depersonalized and seduced the female subject, while Lorna Simpson (b.1960) explored the ways conventions of beauty, including those associated with race and class, placed limits on efforts to construct an individual identity.

Institutional Critique

Other deconstructivist artists turned their attention to the power structures of the art world, including museums, galleries, collectors and critics, revealing its widespread gender-, race- and class-based inequities. In the late 1960s feminist artists began protesting the exclusion of women and artists of color from mainstream art institutions. By the mid-1980s dissent took more subtle forms as a booming economy, along with the rise of large-scale expressionist painting by an international group of male artists, conspired to marginalize alternative voices. An institutional critique emerged, launched chiefly by women artists who were determined to expose society's hidden social, cultural and economic biases and to thereby encourage the art world to tell a more inclusive, less patriarchal story. These artists recognized that the discrimination they experienced was systemic, not personal, and they had the statistics to prove it.

While artists such as Barbara Kruger, Louise Lawler (b.1947) and Jenny Holzer (b.1950) used photographs and texts to examine the mechanisms of cultural power, others preferred to take more direct action. The Guerrilla Girls, an anonymous collective of activist artists formed in New York in 1985, used absurdist humor to send serious messages. The artists donned large gorilla masks, demonstrated at art openings, and presented talks and workshops across the United States and internationally; posters bearing gorilla-masked figures were mounted in public places. Ironically calling themselves 'the conscience of the artworld', they delivered scathing critiques of institutional sexism, racism and corruption in an inimitably engaging style. Their antic multimedia lectures and live performances were designed both to provoke and amuse. The spirit of the Guerrilla Girls is best captured in a 1989 poster

Fig.7 Guerrilla Girls, *Do Women Have to be Naked to Get Into the Met Museum?*, 1989, screen print on paper, 30.5 × 66 cm (12 × 26 in)

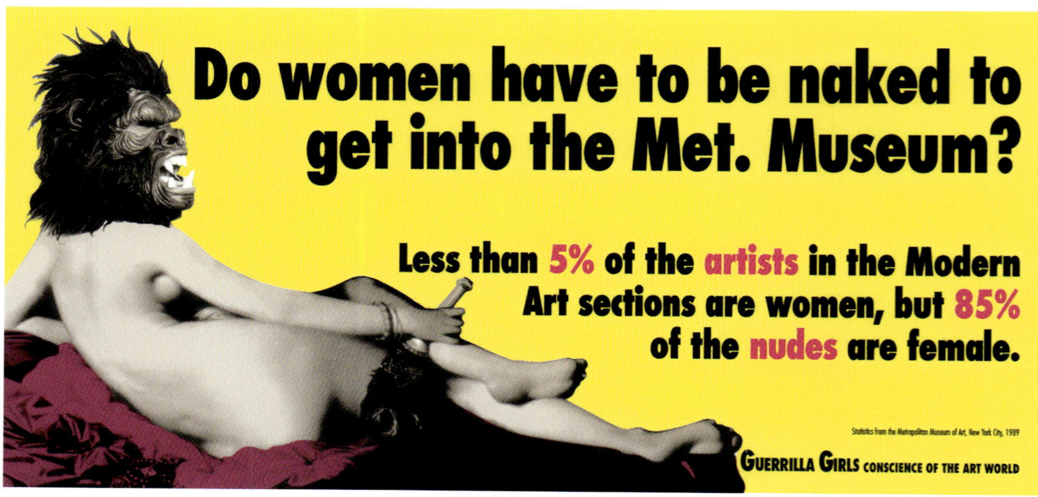

that poses the question, 'Do women have to be naked to get into the Met. Museum?' created in response to the overwhelming number of images of female nudes held in encyclopedic art collections (fig.7). An image of Ingres's reclining odalisque sporting a gorilla mask accompanied their sarcastic query.

Artist Andrea Fraser (b.1965) offers a more decorous, yet no less sharp, critique of the structural biases, social prejudices and economic underpinnings of cultural institutions. In a video titled *Museum Highlights: A Gallery Talk* (1989), Fraser takes us on a tour of the Philadelphia Museum of Art in the guise of a fictional docent named Jane Castleton. Conservatively dressed in a tailored grey suit and speaking in smug, self-important tones, Fraser parodies the language and behavior associated with art museums and their conventions. With tongue planted firmly in cheek she describes the museum and its holdings as the essence of taste, grace, dignity and order, extending her critique to other institutions dedicated to the public good, such as libraries, hospitals and zoos. As the personification of noblesse oblige, Fraser's docent deconstructs the myth of the museum as an egalitarian institution, exposing its codependent relationship with the patron class on whose social connections and financial bounty its existence relies.

Identity Politics

Issues that had been central to performance art since the 1960s, such as identity, visibility and difference, emerged in full force in the mid-1980s and 1990s as artists extended their critique of social inequities beyond the art world. During this time groups that had long experienced exclusion, exploitation and oppression under the dominant culture rose up in resistance. It was a highly fraught, ultimately unresolved political and cultural moment as artists and activists confronted injustices that resonate to this day. Performance was often the medium of choice for those speaking out against multiple forms of discrimination based on gender, race, sexual orientation, ethnicity or social class. Some artists expressed deep concern about such hot-button issues as the HIV/AIDS crisis and abortion access, while advocating for women's rights, LGBTQ rights and multicultural inclusion. Individuals from traditionally marginalized groups, primarily women and gay men, met vulnerability with anger and defiance and encountered a swift backlash. As Barbara Kruger declared, 'your body is a battleground', as the body under threat gained renewed attention.

Feminist artist Karen Finley (b.1956) expressed righteous rage against the patriarchy's domination of women in a spoken word performance called *It's My Body* (late 1980s–early 1990s), releasing her fury over the lives lost prior to the US Supreme Court's legalization of abortion in 1973, since overturned in 2022, in a powerful pro-choice rant. In a related work called *We Keep Our Victims Ready* (1990), she infamously smeared chocolate sauce over her nude body to prompt questions about sexual violence and the degradation of women. David Wojnarowicz (1954–92) chronicled the intense physical and emotional toll and devastating losses wrought by the AIDS epidemic in a range of media, including performance works, videos and writings produced in the years up to his death from the virus in 1992. The artist attributed the spread of the disease in the gay community in part to the government's lethal lack of funding for medical research and to the Catholic Church's intolerance of homosexuality and suppression of safe sex information. He expressed fierce anger and moral outrage through provocative, often apocalyptic imagery and painful yet poetic language. His performance, *All I Can Feel is the Pressure* (1988–9), is a personal diatribe voicing his intense frustration at being diagnosed HIV positive. In his impassioned words:

> If I had a dollar for health care I'd rather spend it on a baby or innocent person with some defect or illness not of their own responsibility; not some person with AIDS says the health-care official on national television . . . I was diagnosed with AIDS recently and this was after the last few years of losing count of the friends and neighbors who have been dying slow vicious and unnecessary deaths because fags and dykes and junkies are expendable in this country . . . I wake up every morning in this killing machine called america and I'm carrying all this rage like a blood-filled egg . . . and at the moment I'm a thirty-seven-foot-tall one-thousand-one-hundred-and-seventy-two-pound man inside this six-foot body and all I can feel is the pressure . . . and the need for release.[20]

Wojnarowicz, Finley and other artists dealing with identity-based content and imagery, including performance artist Holly Hughes (b.1955) and photographer Robert Mapplethorpe (1946–89), became prime targets of the culture wars, a form of political conflict that arose in the United States during the 1980s and 1990s. At that time a number of socially progressive artists were attacked by conservative groups, such as the Catholic League and the American Family Association, who condemned their work as obscene, immoral and / or blasphemous. Right-wing politicians such as Republican senator Jesse Helms, along with the then-chairman of the National Endowment for the Arts (NEA), weaponized the NEA by vetoing grants to artists and disparaging their work. Their attempts to censor artistic expression and freedom of speech had a chilling effect. However, certain artists and their allies pushed back in protest. For his part, Wojnarowicz created an indelible portrait of the artist with his lips, shockingly, sewn shut. This iconic image first appeared in the artist's controversial video *A Fire in My Belly* (1986–7), accompanied by scenes of fire-breathing teenagers and ants crawling on a crucifix, and later appeared on a poster for the AIDS activist group ACT UP, in poignant illustration of their motto 'Silence = Death'.

The Cyborg

Although the politics of difference proved empowering to some, others found categorization by group to be overly simplistic and needlessly restrictive. They believed that identity politics merely reinforced the problematic dichotomies that plagued Western culture and served to strengthen an entrenched patriarchal system. There was a desire to move away from rigid notions of gender, race and class and toward alliances based on affinity or choice. In an influential essay titled 'A Cyborg Manifesto', feminist theorist and science and technology scholar Donna J. Haraway, wrote that the traditional oppositions between men and women, mind and body, nature and culture, human and animal, organism and machine were all conceptually questionable. She used the figure of the cyborg as a metaphor to describe 'how boundaries between the human, animal, and machine had been irreversibly breached'. Haraway identified 'the female body as the site where those boundaries are most vulnerable [citing] the cyborg as an avatar of hybrid identity that signals the beginning of a new, posthumanist, and postgender future'.[21] The cyborg was acclaimed as an icon of feminist freedom and 'a creature in a post-gender world'.[22]

Several artists anticipated or explored the liberating potential of the cyborg, blurring the borders between the corporal and the technological in their performative work. Pioneering artist Laurie Anderson (b.1947) created complex, multimedia events in which she imaginatively integrated her female body with emerging technologies. Her highly ambitious *United States, I–IV* (1983), was a large-scale, four-part work comprised of 78 individually titled segments, including music, spoken word and visual effects. It featured the artist playing an electric violin and using a vocal modulator to technologically transform her feminine voice into a deep, masculine one, thereby assuming the male voice of authority. The eight-hour-long work ironically addressed various aspects of daily life in the digital age.

German performance artist and object-maker Rebecca Horn (b.1944) merged human gesture, animal appendage and machinery to create large kinetic sculptures and installations that appear to have a life of their own. In her *Kiss of the Rhinoceros* (1989), two large, curved metal arms, each tipped with a rhinoceros horn, slowly pull apart and then come back together to form a nearly complete circle. When the horns meet at the circle's top, a bolt of electricity shoots between them emitting a sizzling burst of sparks, suggesting a kiss. In this way, the artist's anthropomorphized object surges with mechanical, sensual and spiritual energy. According to the artist, her cyborgs 'have a soul because they act, shake, tremble, faint, almost fall apart, and then come back to life again. They are not perfect machines. . . . I'm interested in the soul of a thing, not the machine itself'.[23] Elizabeth King (b.1950) also summons the soul of the machine in her stop-frame animation *What Happened* (1991). Her film features a movable figure called 'The Pupil' (a miniature portrait of the artist herself) whose expressive arm, hand and head movements and seemingly responsive gaze evoke intelligence, emotion – even consciousness. This uncannily lifelike hybrid creature probes the line between the human and the machine, strangely confounding the two.

Globalization

Of course, performance artists continued to explore issues of identity, difference and their representation during the 1990s and beyond, as the body, which retreated from view in the 1970s, made a dramatic return. The 1990s were a decade of great social, political and economic change brought about by the emergence of a new global culture and the rise of digital technologies. Globalization described an increasingly interdependent and interconnected world in which the growth of global capitalism after the fall of Communism and the birth of the Internet transformed the circulation of money, people, art and ideas.[24] This stunning increase in the volume and flow of information worldwide combined with the decline of Western systems of domination opened the door for artists from diverse locales, including those from formerly marginalized countries, to gain visibility on the world stage. As a result, there was a significant shift in focus from the politics of personal identity to a critique of local, national and international concerns from a personal perspective.

In the 1990s performance artists from such contested geopolitical sites as the Balkans, Cuba, the Middle East and South Africa drew on their experiences of major upheaval to examine the violence, oppression and dislocation left in its wake. The work of these artists was typically rooted in their birthplaces, yet it forcefully spoke to a wider world. Some of the most powerful works were produced by women. In 1997 veteran performance artist Marina Abramović created *Balkan Baroque I* (fig.8) in response to the brutality of the Yugoslav Wars of the 1990s. At the Venice Biennale that year, the artist sat in a dark basement gallery on top of an enormous pile of raw cow bones, painstakingly scrubbing them with a soapy rag as bloody water stained her white dress. As she scrubbed, Abramović sang Slavic folk songs from her youth and openly wept. Her ritualistic performance was a personal act of mourning for the collective loss and grief suffered by victims of the Balkan conflict and, by implication, victims of every war. But as this intense performance made plain, washing blood from one's hands can never cleanse the conscience or ease feelings of guilt and shame. All involved must be willing to face the past and accept the consequences. Only in this way may an individual, or a nation, transcend prior wrongs and help build a more just future.

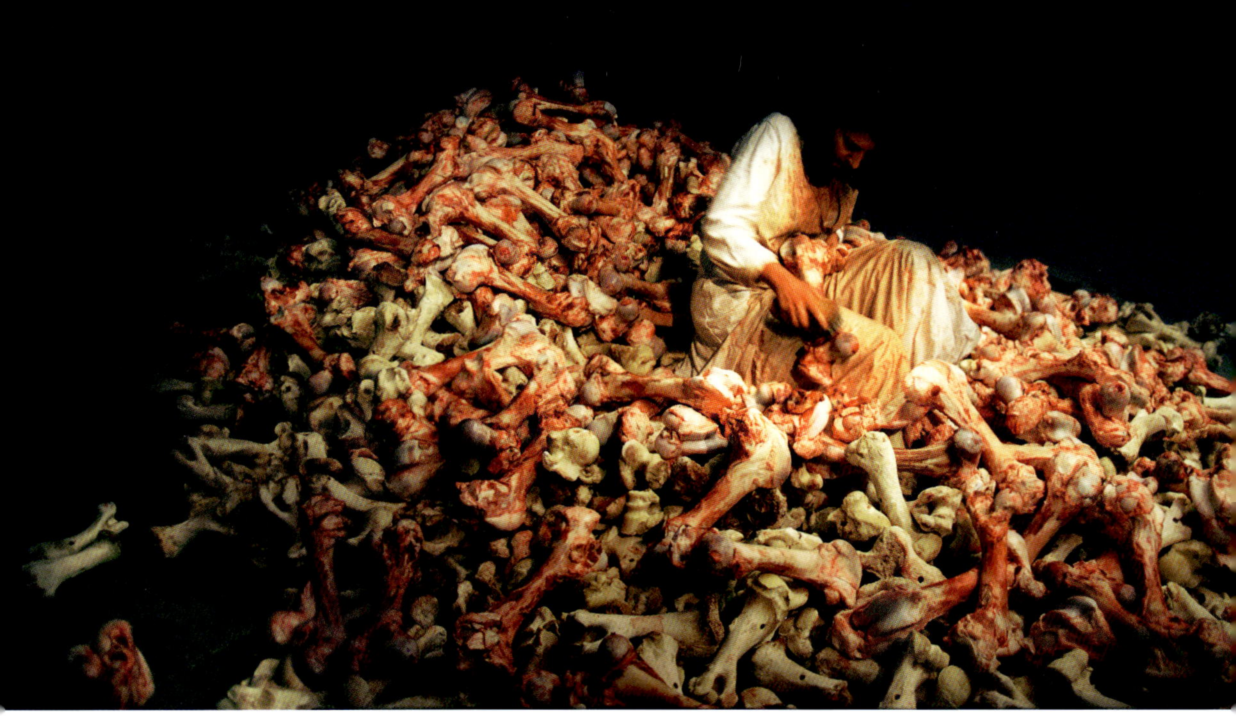

Fig.8 Marina Abramović, *Balkan Baroque I*, 1997, performance lasting four days, six hours a day, XLVII Biennale Venice

Artist Tania Bruguera (b.1968) examines fundamental questions of power and vulnerability in relation to the personal, political and collective body in her conceptually based, socially engaged performances, installations and actions. During the 1990s she created viscerally charged, metaphoric performance works that critiqued life in her native Cuba where the pain of censorship and repression, displacement and exile, was pervasive. Her provocative early works typically featured the artist performing demanding rituals in the nude. Bruguera's physical and psychological acts of endurance recall the work of her compatriot Ana Mendieta, to whom she paid tribute through reenactments of her signature *Silueta Series*, and Marina Abramović, the inspiration for her own extreme, ritualistic performances. Bruguera's works are meant to serve a social purpose. She is committed to the notion that art must be 'completely linked with life – and not a fiction or a virtual reality, but as alive as possible'. She asserts, 'My art has to have a real function for myself, to heal my problems or to help other people reflect and improve'.[25]

The Burden of Guilt (1997–9), Bruguera's quintessential work of the 1990s, is based on a historic tale from the Spanish occupation of Cuba: indigenous Cubans committed mass suicide when, unable to fend off the superior force of the invaders, they decided to resist by eating dirt until it killed them. In her performance, the artist re-presented this solemn act, appearing naked with the carcass of a slaughtered lamb hanging from her neck like a gaping wound, as she repeatedly gathered dirt into small balls and slowly ingested them. This reenactment symbolized the enduring social and political struggles faced by the Cuban people in a place where utopian dreams were shattered by the bitter facts of daily life. She followed her Cuban-themed body-based performances with a series of site-related performance / installations that looked at the political implications of such turbulent international sites as Havana, Moscow, Kassel and Bogota. In the 2000s Bruguera developed a new type of performance called Arte de Conducta, or behavior art, in which human behavior served as artistic material. She staged a series of live events that challenged the audience to consider their personal relationship to power and to respond, not simply observe, thereby transforming passive spectators into an active, engaged community.

Like Abramović and Bruguera, Iranian artist Shirin Neshat (b.1957) is a cultural nomad. She left her native country in 1975 to study art at the University of California, Berkeley, and became stranded in the United States after the Iranian revolution overthrew the Shah's Western-backed government and installed an Islamic regime. Since then she has lived in self-imposed exile, navigating a space between two vastly different cultures and expressing her views from the intersection of multiple, overlapping identities. In 1990 she returned to Iran for the first time since the revolution and found a nation transformed from the cosmopolitan center she once knew into a strict Islamic state. In response, she created a series of performative photographs, followed by films and videos, exploring these dramatic changes.

In the *Women of Allah* (1993–7) series, the artist appears dressed in a black chador, armed with lethal weapons, her hands, face and feet inscribed with Farsi poetry composed by Iranian women. Neshat looks at a range of opposing themes in these works, among them courage and fear, aggression and vulnerability, feminism and fundamentalism. She reflects on these contradictions, stating, 'I was fascinated by that particular intersection of love, faith, and devotion along with an obsession with violence, cruelty and ultimately death'.[26] The artist's self-portraits as a devout Muslim woman bearing weapons of war, clad in a veil that may signify her repression or her faith, are beautiful yet unsettling, both deeply personal and profoundly political.

Intersectionality

The representation of identity and difference grew more complex in the globalized 1990s as the self was by then thought to be the construction of multiple interconnected social, political and personal factors. *Intersectionality*, a term coined in 1989 by legal scholar Kimberlé Crenshaw, describes the ways in which the categories of race, gender, sexual orientation, ethnicity, nationality and class combine to create linked systems of oppression, or in some cases, advantage. This theory provided a framework for understanding the dynamics of discrimination and exclusion and their effects on marginalized groups, taking into account the concerns of those previously overlooked by second-wave feminists, who were typically white, middle-class and cisgender. Artists from diverse backgrounds recognized the power of images to both reinforce and subvert these biases. In response, they created intentionally provocative works that openly expressed their own reality and took charge of the narrative.

Beginning in the early 1990s Catherine Opie produced a series of photographic portraits of San Francisco–area lesbians who engaged in sadomasochistic practices, a community to which she belonged. She also turned the camera on herself stating, 'I thought it was important, if I was going to document my community, to document myself within that community'.[27] Opie's queer, feminist portraits and self-portraits actively assert the visibility of a lesbian subculture often treated with disdain. She bestows her openly transgressive subjects with an aura of dignity, portraying them in a formal manner that recalls the 16th-century paintings of Hans Holbein. In *Self-Portrait/Pervert* (1994), her most confrontational work to date, Opie poses before an elegant black-and-gold brocade fabric, stripped to the waist, masked in a black leather hood, each arm pierced by 23 large metal needles. The word *pervert* is bloodily carved into her bare chest in a bold reclamation of this homophobic slur. A decade later Opie returned to the self-portrait in a far different mood. *Self-Portrait/Nursing* (2004) is a beatific image of the artist nursing her infant son in the guise of a classic Madonna and child. A trace of the scar reading 'pervert' is still visible across her chest – a persistent reminder of gender difference.

Artist Lyle Ashton Harris (b.1965) disrupts our understanding and experience of the gendered, sexualized, racialized body in a series of seductive photographic self-portraits depicting himself as male and female, passive and aggressive, black and white. Essentially, he encourages us to reject these binaries as a means of determining social and political identities, crossing over expected categories of race and gender by occupying multiple subject positions. In his Polaroid triptych *Brotherhood, Crossroads and Etcetera* (1994), the artist and his brother, filmmaker Thomas Allen Harris, appear naked against a red, black and green background reminiscent of the Black Liberation Army flag. In the first image Thomas swoons in Lyle's arms, in the second, they kiss as Thomas points a gun at Lyle's chest and in the third the brothers embrace while directing their guns and their gaze at us. As a gay black man, Harris slyly courts the objectifying male gaze only to subvert its power, destabilize its norms and turn our culture's macho fascination with sex and violence on its head.

Berni Searle (b.1964) uses her body to explore the intersection of race, class and gender from the vantage point of a mixed-race woman living in postapartheid South Africa. She examines the wounds historically inflicted on her country's collective body in performative photographs and video installations that address, and ultimately transcend, their context, evoking the painful emotions associated with vulnerability, erasure and loss. In *Colour Me* (1998–2000), a series of four large-scale photographs, the artist confronts the viewer's gaze while lying naked on her back, her body covered in a thick layer of colored spice. The white flour, yellow turmeric, red paprika and brown cloves that stain her skin allude to the discriminatory system of classification imposed on the nation's so-called colored, Indian and Black populations by the white minority, as well as her own struggle to form a personal identity that exceeds the category of colored. In a related video performance titled *Snow White* (2001), the artist stoically kneels on the ground as flour falls from above and dusts her nude brown body a powdery white. Searle's metaphorical works challenge the fixity of the racially defined body and the values absurdly ascribed to skin color, as she deconstructs the difficult legacy of colonialism in South Africa.

Call to Political Action

Feminist performance has always been interconnected with and responsive to the wider social and political world. In fact, an activist bent runs through the history of this practice. Since the 1970s performance artists have consistently tackled real-world issues, creating works that boldly challenge the established order. As noted, artists such as Carolee Schneemann, Suzanne Lacy, Adrian Piper, Marina Abramović and Shirin Neshat are well versed in the critical art of resistance. At the dawn of the 21st century the call to political action by artists and collectives became even more striking. Influenced by the activism of second-wave feminism and by renewed demands for social justice, and in response to the persistence of political violence, artists from around the globe are confronting a broad range of human rights concerns. They encourage us to believe in our collective capacity to effect change and, in the words of Catherine Opie, 'to create more understanding, equality, and humanity within this world'.[28] It is an urgent and, at times, daunting task given the threats faced on multiple fronts.

Performance artists adopted various strategies to call attention to political injustice and oppression in the new millennium. Tania Bruguera released a video announcing her run in the 2018 Cuban presidential election and urging her fellow citizens to follow suit. She proposed this 'civic exercise' to highlight Cuba's one-party system and envision a time when power will return to the people through free and fair elections. In a dramatic video trilogy titled *And Europe Will Be Stunned* (2007–11; fig.9), artist Yael Bartana (b.1970) created an alternate history of Poland's and Israel's traumatic past as a springboard toward a better future. She borrowed the visual style of early 20th-century Stalinist and Zionist propaganda films to tell the story of a semifictional political movement called the Jewish Renaissance Movement in Poland (JRMiP), tracing the group's progress from its inception at a rally in a Polish stadium through the building of a kibbutz on the site of the former Warsaw ghetto to the assassination of and memorial for its leader. Bartana's JRMiP manifesto calls for the return of over three million Jews to their forgotten Polish homeland in the hope of establishing a new multicultural society free of the destructive nationalisms of the past. Bruguera's and Bartana's visionary projects blend the real with the imaginary to create utopian models meant to spark political action.

Other artists have taken a more directly confrontational approach. Guatemalan Regina José Galindo (b.1974) took to the streets to graphically address her country's long history of political violence and social injustice. In *¿Quien Puede Barrar Las Huellas?* (*Who Can Erase the Traces?*) (2003), Galindo walked barefoot from the Court of Constitutionality to the National Palace in Guatemala City, dipping her feet in a basin of blood and leaving footprints along the way, in memory of the more than 20,000 civilians killed during the Guatemalan Civil War (1960–96). The performance was a protest against the 2003 presidential candidacy of Efraín Ríos Montt, a former military dictator who was responsible for some of the worst atrocities of the war yet permitted to run despite a constitutional ban. In recalling the victims, Galindo's somber work challenges her country's communal amnesia, calling on its people to acknowledge past wrongs and help build a more humane democratic society. More recently, the artist presented a haunting performance in which 28 black-shrouded women appeared in a park at dusk as they were gradually

Fig.9 Yael Bartana, *Mary Koszmary (Nightmares)*, 2007, part 1 of the trilogy *And Europe Will Be Stunned*, 2007–11, one-channel video and sound installation, 16 mm film transferred to DVD color/sound, duration: 10:50 min

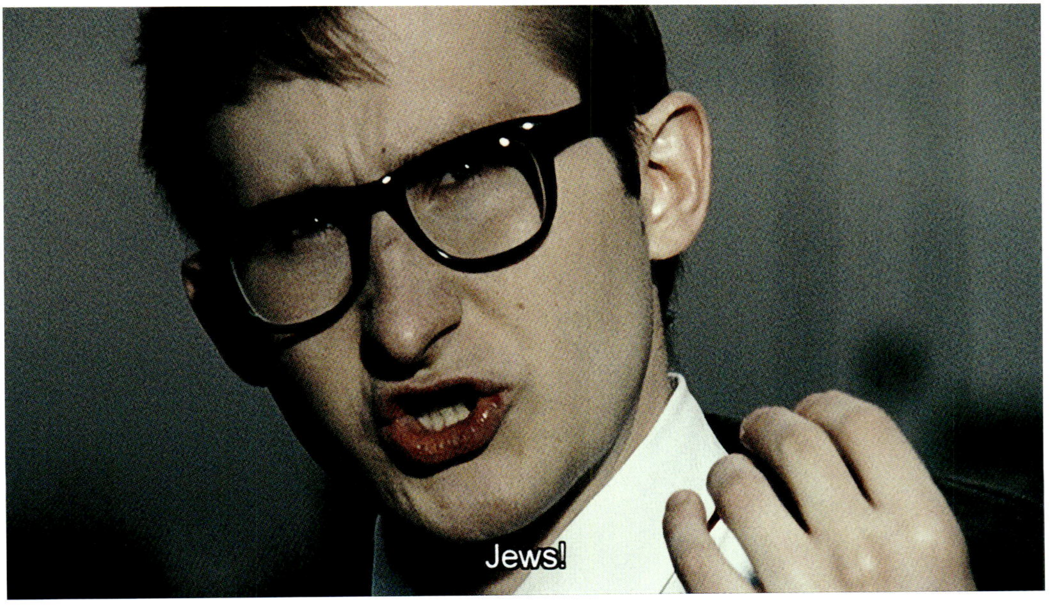

enveloped in darkness. These figures represented the approximately 28 women who vanish in Guatemala each week as a result of femicide, homicide based on gender bias. In *Monument to the Disappeared* (2020), Galindo urges us to remember victims of violence yet again, honoring individuals not typically memorialized in the town square.

For over a decade, Pussy Riot, a Russian, feminist, anti-Putin collective, has been staging courageous, anarchic, disruptive and political performances or actions that attempt to expose the cruelty of Vladimir Putin's authoritarian regime. As a result, they have been subjected to government harassment, detention, forced labor and, most recently, exile. They also have received significant support from the West. The human rights group Amnesty International designated them 'prisoners of conscience' and the pop star Madonna championed their cause during a Moscow concert. The performance that first brought them international attention was *Punk Prayer* (2012), a chaotic, guerrilla action in which several members crashed a service at Moscow's Cathedral of Christ the Savior wearing brightly colored minidresses and knitted balaclavas (ski masks) while aggressively shouting an anti-Putin song. The lyrics opened with a fervent plea: 'Virgin Mary, Mother of God, banish Putin, banish Putin/Virgin Mary, Mother of God, banish him, we pray thee!'

Three members of Pussy Riot were arrested for their efforts and charged with 'disrupting the social order by an act of hooliganism that shows disrespect for society and is motivated by religious hatred or enmity'.[29] They maintained that their protest was not primarily antireligion but against the ways Putin's government uses its alliance with the Russian Orthodox Church to validate nationalist goals and absolve human rights abuses. After undergoing a show trial, artist-activists Maria Vladimirovna Alyokhina and Nadya Tolokonnikova were found guilty and sentenced to two years in a penal colony, while a third member, Yekaterina Samutsevich, was released on appeal after serving eight months. Art critic Sebastian Smee has praised Pussy Riot for creating political art that 'dares to engage in the actual political arena'. He continues, 'It is oppositional, offering clear statements grounded in personal conviction. It understands, through bitter experience, what's at stake. And yet it's made with exuberance, an embrace of the absurd and antic, undaunted joy'.[30] Pussy Riot's Nadya calls its members 'jokers, jesters, holy fools', whose stated mission, undertaken at great risk, is nothing less than transforming the consciousness of their country and ultimately changing the world.[31]

Call for Social Justice

In the United States the call for social justice rose to levels not heard since the 1960s and 1970s as fundamental human rights once again came under attack. In 2019 the FBI reported that bias-motivated killings reached a record high amid a nationwide increase in hate crimes, incidents that sharply rose in the months around the 2016 presidential election. And while the report did not draw conclusions as to the cause of this disturbing trend, the editorial board of the *Washington Post*, in a column titled 'Hate in America is On the Rise' observed, 'It's noteworthy many of the groups against whom crimes rose by double digits were the focus of inflammatory rhetoric by Donald Trump over the course of his presidential campaign', and throughout his presidency.[32] The white supremacist ideology of the radical right fueled these racist, sexist, homophobic, religiously and ethnically based attacks as American democracy shamefully drifted toward authoritarianism. In response, the Black Lives Matter, #MeToo and LGBTQ rights movements sought to address the anger, pain and collective suffering of their members by raising awareness of social inequities and working to make change. They were joined by a diverse group of performance artists who felt compelled to speak out against the forces of discrimination through their socially conscious work.

Artist Tomashi Jackson's (b.1980) archival research into the histories of law, urbanism and social justice animates her multimedia practice. Her paintings and prints serve to explore 'the intersections between the formal languages of visual art (color, composition, layering) and the political languages driving the histories of segregation, voting rights, education, and housing in the United States'.[33] Recently, Jackson recently expanded her investigation to include a series of performative video collages examining distorted color perception and its impact on the value of human life in public spaces. This problem took on special urgency in 2015 with reports of a number of violent acts committed

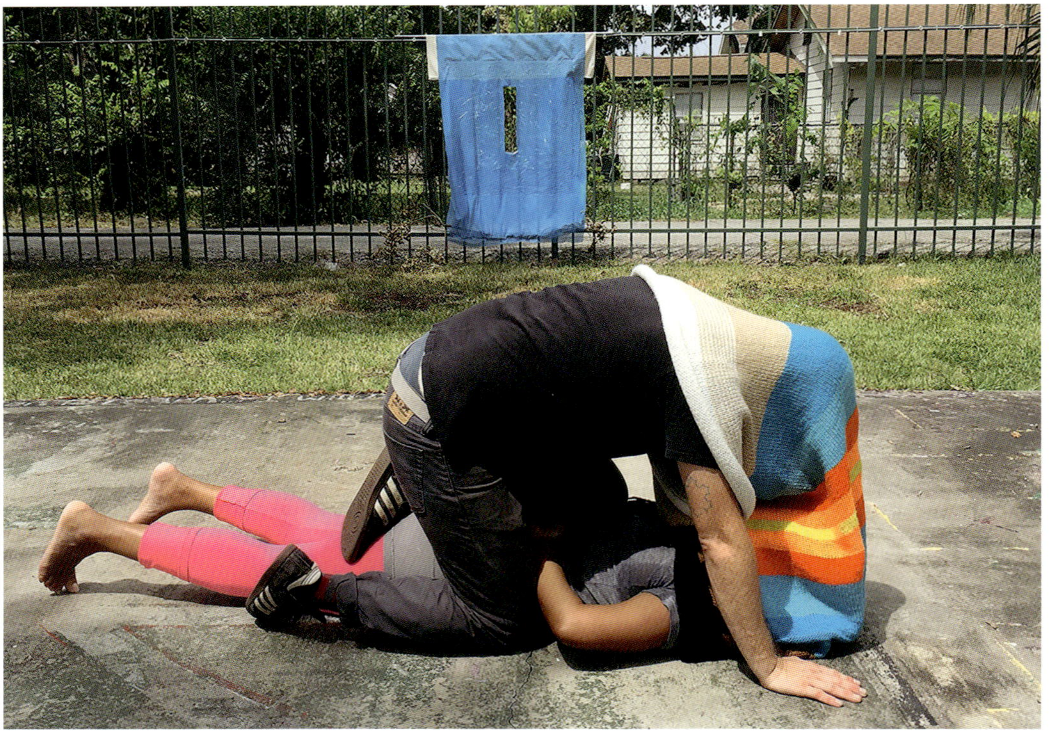

Fig.10 Tomashi Jackson with Naiymah Jackson, Iyonna Jackson, Omar Jackson Jr., Emily Peacock and Patrick Renner, *Vibrating Boundaries (Law of the Land) (Self Portrait as Tatyana, Dajerria, & Sandra)*, 1963–2015, video collage, edition of 3, duration: 13:12 min

against Black women and girls by Texas police. In a harrowing video titled *Vibrating Boundaries (Law of the Land) (Self Portrait as Tatyana, Dajerria, & Sandra)* (1963–2015; fig.10), the artist and her collaborators reenacted the stress positions endured by teenagers Tatyana Rhodes and Dajerria Becton as they gathered for a pool party and by Sandra Bland who died in police custody after being arrested during a traffic stop. The video begins with a woman reading a passage from Joseph Albers's *Interaction of Color* while footage of the pool party assault plays in the background. This collage is followed by a scene of a Black woman pinned face down under a white man's knee as the terrified cries of a woman pulled over during a real traffic stop are heard. According to Jackson, *Vibrating Boundaries* vividly illustrates 'the profiling, resource deprivation, detention, brutality by police and vigilantes, and legalized abuse of entire communities. A terrifying reality in plain sight'.[34]

Artists Nona Faustine (b.1977) and Marisa Williamson (b.1985) examine the institution of slavery and its ongoing legacy through the lens of history, focusing on the abuse and exploitation of the Black female body. For five years, beginning in 2013, Williamson adopted the persona of Sally Hemings, slave and mistress of Thomas Jefferson, in live, interactive performances staged at such key venues as Jefferson's Monticello and the University of Virginia, reimagining and reclaiming the patriarchal narrative from a 'feminist and anticolonial' perspective.[35] Faustine took an even more provocative approach to this troubled history. The Brooklyn-based artist made a series of photographic self-portraits at locations around New York where enslaved Africans were bought and sold, lived and died, posing silently in the nude, wearing only a pair of white heels. In *From Her Body Sprung Their Greatest Wealth* (2013) from the *White Shoes* series (2013–21), the artist appeared naked and shackled atop a wooden block on Manhattan's Wall Street, the site of a former slave trading market and a current financial district. A deep sense of vulnerability, as well as quiet dignity and courageous defiance, pervades the artist's celebration of the Black female body as a living monument to the oppressed and forgotten souls on whose forced labor the American economy was built.

Gay, feminist artist Sharon Hayes (b.1970) probes the ways in which speech intersects with politics, history, identity, love and desire in her performances and multimedia installations. Her work recalls the idealism of 1960s protest movements and their faith in the power of language to change hearts and minds. Her performances often take the form of speeches, protest marches and demonstrations, evoking an earlier time when political views were actively voiced in the public square. In the work *I March in the Parade of Liberty, but as Long as I Love You I'm Not Free* (2007–8), Hayes visited several sites in Lower Manhattan famous for public speaking, including Tompkins Square Park and Washington Square, to express her desires. Equipped with a megaphone, she earnestly recited a love letter written to an absent lesbian partner to onlookers and passersby, using a familiar form of protest to make a public confession of private emotion.

For singer-songwriter and queer performer Taylor Mac (b.1973) and his longtime collaborator costume designer Machine Dazzle (b.1972), the *spectacle*'s the thing, in fact, the more outrageous, excessive and over-the-top, the better. Dazzle employs the familiar trappings of drag and burlesque performance, such as sequins, glitter, feathers, costume jewelry and high heels in combination with salvaged materials and a bizarre array of found objects to create extravagant headpieces, wigs and costumes that exemplify his queer maximalist aesthetic. That aesthetic was on full display in Taylor Mac's *A 24-Decade History of Popular Music* (2016–9), an epic 24-hour drag performance narrating an expansive alternative history of the United States in 246 songs dating from 1776 to 2016. Dazzle provided witty, period-inspired costumes for each decade, appearing onstage hourly as Mac's dresser. For this audacious revue, Mac radically recontextualized 240 years of popular music from a queer perspective, delivering a biting commentary on 'the racism, chauvinism, homophobia, misogyny and white supremacy coursing through the history of American song', with passion and panache.[36]

Queer maximalism, as practiced by Machine Dazzle and Taylor Mac is, essentially, a form of resistance to the social, political and legal constraints imposed on the LGBTQ community, expressed through works of dramatic, eye-popping, liberating excess. As cultural critic madison moore astutely observed,

> [for] queer people, glamour is resistance because of the way it allows you to use aesthetics to seize space on your terms. Glamour as resistance means realizing you're fed up paying into heteronormative systems and structures that were not made for you. With glamour as resistance, you choose the instability and the messiness of queerness, you choose sequins and headpieces, you choose to make beauty out of detritus, and you use style as a tool to explode boundaries and binaries with maximum impact.[37]

Back in Moscow, Pussy Riot mounted a sarcastic celebration of Vladimir Putin's 68th birthday on October 7, 2020, by installing rainbow Pride flags on 'the most important symbols of Russian statehood', including the Supreme Court, the Ministry of Culture and the Federal Security Service (FSB), in protest of the government's continued denial of LGBTQ rights.[38] Member Maria Alyokhina told the press that the group was able to get past government security by posing as maintenance workers and claiming to be in charge of Putin's birthday decorations. This action was accompanied by a set of online demands which included the legalization of same-sex partnerships, an end to discrimination against LGBTQ Russians and an investigation into the reported kidnappings and killings of gay, lesbian, transgender and queer people in Chechnya. As expected, several members were detained for violating statutes prohibiting public demonstrations. *The Pussy Riot Rainbow Flag Action* (2020) made a graphic statement in opposition to the criminalization of same-sex relationships and suppression of freedom in Russia, declaring, 'The state should not interfere in the life of the LGBTQ community. But if it does, then the community can intervene in the life of the state'.[39]

The Political is Personal

A survey of performance from the 1960s and 1970s until today tells the story of an art form that has moved from the margins of the art world to the mainstream. In recent years, for the first time, major museums such as the Tate Modern and the Museum of Modern Art in New York launched departments dedicated to performance art, commercial galleries sold performance works to private and institutional collectors, and performance artists were invited to participate in international biennials and prestigious festivals such as Performa in New York. Yet despite the increased recognition and institutionalization of this once-marginalized medium, performance has maintained its fundamentally radical, disruptive stance. In fact, performance is at the forefront of contemporary art and action, led by a new generation of artists whose work confronts an expanding range of political and social issues. And while the feminist rallying cry 'the personal is political', sounded 50 years ago, still inspires, its converse, 'the political is personal', also rings true for the socially aware, politically engaged performance artists who bravely and consistently put their work, and themselves, on the line.

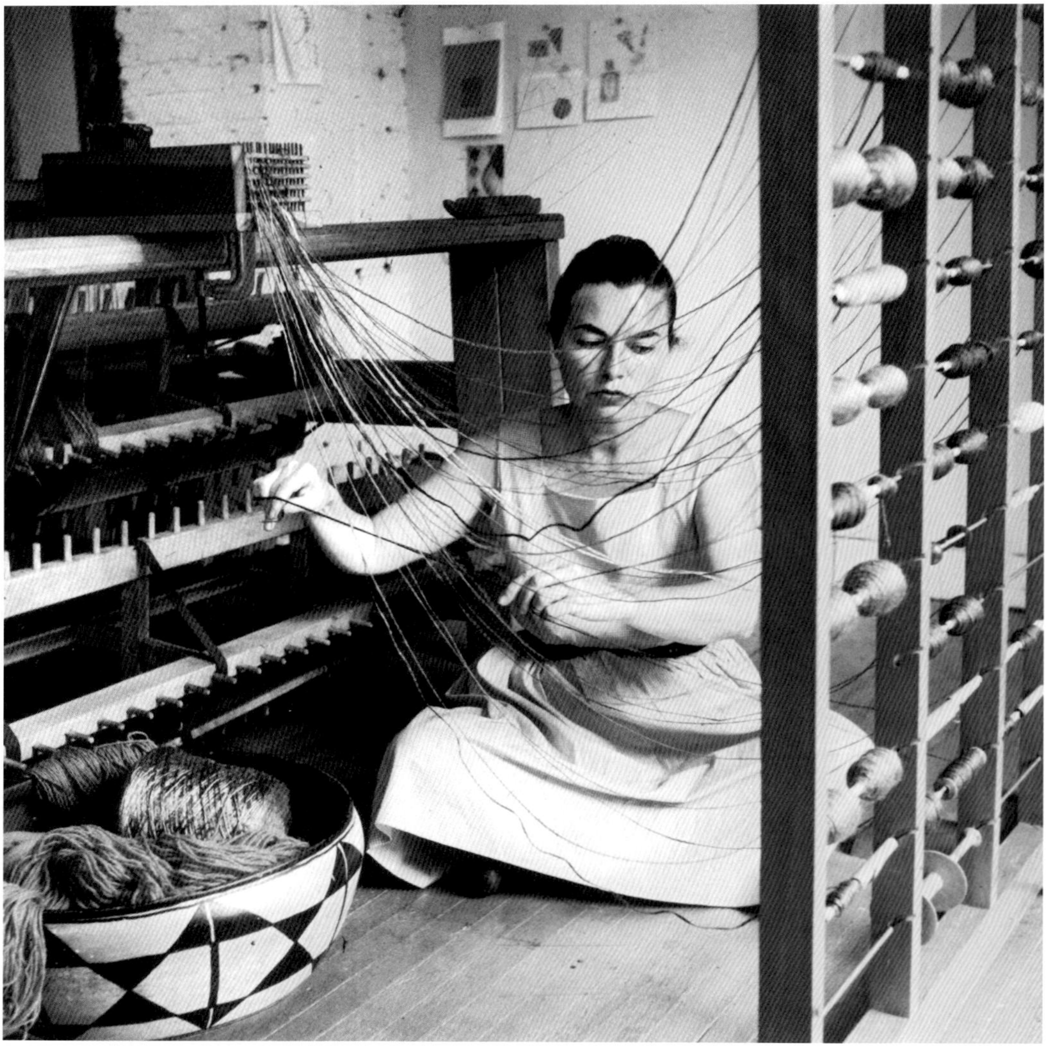

HANDMADE

ART, CRAFT AND FEMINISM

Nancy Princenthal

Like the opposition of women and men, the contentious distinction between craft and art can seem anachronistic – a struggle over the status of positions whose once self-evident integrity has long since been challenged. There is no secure boundary separating high art and handcrafted, useful objects. Similarly, acknowledging that gender is a spectrum, rather than a binary pair, can make feminism seem obsolete. And yet feminism still has work to do. Lots of it. And handmade art – or to use the more familiar but problematic term *craft* – has never offered a more illuminating perspective on visual culture's forms, purposes and meanings than it does now. A focus on the handmade is just as important for clarifying women's particular contributions, many of them long neglected, to contemporary art.

An adjective, a noun and a verb, *craft* is a slippery word, naming a range of materials, processes and products. In the popular mind, it is mostly identified with tactility – with a record of the hands that made it and an invitation, in turn, to be held and used. By tradition, craft is insistently physical. But it can also be associated with performative art – as well as with strains of pedagogy, therapy and activism. For art historian Jenni Sorkin, ceramics is a 'live form', a practice in which women, by both choice and necessity, have been dominant.[1] The writer Julia Bryan-Wilson, who has explored textile arts ranging from sculptures by Harmony Hammond to the Cockettes's glam apparel to the AIDS Quilt, is especially interested in cloth as a medium that occupies a subversively indeterminate position between the useful and the purely expressive – a position she finds particularly germane to the representation of queer

Fig.11 Lenore Tawney in her studio, 27 Coenties Slip, New York, 1958

experience.[2] Anthea Black and Nicole Burisch have explored the labor politics of craft, looking at handcrafted objects produced by makers as diverse as Sabine Gschwandtner, who has led knitting circles based in historical wartime practices, and sellers on Etsy. Noting craft's commodification by the home décor and fashion industries, Black and Burisch observe a descent from 'craftivism', a form of social-justice artwork – one that makes gender equity a priority – to a 'craftwashing', by which corporate culture exploits superficial aspects of both the homemade and the exotic.[3]

Indeed, some of the questions raised by craftspeople and their products are inseparable from those of market value. The history of handcraft over the past century and a half, beginning with the decorative arts associated with the British-born Arts and Crafts movement, reveals inherent confusion over whether its aim was to produce luxury goods or demotic ones. One reason the relationship between the handmade and the manufactured has always been fluid is that tools of one kind or another come into nearly every kind of human-made object except woven baskets and coiled or slab-built clay pots, as David Pye famously observed in 1968.[4] And the work of craft is both individual and collective, involving technologies ancient and novel. As Ezra Shales notes, if we are talking about the handmade, the question is, whose hands count? In particular, do they count least when we're talking about women's work? The rise and fall of the Bauhaus and Black Mountain College show that even where the values of workmanship were prized, some kinds of manual skills were more valued than others. At the Bauhaus those skills held in highest regard (metalworking, woodworking and the fundamentals of architecture) quickly became restricted to men. It would be essential to the feminism of the 1960s and early 1970s that those media (and workshops) relegated to women by Bauhaus leader Walter Gropius – textiles, ceramics – became forms of celebratory provocation.

A premise of art since the postwar period, when the study of art became academicized, is that artists find the tools, mediums and processes that best suit their expressive and conceptual goals, seeking skills on an as-needed basis. With craft, on the other hand, the creator begins and remains in dialogue with the medium – be it clay, textile, wood or glass – and its past. At least that's the traditional ethos of handmade work: a craftsperson submits to the material and is in that sense

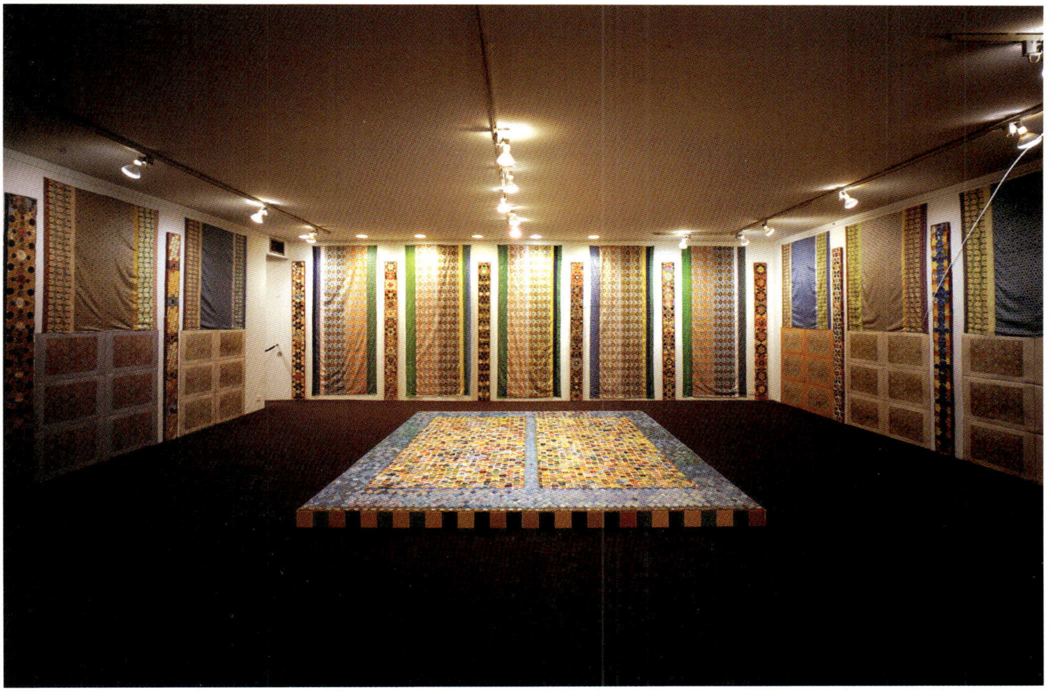

Fig.12 Joyce Kozloff, *An Interior Decorated*, 1978, textiles and luster-glazed ceramic tiles, dimensions variable, installation shown at Tibor de Nagy Gallery, NY, 1979, separate parts sold into private collections, floor owned by the Ludwig Forum for International Art, Aachen, DK

a perpetual student. This attitude comports with a Zen influence that has been particularly strong with potters, both Western and Asian, and that gained considerable traction in the United States in the 1950s. But the Western roots of craft-based art, from regional 'folk' traditions to domestic handicraft, are equally deep and reflect a spectrum of moral and spiritual, cultural and political standards. While not gender-specific, craft-based art has been taken up most energetically and consistently by women.

As is evident in Faith Ringgold's unstretched paintings modeled on Tibetan *thangkas* and Joyce Kozloff's references to Islamic decorative patterns in her paintings, textile hangings and elaborate tiled installations (fig.12), non-Western traditions were an important element of the craft impulse in the 1970s and of the Pattern and Decoration movement in which both men and women embraced opulent decorativeness. The celebration of female Hopi-Tewa potter Nampeyo in the early decades of the 20th century, like the later embrace by the mainstream art world of the remarkable quilts made by Black women in the Gee's Bend community of Alabama, suggest that, more generally, techniques and styles born in Africa and in Indigenous cultures of the Americas and elsewhere have long been crucial to craft-linked art; sensitivity to the ethical complexity of such borrowings has slowly grown. The Seneca artist Marie Watts is one among many contemporary artists to look at that history obliquely, using textiles as a primary medium. It is striking that the exploration of cultural traditions that originated outside of Europe were so often undertaken by women.

As is suggested by unresolved questions about craft's gendered identity and intercultural expropriations, one value of the handmade object is that it is an excellent spanner, holding open space for a host of issues. If craft expertise moves the art impulse from head to hand – if craft is a more intuitive operation than other art processes – is it therefore less conceptual and less intellectually ambitious? Does it then follow that it is, by established prejudice, more feminine? Or is it the wellspring from which the most advanced ideas derive?

Not only conceptual art but illusionism, too, is a defining opposite to craft: with realist painting, the surface is typically meant to be transparent, unseen. Three-dimensional artworks by contrast always engage the conditions of material presence, handcrafted ones most of all. Some particularly painterly sculptors (Medardo Rosso, for instance) have experimented with surface illusions. Some have even undertaken the representation of landscape: Mary Carlson, for one, has recently made a series of small ceramic landscapes, borrowing from a genre invented by painting and, confoundingly, restoring its dimensionality. As figurative art, along with art that foregrounds handwork, has regained critical attention and acclaim in the past decade and more, such intriguing paradoxes have multiplied.

Of course, for millennia all art was handmade, as were all practical goods, from which art was at first inseparable. Ezra Shales writes in *The Shape of Craft*, 'Just as speech preceded writing, craft came before art and architecture'.[5] It follows that, originally, craft – much like the oral tradition in literature – was communal and transgenerational, carried forward by living bodies in communities of shared language. (It is also worth noting, in this context, that the word *textile* shares a root with *text*.) Until the advent of photography in the mid-19th century, the default mode of producing images was handmade painting and drawing; almost all sculpture remained handmade (at least in its initial, precast form) until commercial fabrication arose in the 1960s. Industrial and computer production are, on this timescale, a blink. And the emergence of digital technology is perhaps a less radical break with the past than it seems; the world has been wired telegraphically since the 1840s and telephonically since 1875; radio signals have flown through the air for more than a century. For all its 'clouds' and 'ether nets', the digital realm has an enormous carbon footprint (NFTs are especially mammoth). Moreover, despite digital software's touted powers of calculation and creativity, its products, as we all know, are as fallible – as prone to clumsiness and error – as the humans who create it. Yet it, too, is a defining opposite to handmade art – and sometimes a subversively collusive element of it.

In *Thinking through Craft*, Glenn Adamson argues that craft 'only exists in motion' as an 'active, relational concept',[6] a proposition close to Jenni Sorkin's notion of craft as a 'live form'. As to the imperative that the medium imposes, Shales advises tolerance. 'Craft demands that humans meet material at some middle ground that is not entirely anthropocentric. "Empathy for material" is a much better rule that "truth to material".' Citing George Kubler, who called craft 'an instinct to animate matter', Shales adds, 'There is no one truthful way to use any given material'.[7] Adamson begins his book by suggesting that it may be time for those who care about craft to let it flourish in 'a state of benign neglect', but he goes on to suggest that craft be thought of as a conceptual limit 'which defines modern art by opposition'.[8] In that spirit, it is worth exploring how women artists have predominated in that oppositional workforce, availing themselves of the self-consciously handmade as an incursion into the field of modern and contemporary art, disputing its autonomy and opening it up to a wealth of history and personal experience.

Handing On Knowledge

In *The Craftsman*, sociologist Richard Sennett traces the deep social history of handwork, affirming the value of collective labor and of skills passed literally from hand to hand. From the time of the early Greeks, he writes, craft and community were 'indissociable',[9] deeply esteemed and firmly associated with women. By the Classical era, 'the craftsman's honor had dimmed', Sennett explains, contributing to a 'gendering of skill that produced the word *craftsman*'. But the 'public virtue of women' continued to be celebrated. In Athens 'women spun a cloth, the *peplos*, that they then paraded through the city streets in an annual ritual'.[10] This ascription of feminine 'virtue' – *power* might be another word for women's position in Athens with respect to craft – would be eclipsed for centuries. During this time the production of handcrafted goods was taken over by monasteries and then by medieval guilds in which apprentices, almost all male, learned to 'deal face-to-face with issues of authority'.[11]

Although the guild system was challenged in the Renaissance by its promotion of individuality and originality – which arguably produced a shift from craft to art – few Renaissance artists in fact worked in isolation; the successful 16th-century studio sustained many features of the medieval workshop. Sennett believes this to have been beneficial. While art is presumed to have a single agent and craft a collective one, in Sennett's view autonomy is not equated with a higher position: 'the lone, original artist may . . . be more dependent on uncomprehending or willful power'[12] – for instance the court or the church – than the Renaissance master. Nonetheless, the prestige of art with respect to craft rose in due course: in 1648 Louis XIV established the Royal Academy of Painting and Sculpture, drawing an official line between *artist* and *artisan*. A century later, Denis Diderot and Jean le Rond d'Alembert's encyclopedia placed poetry and painting under the heading 'Imagination' and philosophy under 'Reason' in their first-of-its-kind encyclopedia of the arts and sciences, while carpentry and marquetry, for instance, were merely 'trades'.[13]

The ethos of the medieval workshop was resurrected in the middle of the 19th century with the British Arts and Crafts movement. As industrial production made handcraft obsolete, it became an object of nostalgia. Sennett believes such nostalgia, which paid homage to socialist tenets, romanticized the medieval guilds. Similarly, Adamson writes that the elegiac attitude toward artisanship expressed by the Arts and Crafts movement's wealthy proponents conflicted sharply with their advocacy of revolutionary socialism; he indicts their adoption of a regional vernacular as 'purely symbolic'.[14] On the other hand, curator and museum director Marcia Tucker contended, in a catalogue essay for her 1996 exhibition *Labor of Love*, that the British crafts movement kept faith with its beliefs. Arguing that William Morris, a key figure in the movement, took esthete John Ruskin's 'concern with "good" decoration, tradition, and the dignity of the craftsman to another level altogether, [and] devoted much of his life to workers' rights',[15] Tucker also spoke ardently for the idealism that prevailed among Morris's American followers.

One outgrowth of Morris's initiative was the Omega Workshops, founded in 1913 by Roger Fry and his Bloomsbury artists friends Vanessa Bell and Duncan Grant. Spurning social reform on the one hand and challenges to industrial production on the other, Fry was primarily motivated by erasing the division between 'fine' and decorative arts. Omega products ranged from painted murals and mosaics to furniture and textiles. All were expensive, their only patrons a wealthy few; the workshops shuttered in 1919, not without having made their mark. In the United States, the first major Arts and Crafts statement was an exhibition in Boston in 1897. The movement found fertile philosophical ground in the New England-bred school of Pragmatism and cultural support in the fabled can-do, jack-of-all-trades Yankee ethos – the largely spurious but nevertheless durable belief in the possibility of success for self-taught, self-made craftspeople, free from European restrictions of class, family or guild. The American commitment to equal education for all, another lofty tenet generally ignored in practice, contributed to a faith that acquiring vocational skill was an essential factor in developing civic spirit and a healthy democracy. The influential Pragmatist and educational reformer John Dewey advocated learning by doing, a pedagogy aimed not only at developing expertise in manual trades but also at moral improvement. An essential element of his program was establishing the equality of functional and 'esthetic' objects. In *Art as Experience* (1934) Dewey proclaimed that there was no difference between the fine and applied arts, writing, 'The enemies of the esthetic are neither the practical nor the intellectual. They are the humdrum.'[16] He promoted communal engagement. ('In the degree in which art exercises its office, it is also a remaking of the experience of the community in the direction of greater order and unity', he wrote.[17]) He emphasized the importance of process. ('It is not linguistic accident that "building," "construction" "work," designate both a process and its finished product.

Without the meaning of the verb that of the noun remains blank.'[18]) And he prioritized handwork, telling an interviewer, 'I think the whole problem of understanding should be approached not from the point of view of the eyes, but from the point of view of the hands'.[19]

Dewey has recently received renewed attention from artists and writers who find support in his thinking for social-practice projects. But in the 1920s and 1930s his celebration of simple, homespun forms played into the taste for both Modernist abstraction and vernacular art, which were themselves interconnected. Tucker points out that folk art and related craft work was first 'discovered' by American Modernists (and their collectors) in the early decades of the 20th century and were 'appreciated largely because of their formal connections to the contemporary art they themselves were making and / or buying'. Both folk and craft were 'seen in relation to notions of "the common man," promising freshness, simplicity, honesty, and unselfconsciousness', Tucker writes. But she adds the crucial caveat that the 'authenticity' sought in the ostensibly 'innocent, pure "primitive" other' of poor, rural Americans is 'a metaphor of colonization'.[20] Neither the arrogance lurking beneath American Modernism's adoption of 'folk' forms nor Dewey's utopian vision of a classless community of cultural producers were confined to the United States. American appropriation of native folkways was paralleled in Europe by colonialist uses of tribal art; there Dewey's idealism developed on ground prepared not by Pragmatism but by established efforts to put socialism into practice.[21]

Just as with the Arts and Crafts movement in Britain, the Austrian Wiener Werkstätte, which followed in 1903 (and was active until 1932) emerged from a combination of nostalgia for folk traditions and political commitment to cooperative labor. The Bauhaus, founded in 1919 in Weimar, Germany, additionally sought to achieve for industry the qualities valued in handmade objects and to avert the cultural and social losses associated with industrialization. Its ambivalence about the ascendence of mass-manufactured goods reflected, among other things, horror at the mechanized slaughter of World War I. Walter Gropius, architect and Bauhaus founder, wrote in his prospectus for the famous incubator of modern design, 'Training in a craft is a prerequisite for collective work in architecture. This training purposely combats the dilettantism of previous generations in the applied arts.'

The painter Josef Albers, one of the school's most influential instructors (who immigrated to the US and continued to teach, at Black Mountain College and then at Yale, after the Bauhaus was shuttered by the Nazis in 1933), spoke similarly of the importance of the hand's wisdom. 'You don't watch what the arm does, no', he said, and added, echoing Dewey, 'You go by the feeling within the arm'.[22]

While Albers, who taught the Bauhaus's interdisciplinary Vorkurs, became legendary as a teacher and painter, his wife Anni, a textile artist who worked with him at the Bauhaus, labored in his shadow. She was not alone. In Jenni Sorkin's account, a 'pervasive institutional sexism' prevailed at the Bauhaus, supported by the circular logic that women were dilletantes and as such, Gropius believed, they threatened the school's reputation. His 1923 decision to segregate instruction by gender, excluding females from all but three craft workshops – ceramics, textiles and bookbinding – reflects, Sorkin writes, 'the fear of amateurism that plagued Gropius after many more women than men initially enrolled'.[23] This discriminatory policy had the unintended consequence of abandoning the commitment he had made (that was shared by Dewey) to abolish hierarchies in the arts. 'Rather than eradicating traditional media hierarchies', for which the Bauhaus is often credited, 'Gropius, in actuality, reinforced both the low status and the feminine associations of craft', Sorkin argues, putting it in service to architecture, 'its masculine superior'.[24]

Writing about textiles, embroidery in particular, British scholar Roszika Parker similarly observes that in the much-read book *Foundations of Modern Art*, of 1931, Amédée Ozenfant warned, 'If we go on allowing the minor arts to think themselves the equal of great art, we shall soon be hail fellow to all sorts of domestic furniture'.[25] Ozenfant's ire was aimed, implicitly, at those elements of Dada, Surrealism and Russian Constructivism that, Parker writes, advanced 'women's particular skills and traditional areas of activity in the domestic sphere'. Examples include Sophie Taeuber-Arp, a painter only recently celebrated for her prodigious work in textiles, interior design and other decorative objects, from beaded handbags and puppets to a tea salon in Strasbourg. She introduced her husband, Jean Arp, to embroidery, and he contributed a needlework to the magazine *Dada*, but also a long poem in which he reveals, says Parker, that he valued hand-stitching 'not for its qualities as an artistic medium but for its stereotypical associations with intuition, feeling, and above all with nature'.[26] Extending the Victorian notion that embroidery and the feminine realm to which it belongs are beyond – or beneath – thought and skill, Arp mused, 'Embroidery is more nature than oil painting, the swallows are embroidering the sky for thousands of centuries'.

The artists associated with revolutionary-era culture in the new Soviet Union, in the late teens and 1920s, were also subject to demeaning judgments about the artistic and ethical value of craft and decoration. In 1918 artist Vladmir Tatlin wrote, in response to a surge of folk-inspired clothing design by women, 'The Futurists have been too preoccupied with cafes and various embroideries for emperors and ladies'.[27] The pioneering feminist art historian Linda Nochlin, ever alert to choices that might undermine female artists' self-respect and power, acknowledged these conflicts, writing, in 1971, 'On the one hand for a woman artist to "return" as it were to her traditional role in the minor arts . . . can be viewed as a retrograde step. Yet from another vantage point . . . women artists involved in the decorative arts in the early twentieth century were contributing to the most revolutionary directions – both social and aesthetic – of their time.'[28]

By the early 1930s an increasingly autocratic USSR had turned against vanguard art, and the Bauhaus had come under attack from the Nazi regime (it closed in 1933). But in the United States, an ambitious program of governmental support for both traditional and progressive art was undertaken as part of a massive effort to relieve the deprivations of the Depression, and a notable element was aid for craft and folk art. Particular attention went to artisanship associated with the Southern Craft Revival to which a number of private-sector resources were also directed. Led primarily by civic-minded female philanthropists, most from the Northeast, these efforts supported such enterprises as Allanstand Cottage Industries, founded by Frances Louisa Goodrich in the 1920s, and the Penland School of Handicrafts, founded by Lucy Morgan in 1929, both in Asheville, North Carolina. (The latter remains a lively campus.) Morgan trained as a weaver and began by organizing a cottage industry for local women, providing them with looms and materials and then marketing their handwoven goods. The Penland school soon included other crafts as well. In the 1930s photographer

Doris Ulman documented the work, and workers, of this hardscrabble community where making things by hand met needs for both creative satisfaction and thrift. At this time, craft demonstrations of weaving and pottery arose; predecessors of what are now called 'living history museums', they featured practitioners, often in costume, enacting a form of showmanship that had begun with ethnographic displays in the late 19th century and continued with the spectacle-driven expositions in Chicago in 1933 and Saint Louis in 1934.[29] Craft, art and artifice merged uneasily in these performances. Writes Susan Tallman, 'Rural inhabitants of the Southern Highlands of Appalachia, of tribal areas of the Southwest, and of the Low Country of the Southeast were celebrated for the presumed antiquity of their craft traditions, though many of those "traditions" were invented or modified to please distant marketplaces'.[30] As Sorkin writes, 'The merging of vernacular culture with education reform produced a craft revival that romanticized Appalachia as a keeper of Caucasian national values'.[31]

Along with the tangle of social, political and pedagogical aims and assumptions, these workshops reflected a settlement-house paradigm of relieving urban poverty and assimilating immigrants, a not altogether comfortable fit in a rural Southern setting where conservatism and racism dominated cultural priorities. At the same time, the craft and folk-art workshops of the 1930s reflected the therapeutic purposes to which handcraft had been put during and shortly after World War I, when craft was widely used, in England and the United States, as a clinical tool with which to rehabilitate returning war veterans. (Similar efforts were made during World War II; in 1943, the Museum of Modern Art in New York organized an exhibition called *The Arts in Therapy*. Organized under the Museum's Armed Services Program, it involved an uneasy mix of work by 'both normal and mentally disturbed individuals', both soldiers and civilians, along with assorted others, from Alexander Calder to Louise Nevelson.) The practitioners of this method of healing, like nurses generally, were from the start predominantly women, as were the social reformers leading American settlement organizations. In Los Angeles, Nelbert Chouinard, a former settlement house worker, initiated a vocational training program for returning soldiers in 1921 (it was active until 1972). Her Chouinard Art Institute, the West Coast's first woman-run art school, underwent a number of changes before being renamed CalArts in 1970 and soon thereafter hosted one of the era's most radical feminist art programs. (It is still among the country's most progressive and influential art schools.)

Another powerful model of a woman-led craft school was Marguerite Wildenhain's Pond Farm Pottery, in rural Guerneville, California, north of San Francisco. Trained at the Bauhaus, Wildenhain emigrated, in 1940, to the United States, where in summer sessions she led for nearly four decades, she sustained the German school's lessons. She believed they included submission to the rigorous discipline but also pursuit of invention as purpose higher than technique. Her program was legendary for its insistence that students relinquish attachment to their initial efforts: the pots they executed by the hundreds, in a strict progression of type, weren't fired but instead discarded and recycled. Wildenhain's own work – which often features vessels with simple, graceful faces on their sides – is seldom exhibited, and her considerable influence on the rise of the powerful West Coast school of 'funk' ceramicists little acknowledged. These ceramicists include Peter Voulkos, who epitomized a heroic, manly disregard for tradition and for the assumption that ceramics be functional, a disdain he shared with Robert Arneson, Ken Price and Ron Nagle. By 1952 an annual US Ceramic National exhibition began offering two categories of awards, one for pottery (associated ever more firmly with domesticity and amateurism, and with women) and the other for ceramic sculpture.

A final major episode in 20th-century experimental art pedagogy took place in the 1950s at Black Mountain College, which had opened in 1933 and closed in 1957. Only 20 miles away from Asheville, North Carolina, home of the Southern craft revival, Black Mountain itself glorified neither handcraft nor the achievements of women artists. But among its remarkable students and faculty were both Alberses; as at the Bauhaus, Joseph promoted sensitivity to process and to material. Representatives of the Korean *mingei* movement, which revived traditional, humble ceramics and open, communitarian approaches to their creation, were influential visitors at Black Mountain and also at workshops on the West Coast. Voulkos taught at Black Mountain in the summer of 1953 for a pottery session that also brought the esteemed British potter Bernard Leach and renowned Asian potters Shoji Hamada and Soetsu Yanagi, who helped Zen Buddhism – already a rising influence on the West Coast – gain a foothold in the East.

Today some craft schools still flourish.[32] But for the most part art education assumes the postdisciplinary position that ideas have priority and that students will learn whatever skills are required to realize them.

Centering Women's Work

Among the faculty at Black Mountain was the literature professor M.C. (Mary Caroline) Richards, who availed herself of the college's facilities and instructors to learn pottery, and who became a singular leader in the field after leaving North Carolina. She did so first with an unconventional presentation of her work: a one-evening event held in April 1958 in New York's East Village, with the very long title, 'Clay Things to Touch, to Plant in, to Hang Up, to Cook in, to Look At, to Put Ashes in, to Wear, and for Celebration'. By emphasizing active viewer engagement and staging a spectrum of uses, Sorkin argues, this event challenged the conventional history of performance art, coming one year ahead of Allan Kaprow's *18 Happenings in 6 Parts* (1959) and three years before Claes Oldenburg's *The Store* (1961).[33] In 1954 Richards had helped form Gate Hill Cooperative Community in Stony Point, New York, where she again taught literature; John Cage, whom she had met at Black Mountain, was also a member and reinforced a connection to Zen that Richards also pursued. Later she returned to pottery, and for the last 15 years of her life she lived and taught in rural Pennsylvania in a handicraft- and agriculture-based community for mentally handicapped people, who produced crafts alongside their teachers, all volunteers. Called Camp Hill Village, it was one of 80 such communities worldwide to have been founded by Theosophists and guided by its eclectic spirituality.[34]

Richards is remembered less for her pots than for her teaching, her communitarian spirit and her writing. Her *Centering*, first published in 1962, is a poetic, book-length hymn to the proposition that working with clay is a way to deepen one's spiritual and ethical life; the title's reference to the crucial first step in pottery – centering the clay on the wheel – serves as a governing metaphor. In addition to Buddhism, Richards invoked Jung, Shakespeare and Emily Dickinson, as well as

Quakers and Transcendentalists. Citing Emerson's exhortation 'Do the thing, and you shall have the power', she affirmed, 'We can't fake craft'.[35] Richards encouraged a deep dive into the material. 'We experience the mud, we experience the forces of time and destiny that have transmuted rock into plastic dust', she wrote.[36] But her prose has none of the stern, exacting tone of the Bauhaus. 'We must fill our devotion with the spirit of play, of celebration and holiday. Love-play', Richards advised. 'Unless our ideals of peace and of love are so much cant, we must surely embrace our world in all its daily happenings and details.'[37]

The dubious edict that material has an inherent truth that artists and craftspeople should aim to express had a particular resonance in the United States in the 1950s, when the Red Scare and the equally brutal Lavender Scare put careers and lives in danger, making suspicion – of communists, of homosexuals – rampant, and truth newly precious. A crisis of honesty was front and center in popular culture (witness such television shows as *To Tell the Truth* and *What's My Line?*, both launched in the 1950s). Visual artists responded in many ways, from Pop art's impulse to use coded references to the surfaces of the material world to the contrary impulse, at the end of the 1960s, to bare all in performance art. Richards's version of integrity was grounded in values – of love and peace, Zen and other Eastern spiritual systems – that arrived in the United States first on the west coast. Cage and Merce Cunningham, for instance, were exposed to Buddhist thought as early as the 1930s at the Cornish School in Seattle, and they were among those to bring it to Black Mountain (along with the Asian potters mentioned above). As would Richards, they found in it cultural and social tolerances that Western religion and ethics didn't honor.

In other words, it was no accident that the Summer of Love was a Californian phenomenon. By the later 1960s, the hippie counterculture had spread widely in the United States and abroad, promoting a back-to-the-land self-sufficiency that included such handcrafts as tie-dye, macrame, crochet, beadwork and patchwork, along with ceramics. It was quickly (and often crassly) assimilated into commercial culture, but at the outset it was a powerful source of solidarity and of pleasure. One domain in which it was apparent was in clothing. Writes Rozsika Parker, 'In the 1960s, embroidery suddenly gained a new face. Embroidered suns rose over hip pockets, dragons curled round denim thighs, rainbows arched over backs. For the hippy era embroidery symbolised love, peace, colour, personal life and rejection of materialism.'[38] One woman spoke to Parker about her hippie phase, when she lived in a commune: 'We all embroidered. It had various meanings: pleasure, self-indulgence with colours, a determination to make your clothes beautiful. It also functioned to establish you as a member of a tribe.' Notably, men took up embroidery too, although Parker notes tartly that 'this was less a subversion of sex roles than a longing for the freedom of an idealised image of childhood – mother-loved, anarchic and untouched by daddy's world.'[39] The sources for the new decorativeness ranged widely. The Beatles's eastward-looking involvement with Hindu ragas and Brahmin finery (mirrored and braided vests) spawned a fashion trend as well as an interest in South Asian music. In the United States, the rage for fringed leather and beaded headbands was a mash-up of Native American and frontiersman accessories. And despite its globalist name and Left-leaning politics, the *Whole Earth Catalog*, first published in 1968, supported an emphasis on self-sufficiency and handmade goods that was hardly a property of the Left; the Hobby Lobby, founded 1972 and self-identified as a Christian-owned company, has been associated with extreme conservatism since the start.

For her part, Richards avoided politics of all kinds, including those concerning gender, and in the 1950s and early 1960s was hardly a staunch feminist. Early in her book she followed an anecdote about men's and women's roles in marriage, and in pottery, with the quip that while the husband's ethical and emotional responsibilities ran deep, the wife's concerns were, 'Will it hold water? Can I cook in it?'[40] In a later preface, she rued such statements. But even in 1962 she saw sexual injustices afoot. 'My struggles to accept my nature were the struggles of centering. I found myself at odds with the propaganda of our times', she wrote.[41] Insofar as she expressed her discomfort, she was prescient.

Weaving New Histories

At the same time that ceramics were gaining stature with respect to art, textiles were also rising in art-world esteem. 'It is from fiber that all living organisms are built – the tissues of plants, and ourselves, our

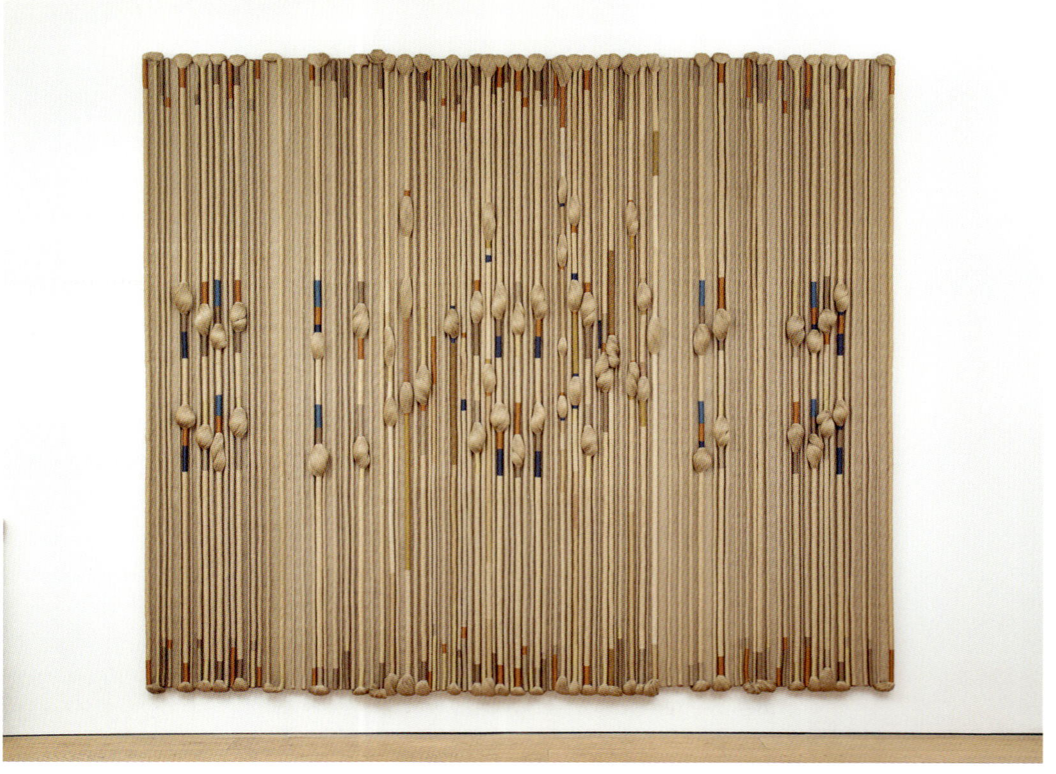

nerves, our genetic code', the Polish artist Magdalena Abakanowicz (1930–2017) said in an early statement about her work.[42] In the late 1960s, she produced great suspended forms from flax, jute, horsehair and hemp that she spun and dyed herself, sculptures that were also containers of space. These 'Abakans' were followed by figurative sculptures made of sackcloth stiffened with resin and, later still, stone and metal. Headless, often bigger than life and generally ungendered, the figures were grouped in menacing standing formations or were seated and bound, potently ominous. But it is the equally powerful Abakans that firmly associated her with a group of abstractionists using textiles who came together in the early 1960s under the heading of a newly invigorated discipline labeled *fiber arts*. Taking up the legacy of Anni Albers and others who used weaving, tapestry stitching and also many off-loom techniques – tying, knotting, wrapping, braiding, knitting, crocheting – they made bold, formally inventive work that often inflected space in a way that would later be called installation

Fig.13 Sheila Hicks, *Textile Fresco*, *c.*1969, linen, silk and cotton, 5 panels, 300 × 340 cm (118 1/8 × 133 7/8 in) overall, private collection

art. At the same time, it was intricate, richly tactile and, inarguably if only tacitly, feminine.

Prominent among fiber artists is Sheila Hicks, a highly skilled artisan who also had a sophisticated education in art. Born in 1934 and still at work in her 90s, she has had a boldly interdisciplinary and international career. After completing two degrees in art at Yale, where she studied under Josef Albers and met Anni Albers, she spent five years (1959–64) in Mexico; since then Hicks has lived in France and has, along the way, set up workshops in Chile and South Africa while also developing commercial woven fabrics in India and tufted rugs in Morocco. Her large-scale public commissions have been realized in the United States, Japan and Saudi Arabia. The work Hicks has made, drawing on textile traditions from all those regions, ranges from intimate, delicately textured and neutral-colored weavings (fig.13) to mounds of vividly colored, baled yarn or skeins of fiber cascading from the ceiling, bearing all manner of objects knotted within. Equally influential for textile art, Lenore Tawney (1907–2007) studied at Chicago's Institute of Design, descended from the Bauhaus, in the 1940s, and she also attended the Penland School of Crafts, in North Carolina. Her work is elegant, linear, sometimes ethereal, suspended from the wall or ceiling and often totemic in overall form (fig.11), though essentially abstract. Using vertical threads in close parallel, sometimes tied with nautical knots that reflect her residence during the 1950s and 1960s at New York's old seaport, she also used braiding influenced by Egyptian headdresses.

The fiber arts movement was heralded by a 1963 exhibition at New York's Museum of Contemporary Crafts called *Woven Forms* (after Tawney's series of that name); it was followed by *Wall Hangings*, an exhibition in 1969 at the Museum of Modern Art (MoMA), curated by Jack Lenor Larsen and Mildred Constantine. Both shows were mainly of work by women, and Hicks and Tawney featured in each; at MoMA they were joined by (among others) Anni Albers and Magdalena Abakanowicz. In a catalogue essay the curators pointed to the Weiner Werkstätte and the Bauhaus, endorsing their shared insistence that 'the physical qualities of materials were consciously explored'. But while the Bauhaus had developed weaving 'in accordance with industrial needs', Constantine and Larsen wrote, things had changed in the postwar era, causing them to change their 'concepts of this craft and view the work within the context of twentieth-century art'. True to form for mid-20th-century American modernists, they firmly distinguished American from European production, judging the latter as derivative of folk art and overly 'weighty, finished and permanent'; even more harshly, they pronounced that in 'the East European countries [i.e., those in the Soviet bloc], where weaving is considered an art of the people',[43] it has not been taken seriously as art. Unsurprisingly, the curators deemed the American work 'more exploratory', displaying greater individuality and invention. In other words, Cold War politics were actively in play.

It has recently been pointed out that the fiber arts movement, with its turn away from machine production, emerged 'just as the American textile industry began its inexorable decline in the face of globalization'.[44] At the same time, visual art was going in an opposing direction, away from handcraft toward machine production. By the mid-1960s, what was eventually called 'post-studio' art (it was introduced as Process art, or postminimalism) was being produced by such artists as Richard Serra, Robert Morris and Donald Judd, who were using industrial means, materials and, when funding permitted, fabricators. Like weaving and pottery, these processes are associated with functional objects. But they differed by status in the postwar American economy and its art world; not coincidentally, they were also differently gendered.

Some observers in the early '60s were at pains to claim for craft materials the rank of high art precisely by holding fast to the difference between industrial and domestic utility, and associating craft with the former. Rose Slivka, longtime editor of the magazine *Craft Horizons*, proclaimed in 1961 that 'the new clay art' (she meant work by Peter Voulkos and his students) had benefited from 'a climate which not only has been infused with the dynamics of a machine technology, but with the action of *men* – ruggedly individual and vernacular men (the pioneer, the cowboy), with a genius for improvisation'[45]. It would be hard to imagine a balder illustration of the macho posturing prevailing at the time, which even women (like Slivka) felt they had to celebrate. So perhaps it is no coincidence that when fiber arts first took the stage as a leading crossover medium from craft to art, it was with work that could compete in scale with the attention-getting art of the period's male artists. In fact, women fiber artists had quietly stolen a march on them.

Speaking Out

It took some time for that incursion to be acknowledged. Although forthrightly socialist communitarianism had driven aspects of the craft movement from the late 19th century on, activist sexual politics didn't take center stage in the promotion of textiles and ceramics until the early 1970s, with the rise of second-wave feminism (the first wave having been the suffrage movement). Rejecting the minimalist and postminimalist mandates that serious art be big, geometric, abstract and made of industrial materials and processes, and that it shun not only emotion and personal history but in fact any content at all, many rising feminist artists also resisted the slick ironies of pop art. Some embraced its barbed humor; Mimi Smith's *Steel Wool Peignoir* (1966), for instance, is a sheer, pink, floor-length item of lingerie trimmed with lace and, abundantly, with steel wool. But most feminist artists of the time preferred materials that were soft, yielding, porous. When critic Lucy Lippard convened a panel in 1975 asking 'What Is Female Imagery?' painter Joan Snyder suggested, 'It has to do with a kind of softness, layering,' and invoked her own use of flocking, seeds, and 'floating objects'.[46]

A signal moment for feminist art in the United States and for its emphasis on handcraft was the 1972 *Womanhouse*, a student project undertaken as part of the Feminist Art Program led by Judy Chicago and Miriam Schapiro at CalArts in Los Angeles. Faith Wilding's contribution was the crocheted environment *Womb Room* (1972), which used a female-associated 'amateur' craft to represent an essential biological marker of femininity. Wilding (b.1943), who had studied fiber arts and trained in weaving and other crafts, was brought up in a utopian community in Paraguay; she embraced the physical satisfactions of handwork as well as its symbolic ramifications. Her *Womb Room* was a spiderweb; a trap; a disordered, unraveling nest; and a soft, tangled refuge, ghostly white against a room painted black. Other installations and performances in *Womanhouse* addressed the drudgery of housework and childcare, the frustratingly limited expectations for women and the unequal distribution of housework between the sexes.

Notable for the courage, invention and sheer work it demanded, *Womanhouse* was not just a reconsideration of domestic arts – the students took on all the manual labor of renovating the derelict mansion it occupied, as well as producing performance and installation work. The project was also a brilliant public relations coup, eliciting local news coverage, an hour-long public TV program featuring Gloria Steinem and a story in *Life* magazine. The prime mover in that respect was Chicago (b.1939), who is best known for her monumental work of ceramics, *The Dinner Party* (1974–9). Its 39 porcelain plates, individually sculpted and painted, each honor a distinguished women from antiquity to the present; all sit on embroidered runners. A group of 400 volunteers, most of them unnamed, were involved in the project's realization; that most volunteers were not credited is a failing particularly noted by those involved in its elaborate textile elements. But collective activism never lacks internal friction; no community is easily defined, much less mobilized, with perfect equality. Now permanently installed at the Brooklyn Museum, *The Dinner Party* remains a landmark of feminist art.

Chicago's colleague Miriam Schapiro, though less in the limelight, has been equally influential for advancing a kind of textile-based work that she called 'femmage'. A hybrid of collage, quilting and painting, her work showcased matrilineal traditions while also taking up a familiar modernist strategy – the repurposing of everyday things – and redirecting it toward narrative, with women at the center of the story. In response to an interviewer's question about how femmage arose, Schapiro explained, 'The knitting, sewing, tatting, and embroidery my grandmother worked at were the first traditional arts I saw. When I was young' – she was born in 1923 in Toronto – 'my parents were part of a bohemian world that valued ethnic crafts. Later in my life it became clear that many of the crafts I grew up with were attributable to women.'[47] Among her best-known works are compositions from the 1970s that are shaped like open fans, revealing glorious fields of pattern, texture and color.

The imperative to bring forward suppressed narratives also impelled the hand-lettered 'story quilts' that Faith Ringgold (b.1930) began making in the early 1980s. Involving sharp, funny and often also heartbreaking stories, they relate episodes of daily life in Harlem, where she was a longtime resident, as well as allegories of America's sordid racial history and wry takes on famous figures of Parisian modernism. *Sunflower Quilting Bee at Arles* (1991; fig.14) shows eight Black racial-justice heroines,

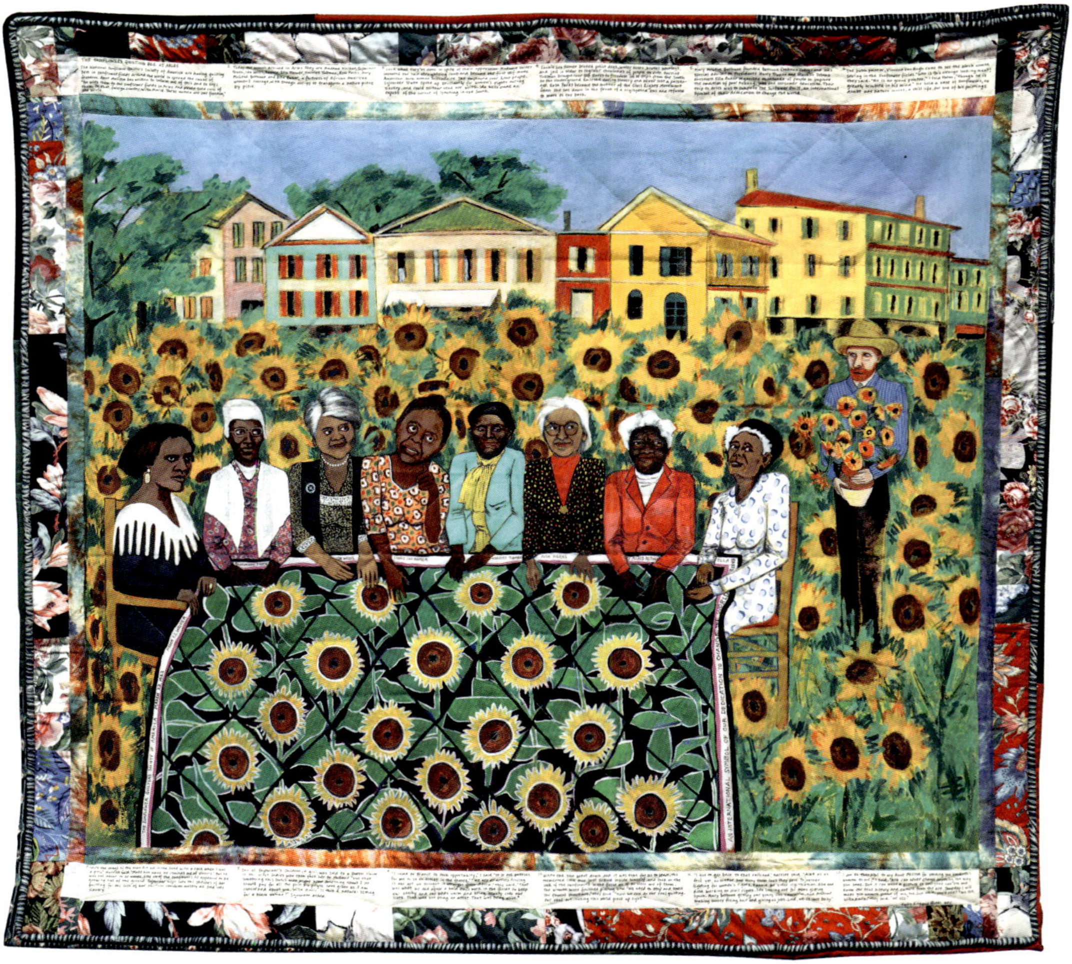

Fig.14 Faith Ringgold, *Quilting Bee at Arles*, 1991, acrylic on canvas with pieced fabric border, 188 × 203.2 cm (74 × 80 in), ACA Galleries, New York

including Sojourner Truth, Ida Wells and Rosa Parks, seated regally around a quilt of sunflowers in a blooming field of the same flowers, while Vincent van Gogh lurks humbly in the background, holding a bouquet. Joyce J. Scott (b.1948) also began by making textile-based work but has, since the mid-1970s, used glass beads to create a hybrid of jewelry and sculpture. Her work's strongest influence, she says, was her mother, who made appliquéd and embroidered quilts – a patched-together form of bedcover that served, Scott points out, those too poor for store-bought blankets. Scott describes her mother's quilts as 'picture books made of cloth'.[48] In her own beadwork, Scott uses a 'peyote stitch' taught to her by an Indigenous woman, sometimes augmenting it with

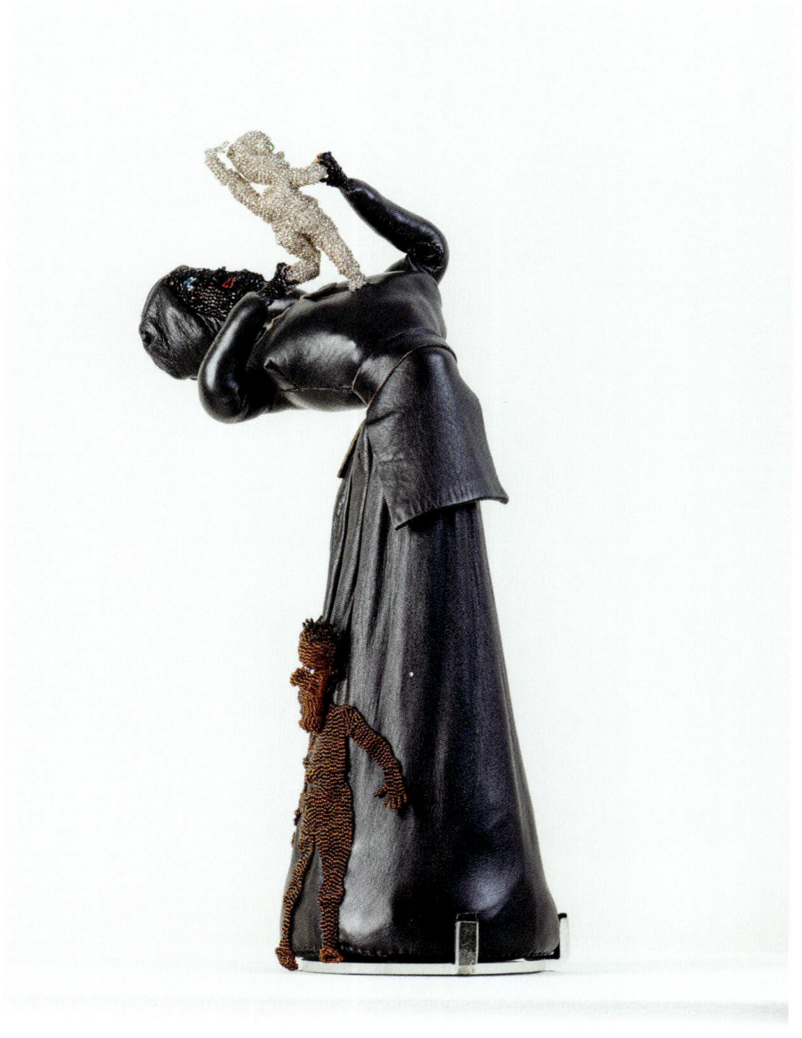

Fig.15 Joyce J. Scott, *No Mommy Me I*, 1991, leather, beads, thread, 38.1 × 15.2× 15.2 cm (15 × 6 × 6 in), Hort Collection, New York

blown glass elements and other materials. Her freestanding sculptures honor the quietly heroic roles Black women have played, from a nurse-maid – shown holding a white baby aloft while a Black child clings to her skirt, beseeching attention (fig.15) – to Harriet Tubman, represented as an extravagantly haloed Buddha, seated in full lotus position and spilling jewels from her hands. There is also a series of small, ferocious sculptures, called *Day After Rape*, acknowledging victims of sexual assault in conflict zones. The delicacy of Scott's beadwork draws viewers in close, sometimes to surprise them with expressions of pain and always to offer unexpected complexity. Along with their beauty, Scott's sculptures, like much work involving highly skilled, fine-boned craft, produce a kind of wonder: it has the persuasive force of commitment shown by any clearly difficult, dedicated labor.

On the other hand, art writer Susan Tallman suggests, handcraft was valued by some feminist artists of the 1970s precisely for the opportunity it offered to celebrate rough edges. 'When Miriam Schapiro and Faith Ringgold took up needle and thread, it was understood as a strategic choice, rich with underdog cultural associations', Tallman argues. For them 'amateurism with regard to artisanship became a mark of professionalism with regard to art'.[49] Subverting the domestic arts by flouting the rules of skilled craft could also be a way of challenging conventional femininity for women expressing their queer identity. Art historian Julia Bryan-Wilson has explored this connection with regard to Harmony Hammond (b.1944) whose *Floorpieces* of 1973 (fig.16) are hooked rugs made from fabric scraps that are coiled into circles, backed by fabric and selectively painted with bright colors, leaving some arcs of the fabric exposed.

Fig.16 Harmony Hammond, *Floorpiece VI*, 1973, cloth and acrylic, 167.6 × 167.6 cm (66 × 66 in), collection of the artist

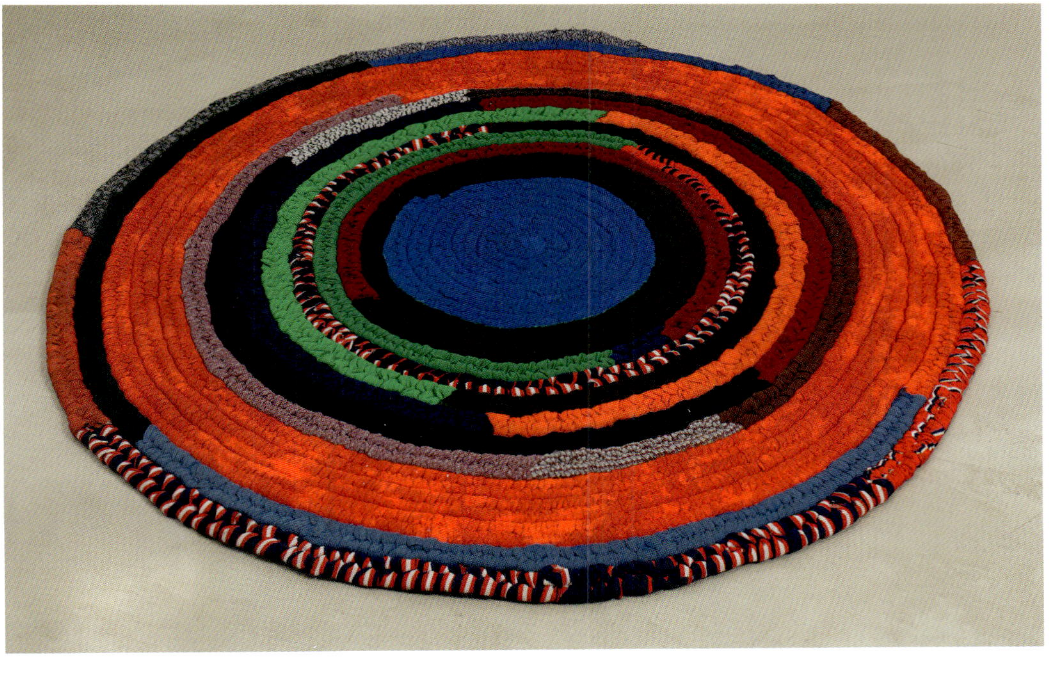

Meant to be placed on the floor, they are, Hammond has said, 'lateral paintings'.[50] Likened to the ringed circular paintings of early modernist Sonia Delaunay, on the one hand, and to Native American coiled pottery and basketry on the other, they have also been compared to the metal tiles Carl Andre placed on the floor. 'To understand the *Floorpieces* as queer craft is to assert a feminist art history that is defiantly lesbian as well as sensitive to class', Bryan-Wilson claims in saluting the work's 'queer orientations'. It is an orientation chosen for subversion. 'Few artists in 1973 were as dedicated as Hammond was to bringing art down while also bringing textile craft up',[51] Bryan-Wilson argues. For her part, Hammond spoke of a 'desire to break down the distinction between painting and sculpture, between art and women's work, and between art in craft and craft in art'.[52] Aligning her efforts with those of local garment workers (she was living in New York's SoHo at the time), Hammond claimed an affiliation also asserted by Andre, who was a founding member of the Art Workers' Coalition and (like Serra) boasted of his blue-collar bona fides. Nonetheless, Andre was appalled when his floor pieces were called rugs, even though he invited viewers to walk on them – unlike Hammond, who made it clear that her work was for viewing, not for using.

Hammond has lived for many years in New Mexico where she was a friend of the painter Agnes Martin, who was also close with Lenore Tawney (Martin was likely Tawney's romantic partner for a time). Against the evidence, Martin adamantly resisted comparisons between her own work and Tawney's, or any other form of weaving, including the Navajo blankets with which Martin's painting has also been linked. Her resistance was as strong as the stakes were high; Martin didn't want to be thought a craftsperson (nor a feminist, nor a lesbian, nor even, she once said, a woman); she was certainly not alone among female artists resisting the label of craftswoman. Perhaps no one better expressed the conflicted feelings roused by these competing identities, voluntary and imposed, than Louise Fishman, a proud lesbian who, after producing a series of stitched, stapled and woven paintings in 1971, introduced a suite of paintings on paper in 1973 that summarized her position at the time. Each painting was emblazoned with the first name of a woman Fishman admired – Djuna (for Barnes), Marilyn (Monroe) and Gertrude (for both Stein and Fishman's mother) – preceded by the word *Angry*. The names are painted mostly in caps and all in slashing brushstrokes.

One thinks of the sharply pointed tools that so many textile artists use, and one thinks of Madame Defarge in Dickens's famous novel of the French revolution, *A Tale of Two Cities*, knitting and knitting and encoding the names of those to be guillotined: a notorious villain but also an avenger raging against the violence done by the aristocracy and the patriarchy against her powerless sister.

Shameless Beauty

Decorous though they are, a spirit of resistance also simmers in the elegantly embroidered and printed wall hangings, influenced by silk Tibetan *thangkas* and hung from dowels, that Faith Ringgold created prior to her story quilts. Textiles can tell stories about cultural exchanges and unexplored formal histories, even when they are not figurative. The highly developed and individualized geometries in quilts crafted by several generations of female residents of Gee's Bend, Alabama, derive from patterns initially made by women who were enslaved and are influenced as well by Native American textiles; they started to gain attention outside the small community of their origin in the 1960s but only found widespread appreciation in the 21st century. While they have, slowly, established a place in encyclopedic and modern art museums, they keep one foot planted in the world of decorative, functional art. Along with their wordless, purely visual content, the Gee's Bend quilts carry a history of resilience and survival and an embrace of invention within the context of deep-seated tradition.

The twist made by the so-called Pattern and Decoration (P&D) artists who came together in 1975 was to convert such content into paintings in a head-on challenge to distinctions between the decorative and 'fine' arts. Their goal, as explained by John Perreault, a critic who organized a 1977 P&D show at New York's then-new art space PS1, was to make work that was 'non-sexist, historically conscious, sensuous, romantic, rational, decorative'.[53] A further aim was to challenge cultural barriers. 'Once we get rid of our cultural bias against Third World art, "decorative" art, and traditional women's art, we may be able to break down the superficial elitism of Western abstract Art', Perreault wrote, adding, 'One characteristic of significant new art is that it calls attention to aspects of the world previously invisible to, or not attended to by consciousness'.[54] He also cited as a precedent Miriam Schapiro's celebration of 'anonymous women fabric designers and homebound needleworkers'.[55] Joyce Kozloff (b.1942), a leading figure in the P&D movement and an inveterate antiwar and feminist activist, affirmed, 'What I learned from the anonymous artist of the past was that decoration at its most glorious can create and articulate centers of sociality for whole communities'.[56] She did so herself in paintings that reflected her interest in the geometric complexity of Islamic patterning she'd seen in mosques on a trip to Morocco. In 1978, responding, she said, to questions she repeatedly received about why she wasn't breaking down hierarchies further – why she was 'taking from crafts and making paintings',[57] thereby confirming the latter's status – she completed *An Interior Decorated*, an installation that spanned the walls and floor with ceramic tiles and fabric hangings in a glorious profusion of pattern and color.

Thirty years later philosopher and art critic Arthur Danto argued that P&D's achievement was to insist that 'from the perspective of meaning, decoration was on a footing with figurative or abstract art, and that the impulse to decorate was the impulse to humanize'.[58] Affirming Kozloff's leading role, and her 'early step into a globalist aesthetics', he added that 'it is a genuine insight to recognize, as Joyce Kozloff did, that there is "a third category of art which is neither representational nor abstract" – the ornament, pattern, and decoration'.[59] Also looking back from 2007, Perreault addressed the group's gender politics, acknowledging that its predominance of female artists explained a reliance on 'women's decorative art traditions' but suggesting that for men, too, 'decoration is the art lover's secret (apparently shameful, and therefore most cherished) love'. Before P&D, Perreault wrote, 'artists lived in fear of having their works called decorative'.[60] It remains a measure of the work's brave risk-taking that such fear has never really gone away.

A 2021 exhibition revisiting the movement suggests its undiminished importance,[61] while also drawing attention to its affinities with the main currents in contemporary art at the time it appeared: a considerable portion of the painting associated with P&D very closely resembles not only weaving but also the grids that are a staple of minimalism. Among the many exceptions were exquisitely complex sculptures by Pat Lasch and fanciful wallpaper by Cynthia Carlson, both made with paint extruded from pastry tubes. If the connection to sweet confections is firmly identified as feminine, the novel gender balance in P&D was certainly one of its most significant features. While the group's energy was driven by pioneering women who had repositioned domestic arts and functional forms – from baking to wallcovering – as fine arts, men were conspicuously numerous, willingly associating themselves with women's concerns, rather than, as in immemorial convention, vice versa. The gender of the fiber arts movement's members had gone unremarked; with P&D, sexuality and gender identity were indisputably in play. The painted imagery by Kim MacConnel and Robert Zakanitch, much of it boisterously floral and suitable for textile design, were important contributions, as were Robert Kushner's outrageous costumes, modeled in runway-type performances by men and women and documented in video. Their legacy is deepened in Nick Cave's glorious, mournful 'Soundsuits', towering full-body garments made of beads, sequins, raffia, twigs and plastic flowers. Initiated as metaphorical suits of armor made in response to the brutal, racially motivated beating of Rodney King, they also express resilience and even joy. Grace and pleasure, humor and even frank hedonism were prevailing motives, too, for P&D. It was a tonic to see, in the 2021 exhibition, Frank Stella's colorful work of the 1970s in its context, where Stella's mandarin self-seriousness was taken down a notch; and it was delightful to find, in a big painting by Sylvia Sleigh, a gender-inverted harem, with portrayals of Scott Burton, Carter Ratcliff and other male friends of the artist lounging naked in a boudoir heavily draped with a myriad of boldly patterned blankets.

Institutions and Identities

Though P&D is rightly credited with bringing attention to global traditions in the decorative arts, the artists originally associated with it were almost all white. But by the mid-1980s there was growing condemnation of cultural borrowings that stripped Asian, African and South American cultural objects of their meaning in the interest of enlisting their visual forms for Western purposes. The Museum of Modern Art's infamous 1984 exhibition *'Primitivism' in 20th-Century Art: Affinity of the Tribal and the Modern* was a watershed in this regard; its presentation of tribal objects as foils for the visual appreciation of European modernist masters was the occasion for a vigorous critical debate between principal curator William Rubin and critic Thomas McEvilley. Henceforth, the spiritual and functional purposes of tribal objects would not be so easily ignored. The exhibition included a contemporary art section, in which women sculptors featured prominently; while the point intended was that these artists used techniques derived in some way from tribal craft traditions and materials – the wrapping of natural fiber around wood in Jackie Winsor's work, for instance, or Nancy Graves's totemic sculptures made of animal skins – their inclusion reinforced a link between the primitive and the feminine that went back at least to surrealism. Elaine Reichek's work of the time literally knit these issues together, bringing 'women's work' to bear on the depredations of colonialism. In a series from 1986 to 1987, she addresses the decimation of natives of Tierra del Fuego by apparently well-intentioned German missionaries, who donated clothing that was infested with germs against which the Indigenous people had no immunity. Reichek represented the Fuegians with knitted silhouettes based on early ethnographic photographs showing them masked and body-painted; the silhouettes were exhibited alongside reproductions of the photographs, generating questions about knowledge, translation and truth.

Other political uses of textile in the 1980s included, prominently, the AIDS quilt, conceived in 1985 to commemorate those who died of a disease that the US government, under President Reagan, refused to acknowledge. The quilt was first displayed in 1987, on the National Mall in Washington, DC. Initially there were 1,920 panels; by the end of a year-long tour, there were more than 6,000. The project drew on a long history not just of memorial quilts but also of cloth banners serving activist purposes, notably during the British suffrage movement in the years around 1911 and again with antiwar protests at Greenham Common in Berkshire, England. From the 1970s through the early 1980s, the Women's Peace Camp there became a center for handcrafted work, including embroidered and appliquéd banners that were directly descended from suffrage pennants. Hung on chain-link fences around the camp, the banners declared, Rozika Parker writes, 'a boundary between femininity and masculinity, between life and death, technology and nature, Good and Bad. Never before had the use of embroidery so clearly demonstrated the place of art in the splitting that structures and controls our society.'[62]

Not all women who engaged with decorative arts in the 1980s were promoting handcraft. Some were reconsidering the power politics of high-style fashion. The provocative cover image of the February 1982 issue of *Artforum*, chosen by editor Ingrid Sischy, showed a slender white woman wearing a dramatic, floor-length black dress designed by haute couturier of the moment Issey Miyake; the open neck of its broad-shouldered rattan bodice plunged to the model's waist. In an ironic counter move, Beverly Semmes fashioned traditionally lacy, velvety gowns with arms and skirts so lavishly abundant that they pooled on the floor. Judith Shea, on the other hand, produced cool gray felt sheaths, shadow-boxing with the power dressing of the eighties, when feminists concerned themselves with the corporatization of visual culture rather than nakedly exposing their own embodied experience. Revisiting the Bauhaus ethos of better living through more streamlined design, Andrea Zittel developed an unyieldingly deadpan line of A to Z clothing and furnishings, its stripped-down functionalism challenging, as did Sischy's *Artforum* cover, the distinction between art commerce and the rest of the retail world. Let's get tough, these women all seemed to say. Or at least, let's be skeptical about celebrating amateurism and its whiff of abjection.

Also reflecting the era's cool ironies, Rosemarie Trockel conflated the commercial and the domestic in her 'knitting pictures': framed monochrome or patterned panels, in various sizes, of machine-knitted wool. This model of hybridization had male proponents too. If Jeff Koons's hyper-inflated appropriations of various kinds of crafty kitsch tip from irony into simple cynicism, other male artists made more complex use of female-identified and/or homespun objects and techniques. Mike Kelley's *More Love Hours Than Can Ever Be Repaid* (1987) is a big, wall-hung assembly of crocheted blankets and stuffed animals that the artist found at thrift shops. The love hours of the title are devilishly ambiguous: do they designate the labor associated with these objects' creation (presumed to be handmade), or the love invested in them (presumably by unknown girls)? In either case, it's not clear whether Kelley was taking on the debt or compounding it. No such coolly stated calculations can be made with respect to Louise Bourgeois's late hand-stitched, plumply stuffed fabric sculptures of the 1990s – baby-doll versions of damaged souls, some locked in harrowing sexual embrace. In this work the association with childhood deepens the adult drama, as does the visible stitching, the painful trail of needles and, in some cases, the cold metal of prosthetic limbs.

The New Museum founder Marcia Tucker's 1996 exhibition *A Labor of Love* presented work that ranged from Liza Lou's full-scale representation of a suburban kitchen, rendered in colored beads (1991–6), to Jane Kaufman's *Embroidered, Beaded Crazy Quilt* (1983–5) to a tiny chair made by self-taught artist Michael Harms from carved soap, popsicle sticks, plastic and Brillo rust (1993). A stalwart feminist, Tucker explained the biases she was aiming to confront in a catalogue essay: 'Many of the skills employed to make the hand crafted, or highly detailed, or labor-intensive and time-consuming pieces in *A Labor of Love* have traditionally been considered women's work', she wrote. 'Because they were made within the domestic rather than the public sphere, were done for love rather than money, or were simply done by women . . . these handicrafts were ipso facto [considered] inferior to fine art.'[63] But her concerns weren't only with gender. Tucker condemned the 'Great White Hunter' attitudes evident in some forums for 'outsider' or folk artists, where such makers are presumed innocent or childlike and unable to speak for themselves. And she called out the troubling paradox that many among those who celebrated traditional crafts and folkways were neoconservatives, even white supremacists, who lumped 'folk' artists and craftspeople with people of color.[64] Astutely, too, she noted that the focus on 'authenticity' in handcrafted and self-taught work 'necessitates the presence of colorful artists' histories'. Hence, she explains, the artists in *A Labor of Love* were asked to write their own biographical statements, which appeared only in the exhibition's catalogue.

All the issues Tucker raised are still germane. In the 21st century, the handmade arts of early second-wave feminism returned in the form of a DIY aesthetic and an epidemic of 'de-skilling' in the arts; backstories that authenticate 'outlier' status (currently the preferred term) have not lost cultural capital. We are now deep in the age of the *artisanal*, a word associated with *craft*; it has coincided with the reign of the *curatorial*, a term born in religion and borrowed, with spiritual authority intact, by art. Curated clothes, and artisanal food and drink, blend seamlessly as companies market the discernment – and whiff of ethical superiority – of the first along with the dedicated labor of the second. The promise is of the ultimate luxury in a time of social distancing (a condition that preceded and will likely outlive the COVID-19 pandemic): attention from real people meeting individualized desires for durable objects providing comfort and pleasure. In a final twist, such objects can be useful for virtue signaling, otherwise known as *craftwashing*: if certified crafted or artisanal, the product is deemed pure, however spuriously. As Ezra Shales points out, the Internet, with its bottomless trove of advice and materials, has (ironically) boosted the capability for DIY craftsmanship.[65] But Shales also observes that the binary between handmade and commercially produced is false; *someone* is always at work, even if by operating a machine, and the consumer's pride in achieving a social good by buying something handmade is groundless. Moreover, ignoring the precariousness of most freelance handcraft plays into the governmental abandonment of social and economic safety nets for the labor force at large (as the art historian Claire Bishop observes in her 2012 book, *Artificial Hells: Participatory Art and the Politics of Spectatorship*). Not least important, the cultural origins of the crafted aesthetic (often ethnic and / or non-Western) are still largely ignored.

This, anyway, is the dark view of contemporary craft in art and in the commercial landscape more generally. But there is an abundance of recent artwork that is visibly, palpably manmade of organic materials that both acknowledges and transforms craft traditions. Arlene Shechet has developed a prodigiously inventive language of shape and color in her ceramic sculptures, while affirming her medium's inescapable link to usable vessels. The busts that Elise Siegel creates in glazed ceramic, while grounded in historical form, are clearly personal, their emotional complexity as vivid as their specificity (fig.17). Siegel's work is also endowed with the equally specific character of clay, its mutability, the unpredictability of glaze, its paradoxically fixed fluidity. Kathy Butterly's send-ups of fine chinaware, beaded and banded, thin-lipped and wasp-waisted, are glazed in the most ravishing shades and then engorged, slumped and slammed into parodies of elegance. Elisa D'Arrigo's ceramic sculptures bring a wry humor to the deformation of form, often incipiently human, that clay undergoes in the process of being built up, bent, propped, fired and glazed – processes whose metaphorical associations are decidedly relevant. The feminine is germane in all this work, not as advocacy but as baseline experience. Independent curator Ingrid Schaffner, who organized an exhibition of contemporary ceramics in 2009, wrote in its catalogue, 'feminism is the context that came up again and again in conversation with artists during studio visits'. Schaffner went on to note that while male and female artists

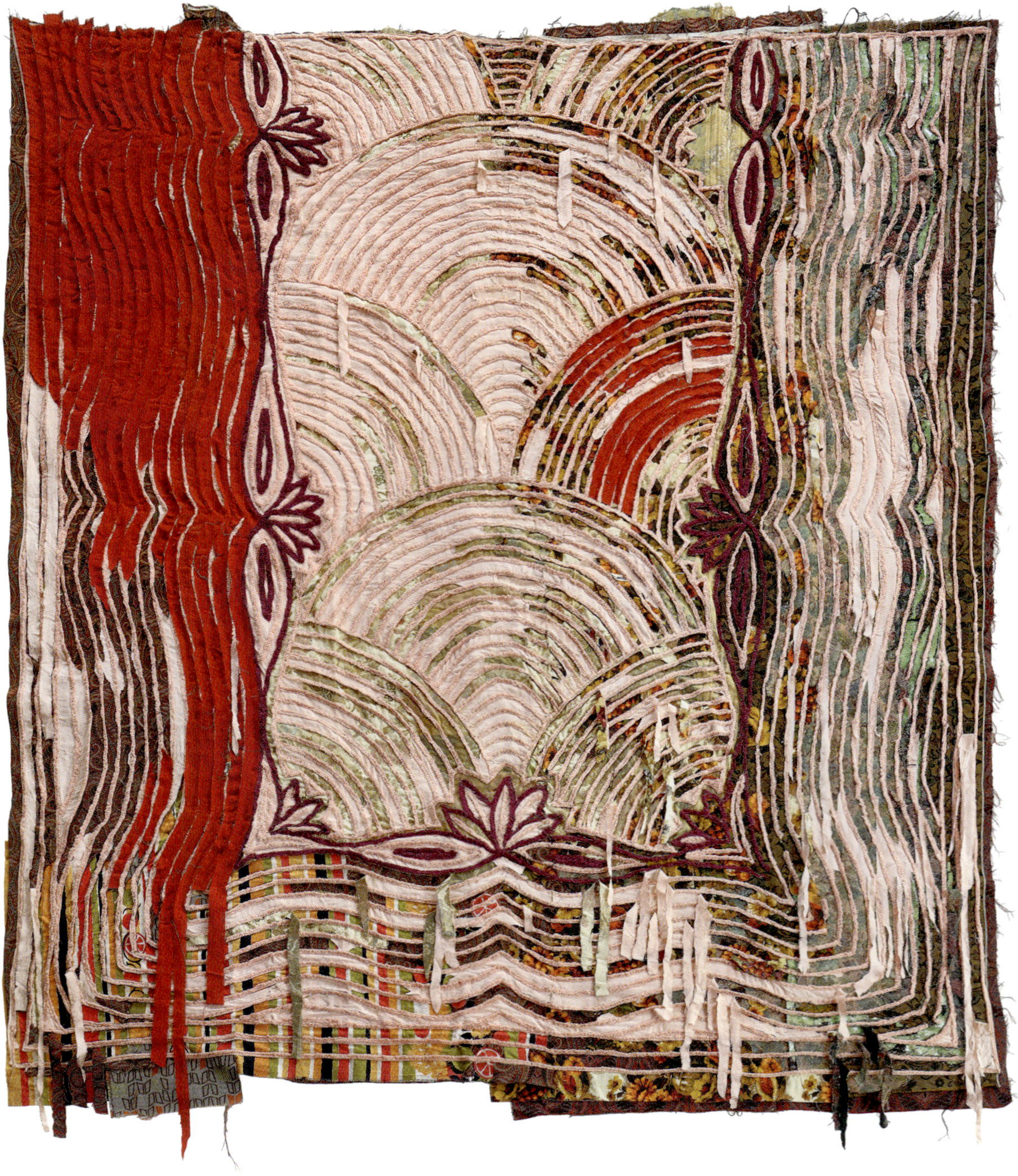

Fig.17 Elise Siegel, *Portrait Bust with Copper and Iron Stripes*, 2017, ceramic, underglazes, 72.4 × 35.6 × 22.9 cm (28 ½ × 14 × 9 in), collection of Ken Aptekar and Eunice Lipton

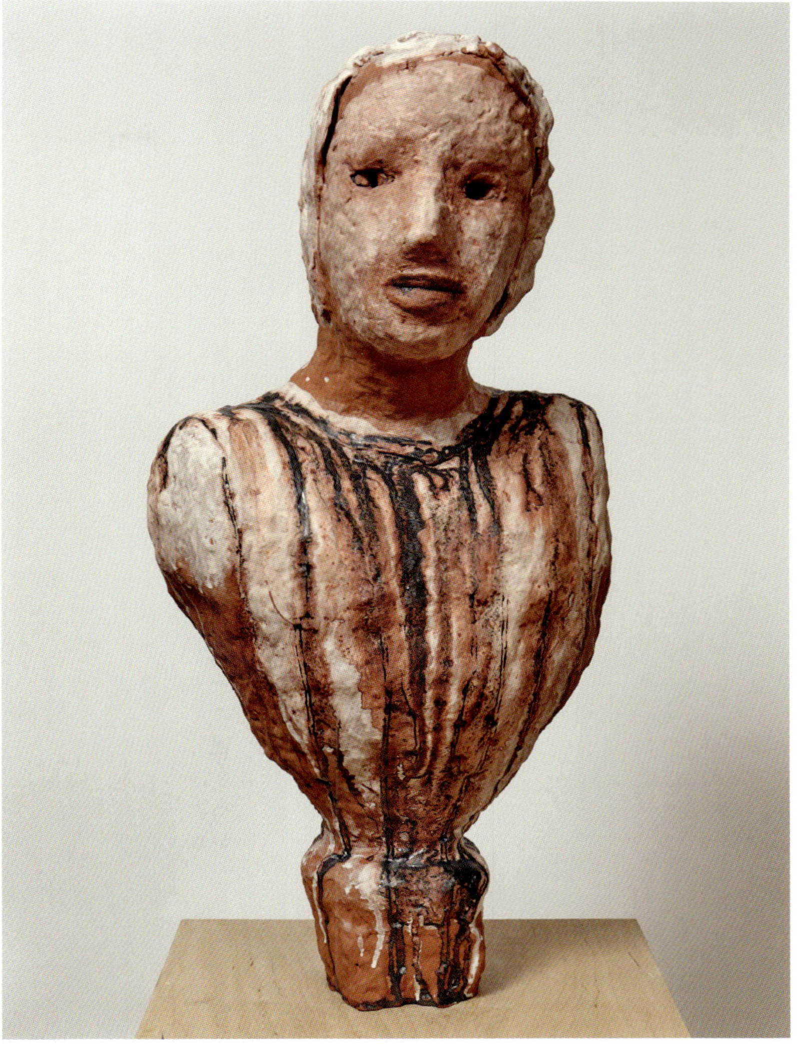

Fig.18 (left) Elana Herzog, *American Pastoral*, 2021, vintage chenille bedspread, mixed textiles, sewing thread, 266.7 × 233.7 cm (105 × 92 in), collection of the artist

alike were deploying strategies pioneered by women during the 1970s, they weren't always acknowledging their sources. 'It's high time,' she concluded, that 'feminists called in their debts'.[66]

In organizing the 2012 exhibition *A Cosmos* at the New Museum, Rosemarie Trockel presented her own multidisciplinary work amid a promiscuous mingling of art and nonart objects, including highly elaborated craft, in a kind of curatorial experiment that has since become commonplace. It can be seen within artworks as well as among them. Jessica Jackson Hutchins, for instance, trounces boundaries between object and image, domestic and public, as by plunking big, obstructive ceramic vessels onto couches and chairs. So does Jessi Reaves in mashups of salvaged furniture, old cars, paint, photographs and hardware. In another kind of compound form, Sabrina Gschwandtner has woven 'quilts' from lengths of salvaged 16mm films, several made by early, forgotten female directors; some filmstrips are from documentaries about textile production. The woven celluloid is shown on lightboxes, and tiny figures are visible in the illuminated frames. Elana Herzog first gained recognition for chenille bedspreads stitched directly into Sheetrock with industrial staples, creating glittering traces of tiny acts of violence; in work of the 2020s, she has been layering, stitching, embroidering and then peeling back various patterned fabrics gathered during her extensive travels, highlighting textile's role as a venerable stock of international trade, and as a register of ethnic, national, familial and personal identity (fig.18). In another, more arch variety of hybrid, this one grafting conceptualism and craft, Alex McQuilkin has stitched, in delicate letters on gauzy pink fabric stretched on embroidery hoops, choice sentences from Sol LeWitt's 1967 *Sentences on Conceptual Art*. Alternately stern, funny, cerebral and mystical, LeWitt's pronouncements are by now as firmly established in American art's roster of aphorisms as any adage sewn into 19th-century samplers.

Along with growing recognition of craft-allied work by young artists, amends have been made regarding older creators who were long overlooked. Suave, graceful pots by Ruth Duckworth, a deeply influential mid-20th-century American ceramicist, have recently regained attention, as have elegant vessels by Magdalene Odundo, a British artist born in Kenya, whose work is widely collected but who hadn't had a show in New York for 30 years before a 2021 exhibition. At the same time, long neglected contributions by craft-skilled women collaborating with their male partners are being recognized, including Patty Mucha's crucial contribution of sewing skills to Claes Oldenburg's early soft sculptures.

Among the most important aspects of the rising attention on craft-based art is its contribution to reconfiguring the contours defining maker, viewer and community. A pioneer in installation that involves active viewer participation, Ann Hamilton has long invited viewer participation in both intimate works and massive installations involving fabric, from *white-cloth* (1999), in which a sheet of silk was made to hover, ghostlike, over a large wooden table, to the billowing curtains that swung and swirled at,

Fig.19 Ann Hamilton, *The Event of a Thread*, 2012, Park Avenue Armory, New York, dimensions variable

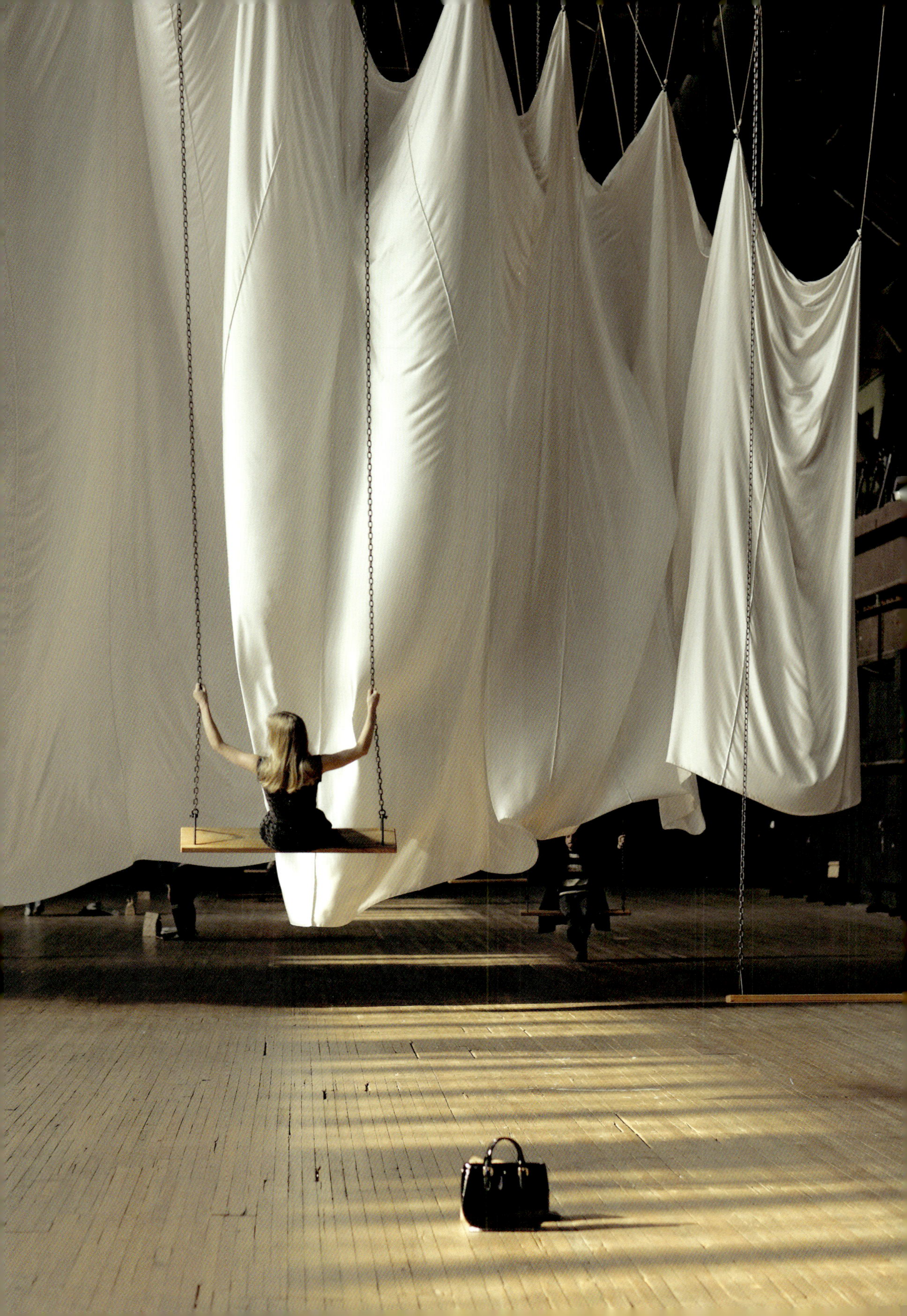

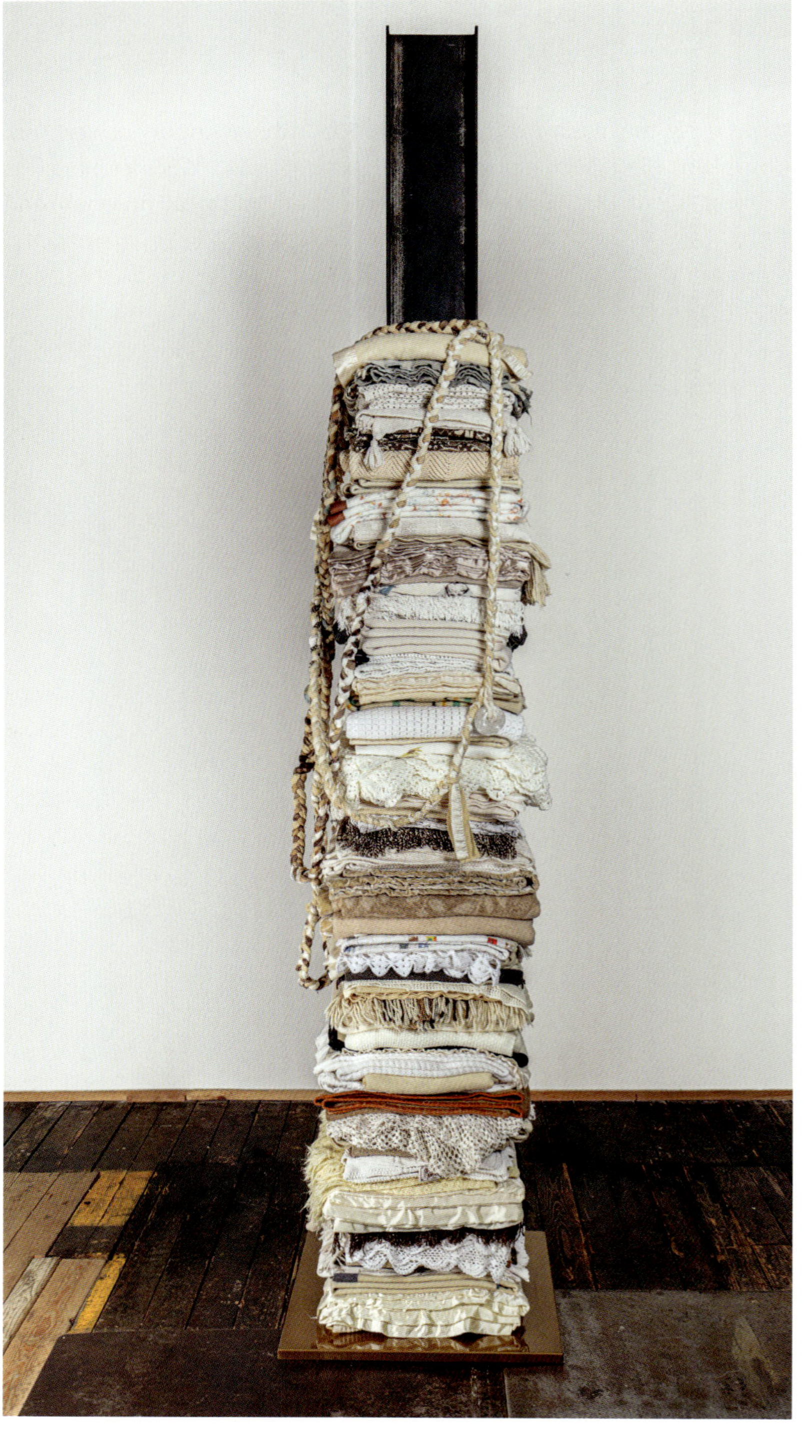

Fig.20 Marie Watt, *Skywalker/Skyscraper (Ghostwriter)*, 2022, steel I-beam, tiger gold base cap, reclaimed blankets, blown glass beads, 383.5 × 76.2 × 76.2 cm (151 × 30 × 30 in), collection of the Detroit Institute of Arts

respectively, the massive drill hall of the Park Avenue Armory in New York City in 2013 (fig.19) and a pier in Philadelphia in 2016.[67] 'My first hand was a sewing hand', Hamilton says, explaining, 'A line of thread drawn up and down through cloth influences how I think about the confluence and rhythms of space and time.'[68] The social pleasure of sewing, knitting and quilting circles has been recaptured by various 21st-century collectives and also by such individually led projects as Nene Humphrey's 'mourning braid' circles, in which participating women jointly form wire braids in multidisciplinary performances that refer to a 19th-century ritual of mourning originally involving human hair. Liza Lou enlisted a community of craftswomen in Durban, South Africa, to create scintillating beaded objects and installations. The Chicago-based artist Theaster Gates has, similarly, brought his Soul Manufacturing Corporation to several urban communities, collaborating with local arts organizations and their members to set up facilities that produce usable ceramic objects. Forging a community composed not so much of makers as of the viewing public, Sheila Pepe and Carrie Moyer collaborated on *Tabernacles for Trying Times* at the Portland Museum of Art in Maine in 2021,[69] integrating furnishings, paintings and webs of cord in an environment conducive to convening and reflection.

Still thriving, too, is the creation of work that puts craft to activist political purpose. Marie Watt, a member of the Seneca Nation whose ancestry is also partly German-Scot, in the early 2000s began making wall hangings and sculptures that employ blankets, some stacked and skewered with pointed dowels or I-beams (fig.20), others embroidered and hung on the wall. All allude to the lethal effects of germ-infested blankets given to Indigenous Americans. The legacy of pennants and quilts deployed by suffragist, antiwar and AIDS activists has recently been taken up by Cauleen Smith, whose big painted paired banners, hung prominently at the 2017 Whitney Biennial at the Whitney Museum, bear indelible images and words. In one example, there is a human eye pierced by a pencil on one side; the other reads, 'I'M SO BLACK THAT I BLIND YOU'.

Perhaps no combination of feminism and craft has recently had more potency than the hand-knit pink pussy hats that bloomed at the colossal Women's March in January 2017, following the inauguration of a US president who boasted of abusing women. The combined energies of feminism, craft and art have a kind and quantity of power that is still gathering force and seems unstoppable.

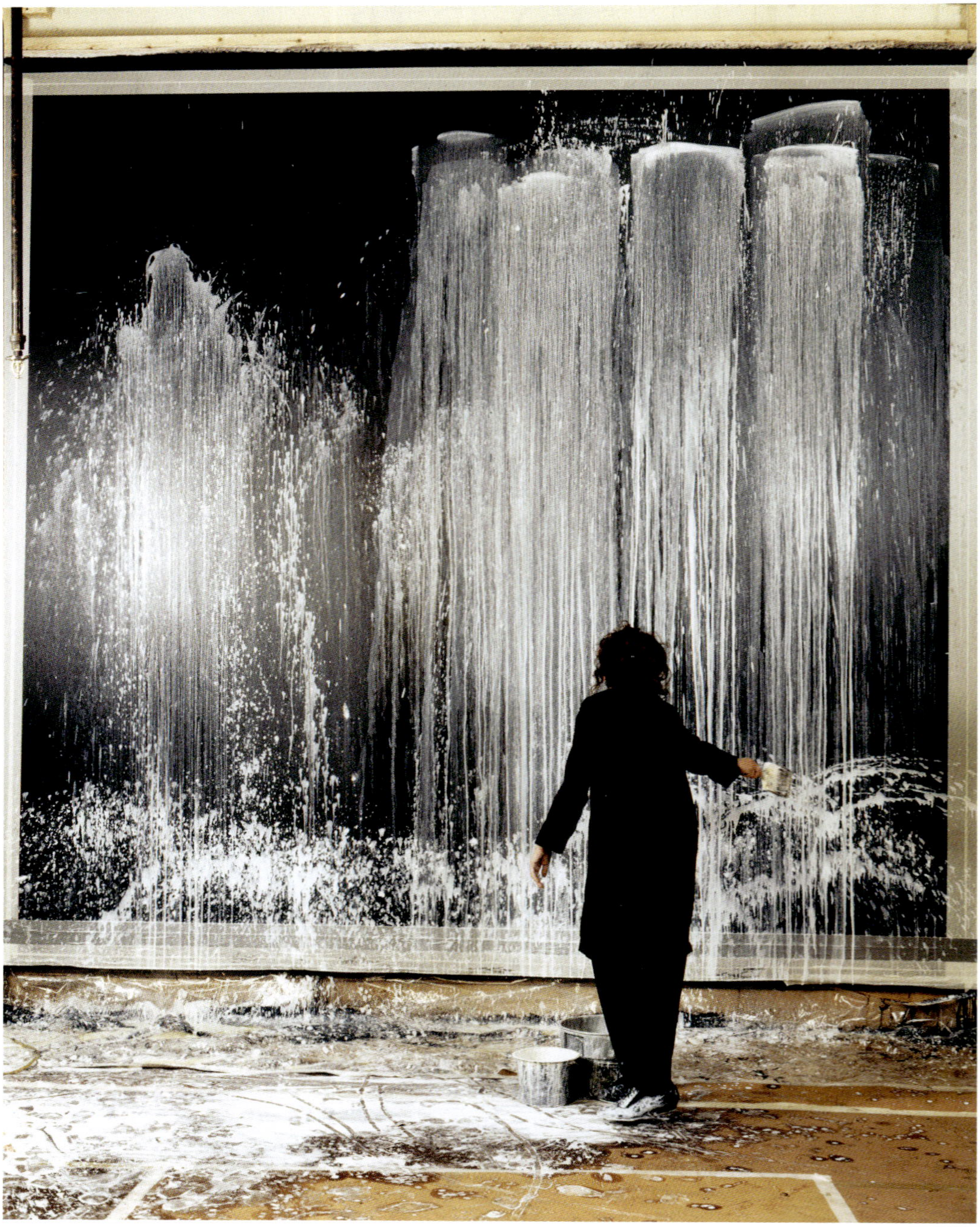

BEYOND TRAGIC AND TIMELESS

WOMEN, ABSTRACTION AND FEMINISM

Sue Scott

I want to reclaim abstract art for women and transform it on our own terms.[1]
—Harmony Hammond

For hundreds of years self-identified women around the world have been making abstract art that varies from the quilting tradition of Gee's Bend, which drew from African and Native American traditions, to the 19th-century spirit drawings of Georgiana Houghton, which were inspired by an astral guide. More recently, the important and comprehensive 2021 *Women in Abstraction* exhibition at the Centre Pompidou brought together abstract work in varied media by a multitude of women artists, spanning generations who were innovators and instrumental in taking abstraction in new directions. This exhibition included dance and photography as well as craft, painting and sculpture. The focus of the exhibition was not on rewriting the origin story of abstraction. The more important question it posed was how were the contributions of these women, so active and vital during their lifetimes, lost over time? And though there have always been women abstractionists working in other media and disciplines, this essay focuses primarily on painting, abstraction and feminism.

Over the years women artists working abstractly were excluded from critical discussions of feminism because, it was argued, their work was not politically motivated, not about making a statement. On the other hand, in her brilliant 1977 essay 'Feminist Abstract Art – A

Fig.21 Pat Steir in her studio, 1990

Political Viewpoint', published in *HERESIES: A Feminist Publication on Art and Politics*, the artist Harmony Hammond (b.1944) observes that for most critics and writers, the feminist sensibility stems from personal experience questioning larger political implications. She laments that most criticism focuses on these political issues or historically misogynistic attitudes and social mores rather than looking at the creative process itself and the meaning embedded within. So how do we discuss abstraction in a feminist context, if content is essential to feminist art? Hammond offers a solution.

'If', Hammond writes, 'women continue to respond to abstract art as "apolitical," they are reinforcing and maintaining myths established by men. It is the marking, making, language and repetition that women can not only connect with the tradition of women's work but also claim the process for themselves'.[2] In other words, innovation and invention are their own forms of feminism.

In the late 1970s the definition of feminist art was still being negotiated. In 1977, Ruth Iskin, Arlene Raven and Lucy Lippard organized an exhibition at the Women's Building in Los Angeles, asking artists 'What is Feminist Art?' The responses were as varied in medium – drawings, collages and written or typed statements on pieces of 8-by-10–inch paper – as they were in content. Titling her response, 'What feminist art is or might be . . .' Martha Rosler (b.1943) wrote, 'I think feminist art is, most fundamentally, a means of provoking critical awareness'. Joan Semmel (b.1932) saw it differently. 'Feminist Art for me is art which in some way expresses a concern with feminine consciousness. Paradoxically enough that very consciousness might be totally unconscious. How then can one define it? One cannot clearly do so.'[3]

Today the Museum of Modern Art in New York defines feminist art as art 'that seeks to challenge the dominance of men in both art and society, to gain recognition and equality for women artists, and question assumptions about womanhood'.[4] If abstraction does not fit neatly into any of these three categories, where does it fit? And how does it intersect with feminism? Is there a gendered aspect to abstraction? And if there is, what language can we use to discuss it? The changing answers to these questions over time help explain how the contributions of so many important women artists have been overlooked or lost.

As different as the two responses by Rosler and Semmel appear, taken together they offer insight for the discussion of feminism and abstraction. If, beyond the accepted notion of the personal and political, feminism can also be discussed in terms of breaking down the boundaries of ego and higher consciousness to get to the source of creativity (and if that source evokes critical awareness), perhaps we have a starting point for the discussion. This discussion has more to do with how the artist sees herself in relation to the universe and sees her art as a way of making connections, rather than reacting and commenting on societal interactions and hierarchies.

Certainly, abstraction is not the only place female artists have been innovators. As shown in the other essays in this volume, women were pioneers in the development of ecofeminism and in establishing it and performance art as viable art forms. And although restricted to the allowed pursuits such as pottery and weaving at the Bauhaus – not architecture, wood or metal working – Lenore Tawney found a way within these limitations to redefine fiber arts, moving it into the realm of fine art.

But painting remained the sphere of male artists. Women seeking to innovate or experiment with abstract painting were not so much staking out new territory or working within the confines allowed them (textiles, still life paintings), but instead by challenging established tradition, they were taking on the patriarchy and, in some cases, intentionally subverting convention. Abstraction in particular enabled women to challenge male ideas about authority – how it's expressed, who can claim it and where inspiration comes from.

'Why Have There Been No Great Women Artists?'

'Our research', the feminist art historian Griselda Pollock wrote, 'revealed that it was in fact only in the 20th century, with the establishment of art history as a widely taught, institutionalized academic discipline, that women artists were mathematically obliterated from the record'.[5] And as Linda Nochlin insightfully pointed out in her groundbreaking essay 'Why Have There Been No Great Women Artists?', men controlled the critical conversation and portals to education.

The simple decision of who gets included and who is left out can have devastating results. The now infamous 1951 *Life* magazine photograph of the leading lights of abstract expressionism, 'The Irascibles', featured only one woman, Hedda Sterne, who arrived late and was told by a member of the staff where to stand, ending up above, but apart from, the men posed below her. The rationale used by the male artists for this exclusion was that abstraction was such a foreign concept for the public to accept that men should make it first and the women could follow. 'They all were very furious that I was in it because they all were sufficiently macho to think that the presence of a woman took away from the seriousness of it all', Sterne said years later.[6] Lee Krasner (1908–84), a woman arguably more central to the vanguard movement than Sterne, was excluded. Unfortunately, the image in *Life* magazine became etched in the public's mind, and it was years before Krasner was acknowledged for her important contributions to abstract expressionism.

Another, perhaps more subtle, exclusionary factor is that, often, incorrect labels were applied to innovations or styles, and then the women were faulted for not meeting the labels' mandates. Take for instance Anne Truitt, who though she didn't consider herself a minimalist, was dubbed one by the critic Clement Greenberg and then criticized for not complying with the minimalist credo of hard-edge and machine-made materials. This is particularly egregious during the era of abstract expressionism and minimalism, when critics such as Greenberg and Harold Rosenberg held sway, but it is repeated throughout the later 20th century as well.

The Af Klint Effect

Consider the Swedish artist and spiritualist Hilma af Klint (1862–1944; Fig.22). Like her contemporaries Kazimir Malevich (1879–1935), Piet Mondrian (1872–1944) and Wassily Kandinsky (1866–1944), the acknowledged fathers of abstraction, af Klint was grappling with ways to connect consciousness or materiality with spirituality, a quest that was moving them all in the direction of abstraction. She made her first abstract paintings in 1906, several years before Kandinsky. Yet while these men were canonized, af Klint was essentially ignored for a century. She only

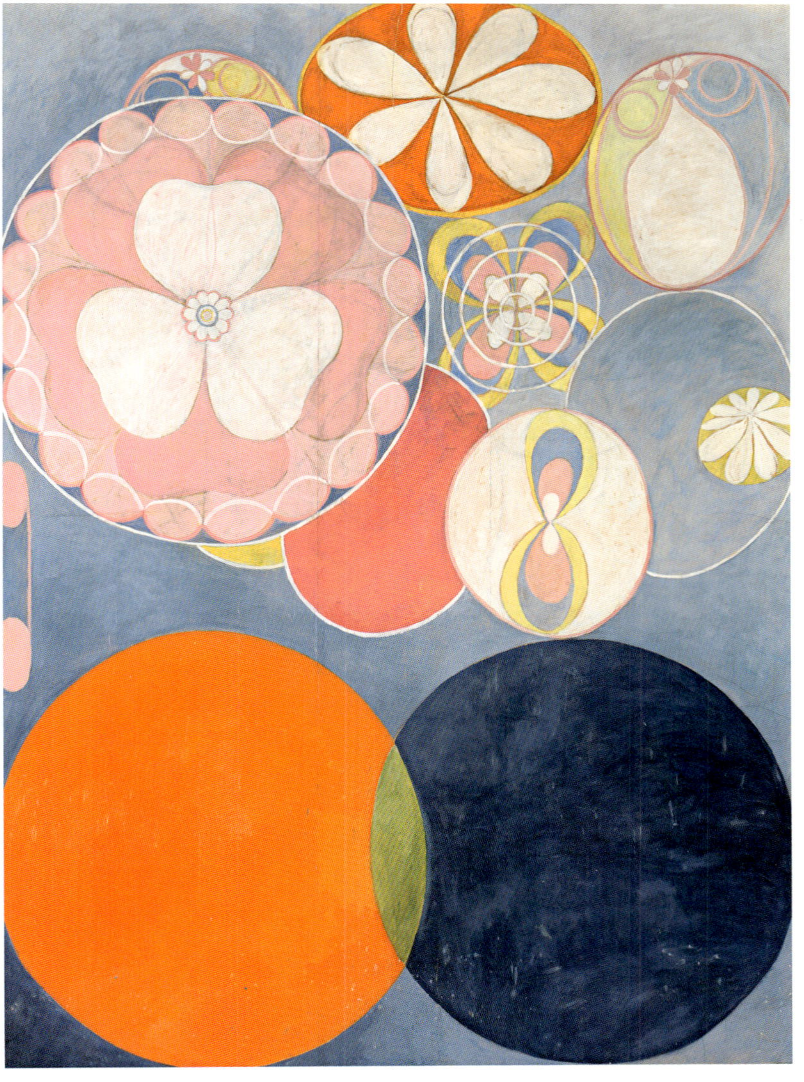

Fig.22 Hilma af Klint, *Group IV, The Ten Largest, No. 2 Childhood*, 1907, tempera on paper, mounted on canvas, 315 × 234 cm (124 × 92 in), Hilma af Klint Foundation, Stockholm, Sweden

came to the attention of the art world in 1985, when she was included in the exhibition *The Spiritual in Art: Abstract Painting 1890–1985* at the Los Angeles County Museum of Art.

Though af Klint was given prominence in *The Spiritual in Art* exhibition and catalogue by the curators, she was disparaged by the likes of *New Criterion* critic Hilton Kramer, who wasn't content just to dismiss af Klint's work as 'essentially colored diagrams' not worthy to be placed alongside Kandinsky, Mondrian, Malevich and Kupka. He further dismissed af Klint stating, she 'would never have been given this inflated treatment if she had not been a woman'.[7]

Yet af Klint was active in the Swedish art world and had graduated from the Royal Academy of Fine Arts with honors. She was aware of many advancements in science and art. She knew Rudolf Steiner (1861–1925), the philosopher and president of the German Theosophical Society, met Kandinsky and attended lectures by Annie Besant (1847–1933), leader of the Theosophical Society after Madame Blavatsky.

In 2018, 70 years after her death, af Klint finally received a comprehensive retrospective at the Guggenheim Museum in New York. For *Hilma af Klint: Paintings for the Future,* her paintings and drawings occupied the spiral interior of the museum as if they were made for it. And perhaps they were. When af Klint was instructed by her spiritual guides to make the 193 *Paintings for the Temple* between 1906 and 1915, she was told they would one day fill a circular alabaster temple, an apt description of the interior of the modern-day white ziggurat on Fifth Avenue.

The exhibition broke the museum's attendance records and catalogue sales. The works were fresh and generated a sense of discovery in the audience. What exactly made them so radical? First, the scale: *The Ten Largest* were painted on the floor as if anticipating later abstract expressionist work, which took painting beyond the easel. Even with their abstract imagery, the individual titles of *The Ten Largest* have a deeper meaning in the way they allude to the stages of life: childhood, youth, adulthood, old age. Second, the palette: childhood in its rich blues and pinks, early adulthood a strong terracotta and later adulthood fading to a paler palette. Third, the space is flat, nonillusionistic, without a single point perspective, which af Klint was certainly capable of executing as she had shown in her representational work. Finally, hidden spiritual messages, looping words with real or made-up meaning, Rosicrucian imagery and planetary and astrological symbols and diagrams put the following question front and center: How is it that af Klint wasn't considered a pioneer of abstract painting?

Clement Greenberg, Jackson Pollock's first critic and the most important critic in the postwar era, argued in the 1950s that contemporary art was moving teleologically toward two-dimensionality. His formalist theory stressed the importance of the flatness of the picture plane, promoted pure open color and space as content, and dismissed figuration and meaning. He praised artists such as Helen Frankenthaler, Morris Louis and Ken Noland for their use of thinned acrylic paint on unprimed canvas because when it soaked into the weave of the painting, this flatness was accentuated. Even as Greenberg's influence has diminished over the years, this notion of purity has haunted our understanding of abstraction.

A deeper understanding of abstraction causes us to ask: doesn't the intertwining of meaning and form make the work more complex and layered, but no less pure? As Helen Molesworth notes in the introduction to the af Klint's retrospective catalogue, 'One can be an artist and make something that looks and behaves a lot like a painting, but it might also be functioning as something else as well'.[8] Automatic drawing and trance states are revelatory and can be confusing or challenging to decipher, even by the recipient. It is interesting here to consider when the sources are external and when they are internal.

In a sense, af Klint gave up authorship to someone outside herself, becoming both medium and artist. The paintings were channeled during séances and automatic writing from directions given by her astral teachers Gregor, Amaliel and Ananada. Af Klint worked collaboratively with four other women, a group called De Fem (The Five), for more than a decade with weekly séances, which yielded automatic writing sessions. She had clearly developed a technique for tapping into her creativity, for finding the inner fountain of inspiration almost at will.

In the same catalogue, the artist Amy Sillman (b.1955) makes an interesting point regarding af Klint's direct link to the other world by addressing the question of who has the authority to create something new, something different. 'If you're dealing with sexism, which clearly would have been the case in the early 1900s, you're always being minimized and marginalized. I get the feeling that Hilma turned that into a productive form of privacy, and her mysticism is a flip on modernism: she says, "I received this," rather than "I invented this."'[9] For af Klint, this authority couldn't be questioned; it was coming from a source greater than herself, connected to the universe.

Thought Forms, published in 1905 by Theosophist leaders Annie Besant and C.W. Leadbeater, argues that specific thoughts take on forms and that one can be taught to see, or read, these forms. The authors illustrated forms that they believed were generated by thought:

intellectual connection can be seen as a thought-form that is a yellow cloud; ambition is orange and spiky; feelings of devotion are blue and hazy or hard-edged depending on the piety of the thinker. Kandinsky had a copy in his library; af Klint was a Theosophist and most certainly knew the book. Without publication of *Thought Forms*, abstraction may not have developed when and how it did.

Af Klint 'was already exploring gender shifts', with Anna Cassell, one of the younger members of De Fem, according to Julia Voss in her excellent biography of Hilma af Klint.[10] It's interesting that the imagery of the snail, both a hermaphroditic motif and a symbol of creation, was repeated often in these early drawings and appears in later work. As she and Cassell made drawings and notes, af Klint referred to herself as 'Asket', a male name, and Cassell was 'Vestal', a feminine name.

Af Klint spent the remainder of her life cataloging and analyzing the abstractions she had channeled and desperately seeking an audience for the work, not for the purpose of sales but as work to inspire 'fellow seekers'. As much as she tried, af Klint never found that audience, nor saw the temple built. Eventually she mandated that her paintings not be shown until twenty years after her death, a time when, she hoped, her paintings would be better understood and accepted. This embargo turned into forty years as the paintings languished in the attic of her nephew Eric af Klint. By the time any of the works were shown, the canon was set.

The systematic erasure of the contributions of women is also endemic in the sciences. Science historian Margaret W. Rossiter's essay entitled the 'The Matthew Matilda Effect in Science' describes this bias that denies or downplays the achievements of women scientists.[11] The name recognizes abolitionist author and suffragette Matilda Joslyn Gage, who in 1883 wrote an essay entitled 'Woman As Inventor' in which she enumerates inventions by women for which they were neither credited nor compensated.

Gage's conclusions about women in science anticipate Nochlin's observations about the art world 80 years later. Gage writes,

> While, as has been shown, many of the world's most important inventions are due to woman, the proportion of feminine inventors is much less than of masculine, which arises from the fact that woman

> does not possess the same amount of freedom as man. Restricted in education, industrial opportunities, and political power, this is one of many instances where her degradation reacts injuriously upon the race. Most inventions are the result of much consideration and self-reliant thought. Inventors must not only possess full freedom to exercise their powers, but there must also be a certain welcome and protection to their ideas. Deprived, as woman is, of political power, she has to face contempt of her sex, open and covert scorn of womanhood, depreciatory allusions to her intellectual powers, – all tending to hamper the expression of her inventive genius.[12]

Women's inventions have been important contributions to science and the economy. Betsy Metcalf was twelve years old when, in 1798, she made a straw hat that spawned an entire industry in Massachusetts. Sarah Mather was granted the patent in 1845 for the first glass-bottom telescope for viewing sunken ships and the ocean floor. In 1891 Margaret Knight not only invented a machine for manufacturing the satchel-bottomed bag but she also held the patent and formed her own production company.

Erasure

Certainly, there is an 'af Klint effect' in the art world, where the contributions of women artists are either marginalized, not considered or lost to the sands of time. Consider the nuances of erasure as they affect accomplished women artists. Helen Frankenthaler (1928–2011; fig.23), Joan Mitchell (1925–92) and Grace Hartigan (1922–2008) were active from the early 1950s during an extremely fertile, prefeminist time in the New York art world as it grappled with the breakthroughs of abstract expressionism. As young artists, Hartigan and Frankenthaler were included in an important exhibition in 1951 at the Tibor de Nagy Gallery called *The New Generation,* which was a more apt description than 'second generation', which connotes a follower not an innovator.

'Frankenthaler, Hartigan and Mitchell achieved critical and curatorial esteem because of their artistic accomplishments', Daniel Belasco notes in his essay 'The Best of Everything: Women in the New York School', 'and also because, as women, they exemplified their generation. Many

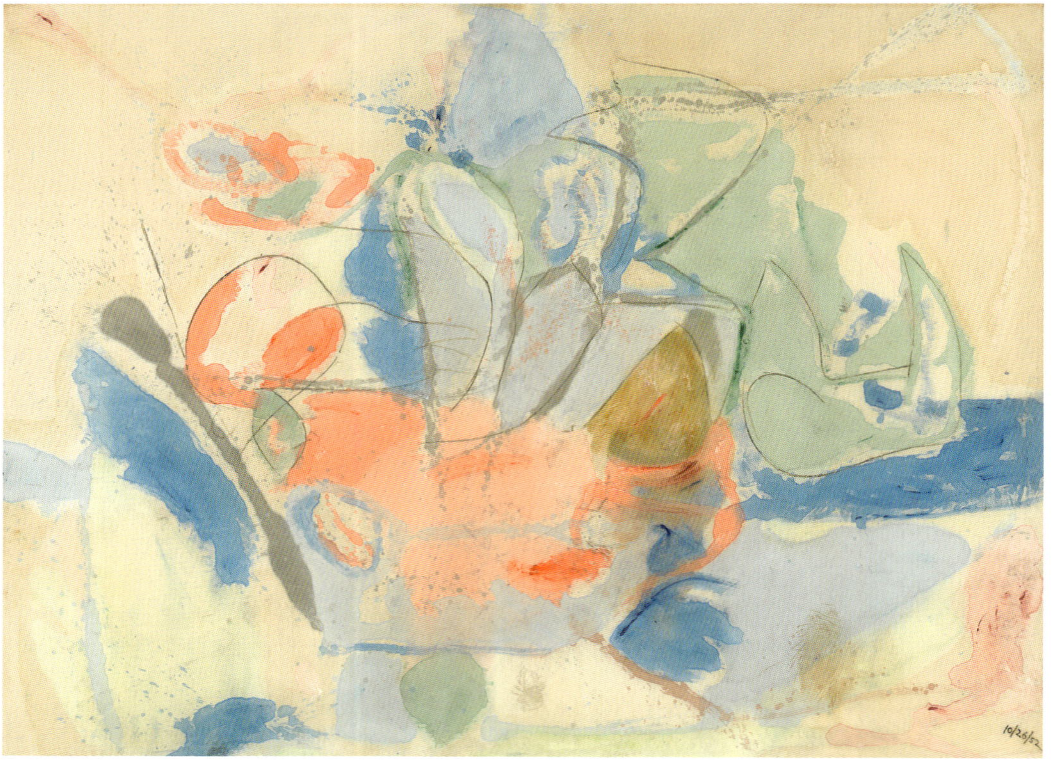

critics perceived the painting of the entire second generation – men and women – as emotional and intuitive, and thus female'. But he goes on, 'The feminist art movement of the 1960s developed in the United States simultaneously with the canonization of Abstract Expressionism and elimination of women from its history. This was not a coincidence'.[13]

Frankenthaler was 23 years old when she made her breakthrough, iconic painting *Mountains and Sea* (1952). What is so radical, so inventive, about this painting that to this day is acknowledged as one of the great paintings of the 20th century? Frankenthaler first built a structure using charcoal drawings. The drawings are overlaid with washes of turpentine-thinned paint, 'soak stain' as Frankenthaler called it, in the palest, most delicate, feminine colors of rose pink, sage green and robin's-egg blue, that both delineate and layer space. Raw canvas frames the forms. The process came out of concepts Frankenthaler had been thinking about for months, and the imagery – clearly references to cliffs, sea and sky – came from numerous watercolors she had made during a trip to Nova Scotia in the summer of 1952.

Fig.23 Helen Frankenthaler, *Mountains and Sea*, 1952, oil and charcoal on unsized, unprimed canvas, 219.4 × 297.8 cm (86 3/8 × 117 1/4 in), Helen Frankenthaler Foundation, New York, on extended loan to the National Gallery of Art, Washington, DC

The painting is both abstract and referential. The blue washes of color recall the ocean, the triangular green shapes the cliffs above. It was Frankenthaler's subversion of the tenets of abstract expressionism – her use of unprimed canvas, the staining and her references to landscape – that inspired Morris Louis's oft-repeated statement that Frankenthaler was a bridge between Pollock (1912–56) and what was possible. Not Pollock's 'I am nature' but the dissolution of nature, a reinterpretation. There is bravery in the way Frankenthaler negotiates between deliberation and accident, understanding there is no turning back once the paint is poured.

While Pollock's work was proclaimed heroic, Frankenthaler's was described as lyrical, both for the soft-edged forms and the pastel palette she often favored. This was not an incorrect description, unless lyrical represents feminine and feminine is considered lesser. Unsurprisingly, Frankenthaler resisted the categorization. 'Looking at my paintings as if they were painted by a woman is superficial, a side issue, like looking at Kline's and saying they are bohemian. The making of serious painting is difficult and complicated for all serious painters. One must be oneself, whatever.'[14] And being herself was what Frankenthaler did for her entire career, continuing to make paintings on a massive scale, soaking the canvas with color to make form. Yet this was not without costs.

In writing about Frankenthaler's work in 1969, Harold Rosenberg unwittingly draws a parallel with the mediumistic genesis of af Klint's work. 'With Frankenthaler', he wrote, 'the artist's action is at a minimum; it is the paint that is active. The artist is the medium of her medium.'[15] What exactly is he saying? Was this a handy way to divorce the artist from the action of making the painting, setting up a stark contrast between Frankenthaler and the masculine gestures – the action painting – of Jackson Pollock and Willem de Kooning? Whatever his intent, the opposite seems true. In acting as 'medium' for the paint Frankenthaler maintains authorship of the work.

What of the notion that Frankenthaler's staining and dripping on raw linen references the monthly bleeding of women? John Elderfield's essay entitled 'On Frankenthaler's Decisions' offers insights.[16] It was Eugene Goossen, who noting this staining on linen, observed that 'Frankenthaler's paintings are manifestly that of a woman' and feminist art historian Lisa Saltzman who decades later claimed Goossen's reference was literal: 'She bled on the sheets'. Elderfield notes that although this was not how critics interpreted Frankenthaler's work in the 1950s, others glommed on to it later, retroactively and metaphorically, to see the work through this lens. It was coded language, an association perhaps meant as derogatory, as opposed to interpreting the drips of Pollock as machismo and in stark contrast to the masculinity of hard-edged minimalism. Frankenthaler wasn't interested in having her work seen through this feminine lens, once telling a colleague that if she stained, then a lot of men did too. Yet it's through the cycles of menstruation that women realize the ultimate creation: life.

Perhaps the basis for this criticism had deeper roots. 'The development of this trope may be a sign of the critics' discomfort with the ascendance of women artists', Elderfield writes, 'which began in the years after the war but was only widely acknowledged in the late 1950s, and particularly at the end of the decade – the same period when the metaphor of staining began to appear'.[17]

But the fact remains there would have been no Color Field painting without Frankenthaler.

Exclusion

The story of exclusion is told not only through gender biases but also racial and socioeconomic challenges. A Black woman, Alma Thomas (1891–1978; fig.24) certainly experienced the limitations of racial and gender inequality throughout her life. But she continually transcended those limitations. Against all odds, Thomas escaped the Jim Crow South to become a celebrated artist. In 1907, when she was 16, her parents left Columbus, Georgia, for Washington, DC, because of limited educational opportunities. In Washington Thomas attended a segregated Black high school, graduated from the University of the District of Columbia and began teaching.

In her thirties, Thomas returned to school and became the first graduate of Howard University's art department in 1924. Thomas taught art at Shaw Junior High School in Washington for the next 35 years. She pursued her own painting on the side and was active in the local art scene and salons, organizing shows and taking graduate art courses at

Fig.24 Alma Thomas, *The Azaleas Sway With the Breeze*, 1969, acrylic and graphite on canvas, 162.6 × 127 cm (64 × 50 in), collection of halley k harrisburg and Michael Rosenfeld, New York

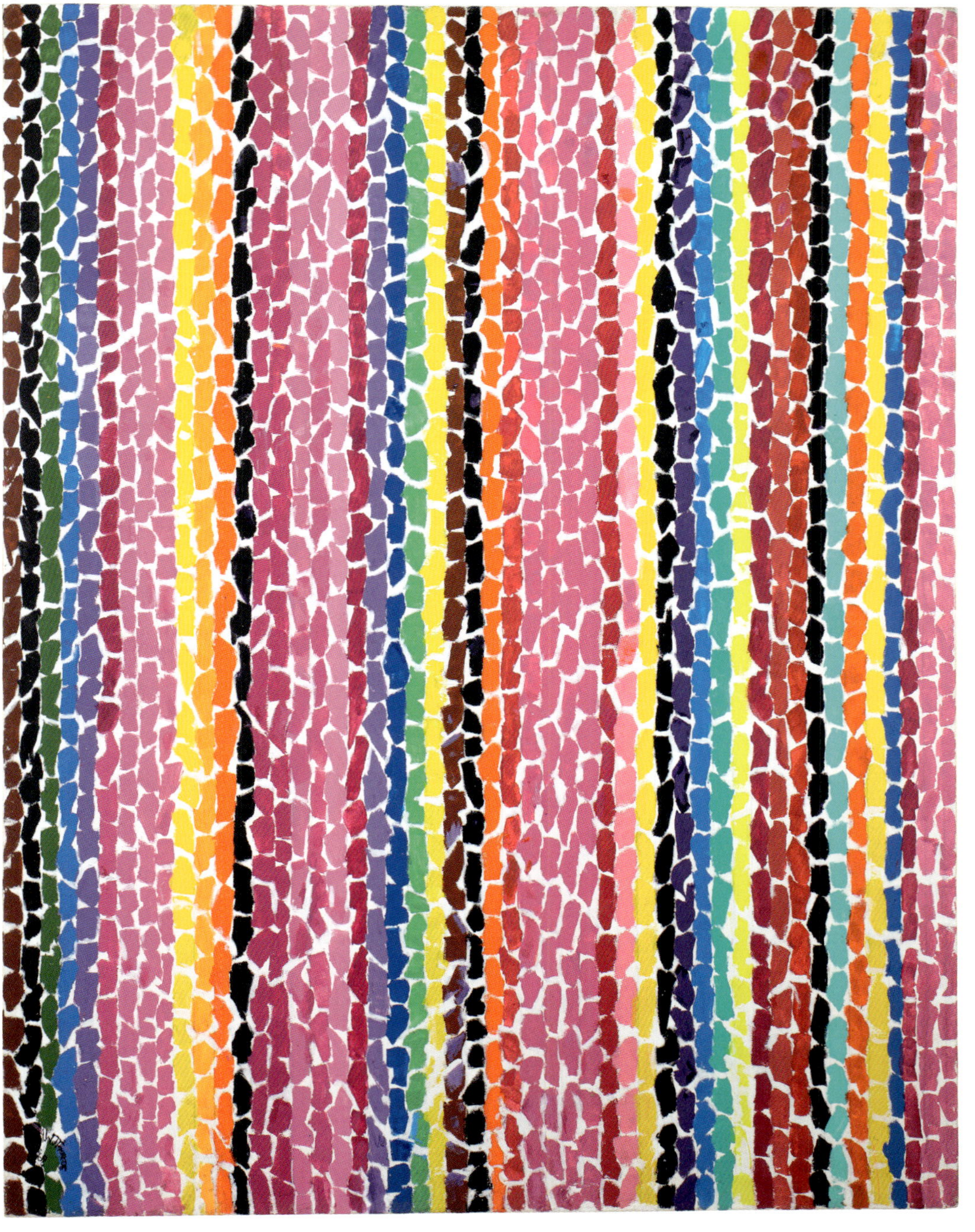

American University. She lived in her childhood home her entire life and never married. Thomas was 69 when she finally retired from teaching in 1960. Suffering from arthritis, she contemplated giving up painting but was offered a retrospective exhibition at Howard University. In preparing for the show, she developed a unique style of abstraction that referenced both the light and nature of her surroundings. She was clearly influenced by the bold, colorful targets and stripes of the Washington Color School painters – Morris Louis, Kenneth Noland and Gene Davis among them – artists who were making names for themselves as Thomas was retiring.

Equally influential was an exhibition of Henri Matisse's gouaches Thomas saw in 1961 at the Museum of Modern Art in New York. Thomas's paintings have been compared to mosaics or a form of enlarged pointillism. One can also see echoes of Matisse's colorful late cut-paper collages in Thomas's quick brushstrokes, spaced in uneven patterns of circles or columns. Like Matisse, whose mobility was limited when he made these collaged gouaches, Thomas's struggle with arthritis may have had a hand in her decision to move into this limited gestural abstraction.

Despite the inherent limits of using her kitchen as a studio – her work was small in scale relative to most other contemporary abstractions – Thomas took full advantage of the changing light and color that she saw from the window. 'I discovered that it was the light glittering through a holly tree near the bay window at my home that attracted my fancy', Thomas said. 'The colors are the children of light and the light reveals to us the spirit and living soul of the world.'[18] Her intimacy and connection to nature shine through.

Thomas can be credited with many firsts, remarkable for an artist who came into her signature style later in life. In addition to being the first to graduate from Howard University's art department she became the first African American woman to be honored with a solo show at the Whitney Museum of American Art, in 1972. When her painting *Resurrection* (1966) was acquired and installed in the Obama White House in 2015, she became the first African American woman to have her work enter the collection.

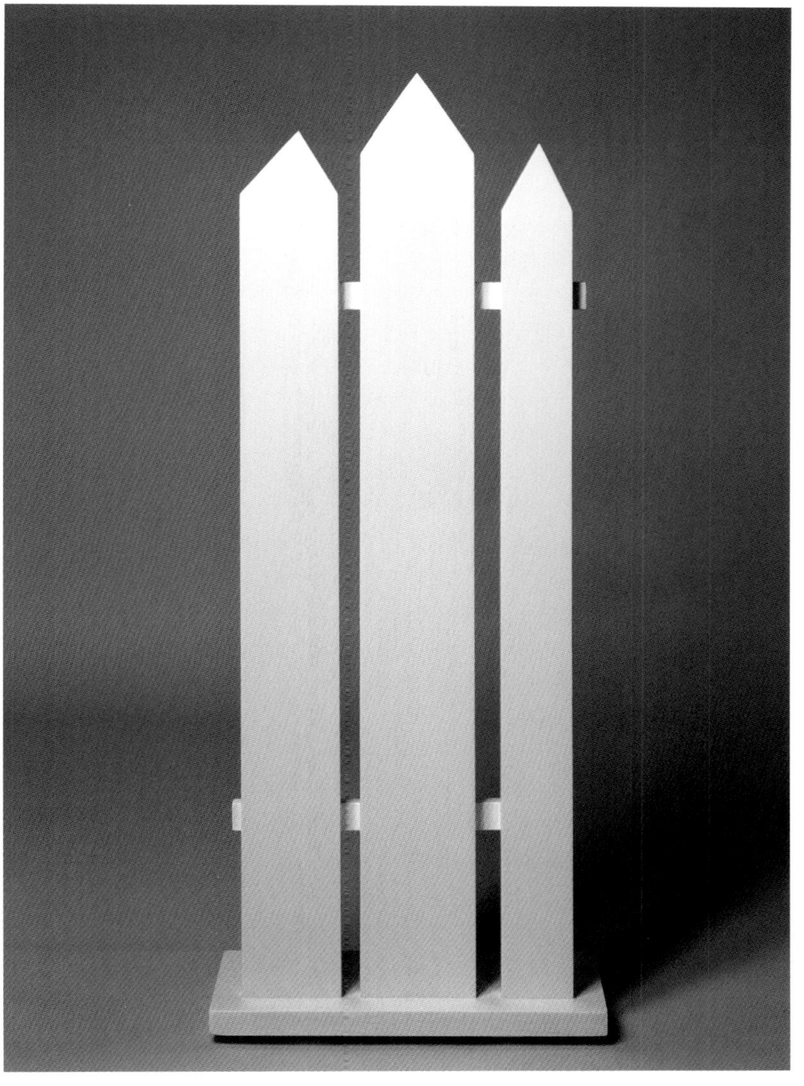

Fig.25 Anne Truitt, *First*, 1961, latex semi-gloss enamel on poplar wood, 111.8 × 43.2 × 17.8 cm (44 × 17 × 7 in), Baltimore Museum of Art, Maryland

Sidelining

Anne Truitt (fig.25) presents a telling case study of a young female artist caught in the perfect storm of a chauvinistic art world. After her groundbreaking exhibition at André Emmerich Gallery in 1963, Donald Judd, at the time known more as a critic than an artist, dismissed the work as looking 'serious without being so', comparing the 'thoughtless' installation to tombstones and fences which the works resembled.[19] Truitt had not done the installation – it was overseen by Kenneth Noland, William Rubin and Clement Greenberg. Later Truitt noted, 'They discounted me, more or less. I think they thought, "Oh, this is a new kind of work. Let's see what we can do with this one and how it will work out. Put this one here, and that one there, and does that one balance this?" That's the way they talked.'[20]

Truitt's *First* (1961) comprises three slats of wood with pointed tops attached to a base, painted white and for all the world resembling a picket fence with its connotations of hearth and home, emblematic of the American dream. Yet the literal reading of this particular sculpture was a catalyst for what Truitt was searching for, and found, in her later work. In *Daybook: The Journey of an Artist,* Truitt writes,

> Having taken off from the houses, fences, trees and fields of my childhood in my work of late 1961, I very soon found that I was leaving the literal objects behind. By simply going ahead with whatever presented itself to me in my inner eye, I discovered what really interested me was proportion which soon led me into the fascinating reaches of counterpoint between form and color, and ultimately to the work I am doing now, at once more austere in structure and more expressive in color.[21]

In spite of leaving Truitt feeling discounted, Greenberg proclaimed her the 'first' minimalist. The six sculptures in the show made of hand-painted poplar were simple, straightforward and pared down. Perhaps Truitt was dismissed by Judd, Morris and Flavin because of Greenberg's support (though he later dropped her), but it was more likely because of their differing philosophical approaches. If Judd celebrated artificial materials and espoused work that was machine-made, void of reference and content, Truitt's work was handmade and based on biography and memory. Yet there were superficial similarities, and as James Meyer points out, the resemblance may have been too much for Judd, who needed to delineate the differences between himself and Truitt.

> Both admirers of Newman and Noland, they had developed three-dimensional objects based on a reading of a painting. But where Judd developed the literalist implications of this move, Truitt

> explored its semantic potential. Where he made objects to be seen for their own sake, she made works that transcended their objectness. And while he removed his hand from making, she was still, unapologetically author.[22]

It was Judd and Morris who defined the movement and surely this reference to emotion and memory made them shudder. But this disservice seems to be more about the umbrella of minimalism under which her work was put and then judged rather than her singular and original contributions as an abstract sculptor. Greenberg introduced the idea of minimalism to a broader audience in terms of gender, implying that Truitt had a feminine approach and the male minimalists another. 'Truitt was', Greenberg wrote in *Vogue*, 'willing to stake herself on the truth of her sensibility'. To Greenberg, that sensibility had the 'power to move and affect'.[23]

The 1970s and Second-Wave Feminism

'If feminism is a methodology, a structure, a way of thinking, as well as a set of contents, then what might feminism do to the category of painting?' Helen Molesworth asks in her essay 'Painting with Ambivalence' for the *WACK! Art and the Feminist Revolution* exhibition catalogue.[24] Molesworth points out that women who painted abstractly are situated in an odd nether region, dealing with the contradiction of continuing the patriarchal lineage of painting while identifying as feminists. But she opens a line of thinking. What can and did feminism bring to abstraction, particularly during a time in history when more and more women were establishing themselves as artists in the New York art world?

Joan Snyder (b.1940), Jennifer Bartlett (1941–2022), Mary Heilmann (b.1940; fig.26) and Pat Steir (b.1940; fig.21) arrived in New York City in the 1960s and early 1970s, art degrees from prestigious art schools in hand, just as second-wave feminism, a reaction to the stifling domesticity of post–World War II America, was taking hold. This push resulted in the founding of *Ms.* magazine in 1971 and the passage of Title IX, a federal law mandating educational equality for women in 1972. Even

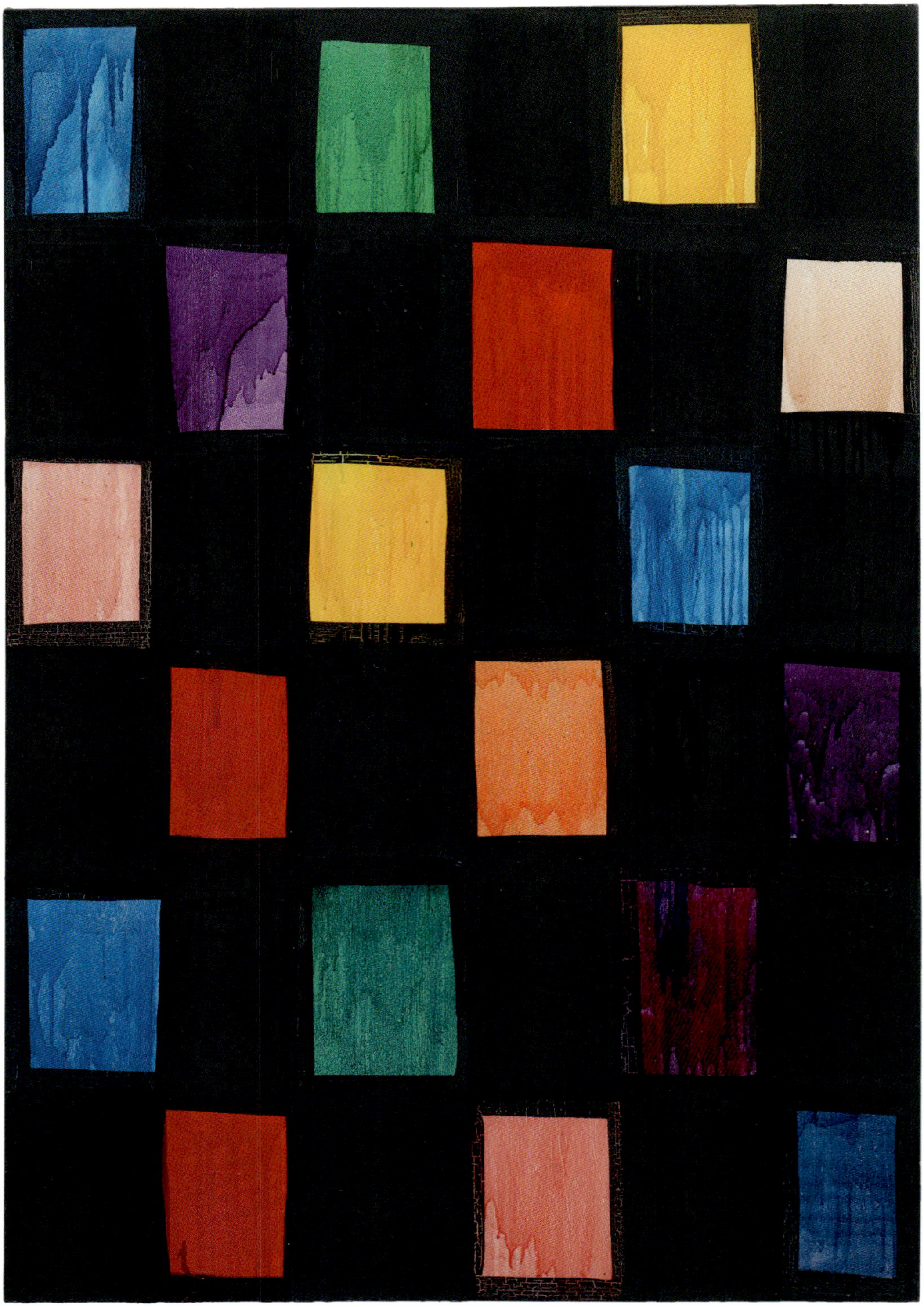

though these women didn't necessarily fully embrace feminism or call themselves feminist, their art was a feminist response to the male establishment that dominated the art world.

At the same time, the feminist art movement was being defined. The Heresies Collective, which published *HERESIES: A Feminist Publication on Art and Politics*, was founded in 1977. Abstract expressionism was starting to wane. The strictures of the minimalist ethos and the importance of the hard edge and the grid were firmly in place. Conceptual art was on the rise. In 1968 Lucy Lippard predicted the dematerialization of art and the death of painting.

Notably, these four artists were born only 12 years after Helen Frankenthaler, less than a generation's difference but a world apart, considering the accelerated cultural shifts in the social fabric between the 1950s and the 1960s. Whether they identified as feminists or not, they believed it was possible for them to achieve what Frankenthaler had: being included in the critical conversations and exhibitions of the day, accepted as working, professional artists, being shown in galleries and museums and, yes, being chosen to represent the United States at the Venice Biennale, as Frankenthaler had in 1966.

If painting was 'dead', then each one of these artists would help resurrect it by finding her own way to introduce 'impurity' into the pure aesthetics of formalism by revealing personal / subjective / spiritual content or by deliberately mixing representation and figuration with abstraction. But at that time the path to resurrection lay with the grid and beyond.

In a highly influential essay in the late 1970s entitled 'Grids', Rosalind Krauss discusses the importance of the grid, its dualistic nature as something both structural and transcendent. It is both contained within the frame and alludes to the space beyond, a continuance of the matrix. Mondrian and Malevich, for example, saw the grid as the pathway to the spiritual. 'The grid's mythic power is that it makes us able to think we are dealing with materialism (or sometimes science or logic)', Krauss writes, 'while at the same time it provides us with a release into belief (or illusion or fiction)'.[25] In a sense, the grid is the antithesis of nature, of nurture. Snyder, Bartlett, Heilmann and Steir believed the integration of the grid into their work was as important to them as any consideration of feminism. If the minimalist grid served

Fig.26 Mary Heilmann, *The Thief of Baghdad*, 1983, oil on canvas, 152.4 × 106.7 × 4.4 cm (60 × 42 × 1¾ in), private collection

as a departure point, it was also a means to the end of finding an individual style using systems, process and gesture, or a combination of all three.

Joan Snyder received her MFA from Rutgers University in 1966 and by the early 1970s was making what are now referred to as her stroke paintings, paint-laden textural strokes laid across and, in a sense, obliterating the grid. By the late '70s Snyder had abandoned the grid in favor of pure paint applied thickly in dabs or strokes, incorporating symbols and texts, and exploring metaphysical properties of the paint.

'During the late sixties, my work was definitely about structure', Snyder said.

> About lines and strokes, about painting paint strokes, telling a story, using the grid, moving from figure and landscape space, making the work narrative, isolating strokes, thinking about the anatomy of a painting . . . being able to see the process the painting went through, the ground, pencil lines, paste, gel, paint. It was not play for me. It was about order and then letting go, speaking, creating a language or a structure to speak.[26]

If thought has form as referenced in the 1905 book *Thought Forms,* does imagery have a gender? 'You made this beautiful claim', Lucy Lippard said in an interview with Synder, 'which maybe all of us feel but are afraid to make that you can tell women's art from men's art. How?' To which Snyder replied,

> It has to do with a kind of softness, layering, a certain color sensibility, a more expressive work than a man is going to do right now, and a repetitiousness – use of grids, obsessive in a way. When I look at women's art, I look for ideas and images that not only move me visually, but tell me something about who the artist is, what she's trying to say. I'm not interested in art so mysterious that it doesn't tell me a thing.[27]

Originally from the West Coast, Jennifer Bartlett graduated from Yale University in 1965 with an MFA and moved to New York full-time in 1972. By 1976 she had created and shown her tour de force work *Rhapsody*

(1976) at Paula Cooper Gallery, now in the collection of MoMA. Contained within a large minimalist grid, *Rhapsody* is made up of 987 machine-made one-foot-by-one-foot steel plates, themselves divided into painted white with baked enamel and silkscreen with a one-by-one-inch grid. The installation is over 150 feet long and is at once monumental – it occupied the entire Cooper gallery – and intimate, enabling each steel panel to be read separately. It is both large-scale and intimate, portable and mural-like. The imagery is a primer on painting – color, shape, realism and abstraction – following systems of thought. Reading left to right reveals thematic sections – mountain, line, house, tree, shape and ocean. A triangle is a mountain in one square, the roof of a house in another. Clouds float through the plates, offering up a softness and contrast to the linear grid. Curvilinear lines weave through a structured, geometric background. Some imagery is contained within a single plate; others bleed across several plates.

Rhapsody was radical in its day, not only because of its sheer scale and novel take on minimalism but because it explored the fluid relationship between abstraction and figuration by introducing color and a narrative subject matter to the male monochromatic hard-edged grid. *Rhapsody* is considered, as critic Ken Johnson noted, 'one of the most celebrated single works of late 20th century American art'.[28]

Bartlett was an iconoclast in her art making as well, not identifying as a Process artist, a minimalist artist or conceptual artist but embracing all three, picking and choosing what served her ends. She painted representationally and abstractly, much to the consternation of the hard-liners in each camp. She also didn't want to be labeled. About anything. 'I'm not naturally the feminist type,' Bartlett once said. 'I just wanted to be an artist.'[29] Yet wasn't what she and the others wanted and expected – the opportunity to be taken seriously as artists and to make art on one's own terms – explicitly feminist?

When Mary Heilmann moved to New York City in 1968 from California, a graduate of the University of California, Berkeley, she not only had to contend with what she has described as a 'boy's club' but the repeated mantra that painting was dead. Heilmann's brilliance – and the very thing that worked against her in the early days – was a direct attack, often with subtle humor, on the monochrome, the grid, the rectangle, the precision and rules held so dear by Donald Judd and others.

Heilmann's palette can be garish, with pinks and acid green; the hand of the artist is revealed in the loose, sometimes watered down, sometimes thickly applied, brushstroke. Heilmann began as a ceramicist, a hands-on practice; so it follows that she would use her fingers instead of a brush to create wobbly and off-angle lines that have a handmade, craft-like feel. But if judged under the strict rubric of minimalism, Heilmann seems more a daughter of Anne Truitt than an adoptee of minimalism. Like Truitt's, Heilmann's titles are picturesque and evocative – *Surfing on Acid* (2005) and *The Thief of Baghdad* (1984; fig.26), for instance.

Looking at *The Thief of Baghdad* one can see the reference to minimalism with her geometric forms, loose grid and repeated patterning. Yet the artist's hand is apparent. Color shifts and moves across the picture plane. The window-like squares that peek out from the brushy and uneven grid seem to drift to the upper left. The abstraction is at the same time oddly representational, evoking buildings with multicolored lit windows in the city or, conversely, moving traffic. Why title a painting after an *Arabian Nights* adventure that involves the antics of a thief, a prince, a princess and an evil genie? Look again and imagine the space flattening. There is no longer a vertical building with windows lit but a tilting magic carpet about to take off.

'There's more going on there than what you see; it's about the backstory', Heilmann said. 'But what you see will always make you think of other things. In a way, it's a dialogue.' But Heilmann isn't trying to be literal as much as referential. 'Each of my paintings can be seen as an autobiographical marker', she said, 'a cue by which I evoke a moment from my past'.[30]

Can the artist who pokes the bear be dismissed? As critic John Yau sees it, she can't. He writes,

> By using anonymous images (rectangles, bars, curved forms, and elongated clouds) to introduce metaphor and the wide range of memories and associations it evokes, Heilmann basically stood Minimalism on its head, enabling the viewer to complete the painting with his or her own personal experience. She rejected Minimalism's authoritarian attitude, which was famously expressed by Frank Stella's credo, 'What you see is what you see.'[31]

Early on, Pat Steir had an interest in exploring the spiritual in art, a connection which only deepened over time. If Stella's comment became the unofficial credo of purity, Steir's belief that painting was more than pure plastic form altered the trajectory of abstract painting. She studied painting and philosophy at Boston University, and then graduated with a BFA from Pratt Institute in 1962; within a year she was included in museum shows around the country.

Art historian Robert Rosenblum's classic book *Modern Painting and the Northern Romantic Tradition*, chiefly the chapter on abstract expressionism, provided an early and unlikely inspiration for Steir's early development. Like af Klint who faced the dilemma of expressing the sublime without representation, Steir found her source of inspiration, of authorship, in nature and in the sublime.

Even in the early 1970s as Steir was working on raw canvas that contained the pencil-gridded minimalist background; the work also included naturalistic imagery – drawings of birds or clouds or rain. When, in the late 1980s, Steir began making her now iconic waterfall paintings, she had discovered the means for making paintings that went beyond language, beyond theory. To this day, Steir retains the grid in her site-specific installations – beginning with many layers of paint on the wall, over which a grid is drawn before the paint or imagery is applied.

Dragon Tooth Waterfall (1990) is a classic example, and one of the earliest, of the waterfall paintings in which Steir loaded a large brush with paint, held it in place and let the paint flow in its natural trajectory down the surface, like water falling. Using a form of a Chinese flung-ink method called Haboku, Steir flings the paint across the bottom of the painting to resemble splashing water or across the top of the painting to suggest celestial heavens. In both cases chance is the determining factor. The viewer experiences the essence of the paint as opposed to direct imitation or depiction. Steir channels nature through the act of painting, plays with notions of alchemy and, through this alchemical act, transforms the paint into the phenomena depicted. She has fused conceptual art with painting by arguing that a brushstroke, color as it relates to meaning, space and the illusion of space are all content.

'I want the paint to tell me something about the nature of art, about the secret of art, the secret of nature, about the universe that we exist in,' Steir once said. 'I'm not sure what that something is. Maybe everyone who makes art has the same feeling. That's why I let the paintings make themselves.'[32]

Steir's art is not overtly political or feminist; nevertheless, she has been and continues to be an activist.

> We have to be careful how we talk about art, define art. Work that aspires to beauty has political implications, too, not just work that is terrifying and about terrifying subjects. But if you really want to be political, do as John Lewis said. Go march. Pick up people and make them march with you, now. And continue to march. Then you will have real impact.[33]

Postminimalism and After

Lynda Benglis (b.1941) arrived in New York City in the mid-1960s and by the end of that decade had emerged as one of the key figures defining postminimalism. While taking night classes at the Brooklyn Museum in 1964, Benglis was introduced to minimalist art. However, from the outset, she rejected minimalism's grid, industrial materials and lack of emotion or drama. Instead, she sought a process that would incorporate theatrics and the body, using a material that acted like paint but did not require a canvas and frame for support. Benglis eventually mixed pigment into latex liquid and poured the viscous substance directly onto the floor, in distinct but overlapping bright colors to make what would be described as both poured sculptures and fallen paintings.

In 1969 Benglis produced a floor piece entitled *Odalisque (Hey, Hey Frankenthaler)* which is not only an homage to the way Frankenthaler worked but can be seen as a nod to Frankenthaler's accomplishments. The overlapping pours of orange and green with veins of blues and red reject the angular forms of minimalism, while serving as a residue of Benglis's performance. These pours demanded a physicality. The tubs of paint weighed five pounds or more, and the movement required was more of a heave than a gesture. In addition to the poured latex, Benglis experimented with many other unorthodox, often malleable, materials such as plaster, foam, enamel, lead and ceramics as well as video and photography. Often underlying references to sex or bodily functions purposely went beyond the bounds of what might be considered 'good taste'.

'The fact that innovative form is so feared by the male establishment shows that like content it has a power of its own', writes Harmony Hammond. 'If our lives and our art are connected, and if "the personal is political," in the radical sense, then we cannot separate the content of our work from the form it takes.'[34]

Curator Lynn Zelevansky's 1994 exhibition at MoMA *Sense and Sensibility: Women Artists and Minimalism in the Nineties* laid out a line of descent from minimalism to postminimalism. It was one of the earliest museum shows to contextualize the feminist contribution to postminimal abstract art. The seven women chosen for the exhibition varied widely in their use of unorthodox materials including cosmetics, fabric and copper panels. But what they shared was the freedom to explore minimalist methodology and elements of geometry such as the grid, hard edge and repetition without being restricted by dogma. In other words, they could expand or contract on the minimalist work and writings that had come before them without repercussions. And this clearly was a result of the contributions artists such Snyder, Bartlett, Heilmann, Steir and Benglis had made in the previous decades.

A standout in the exhibition was Polly Apfelbaum (b.1955; fig.27) whose piece *Splendor in the Grass, Glory in the Flower* (1993) was made from individual pieces of crushed synthetic velvet dyed in an array of colors and patterns and arranged on the floor as a single piece. MoMA curator Kirk Varnedoe once described Apfelbaum's work from the 1990s as 'fallen paintings', such an apt description that the artist began using the term herself. Stripes, polka dots, biomorphic blobs of color, serial repetition of lines, ovals and squares all result from the artist blotting, pouring or stamping fabric dye onto the synthetic velvet. Because the material is porous, the dye seeps in, creating soft edges and mottled and blurred patterning. The staining is an homage to Frankenthaler, both the way she worked on the floor, and the pouring of thinned paint that soaked into the weave of the unprimed canvas.

But the effect is different here, the overall feeling disorienting. The work is colorful and patterned like a rug but melded into the floor. Because the pieces are not fixed, they have a temporal feel, a vulnerability unlike sculpture made from steel plates, pieces of Plexiglas or

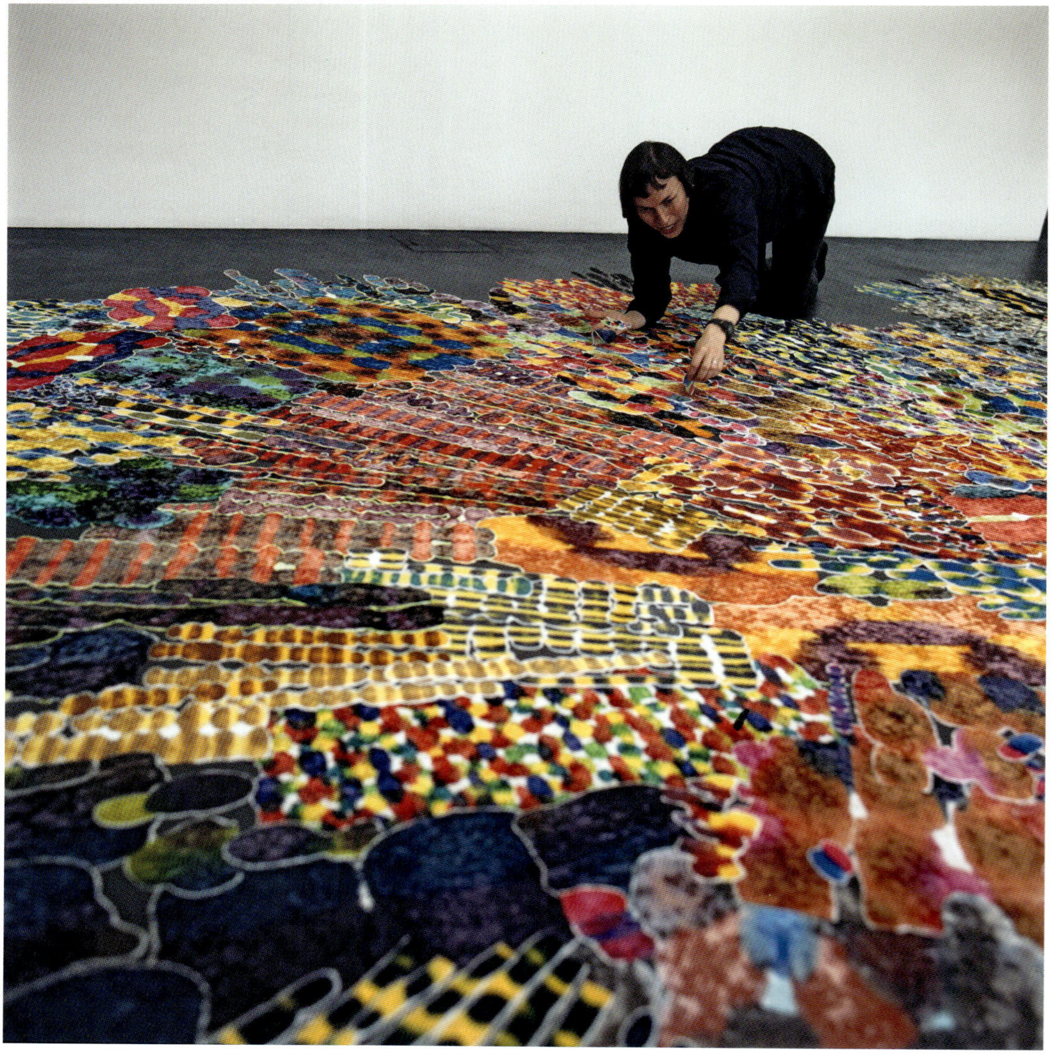

wood. And unlike steel, Plexiglas or wood – hard-edged, impermeable, male – crushed, colorful velvet is distinctly feminine, light-hearted and fun. There is an unapologetic girliness to the vibrant colors and exotic patterning of the pieces of velvet, an embrace of the feminine.

Fig.27 Polly Apfelbaum with *Reckless*, 1998, synthetic velvet and dye, dimensions variable, Buffalo AKG Art Museum, NY

Her work occupies a place somewhere between installation, painting and sculpture. 'Sculpture for me is certainly not about commemoration or monumentality', she has said, 'but it involves memory. *Reckless* (1998) is the opposite of monumental – it has no fixed form and changes every time it is installed. It has a promiscuous relationship to time. *Reckless*, as the word implies, is a reckless disregard of history and categories.'[35] The fabric is malleable and can adapt and morph to different sites. *Reckless* is more than the sum of its parts. The material is tactile and has a fluidity of form though it also has a certain geometry. As the artist notes, 'Not everything has to be big and tall and erect'.[36]

Nochlin Redux

It's worth circling back to Linda Nochlin and her observation of the formidable barriers in place that prevent women from participating at the highest levels of the art world. What happens when these social structures change? She notes in her 1971 essay, 'The making of art involves a self-consistent language of form . . . given temporally defined conventions, schemata, or systems of notation, which have to be learned or worked out, either through teaching, apprenticeship, or a long period of individual experimentation'.[37] The generation of women artists entering the art world in the late 1970s and early 1980s expected the promise of feminism and gender equality to be fulfilled and to take advantage of educational opportunities, studio assistantships and mentorships.[38]

Two artists from this generation exemplify Nochlin's vision of art making. Amy Sillman (b.1955; fig.28) and Suzanne McClelland (b.1960; fig.29) came to painting with an educational foundation and a critical, sophisticated understanding of art making. They came through the conceptual backdoor, reaching past minimalism to harken back to the gesture of abstract expressionism, while exploring the interplay between representation and abstraction.

Sillman is an artist, writer, teacher and maker of zines and animation. She collaborates with poets, writers and other artists to dive deeply into the life of an artist as a maker of things. She's as influenced by 1960s cartoons like *Rocky and Bullwinkle* as she is by the history of art. Sillman studied at the School of Visual Arts (SVA) after arriving in New York City in the 1970s to study Japanese at New York University. At SVA she studied with women painters, among them Elizabeth Murray and Pat Steir, the latter of whom she later worked for as a studio assistant. Sillman spent much of the 1980s, when painting was exploding in New York, drawing in her studio. The notion of proprioception, the sense

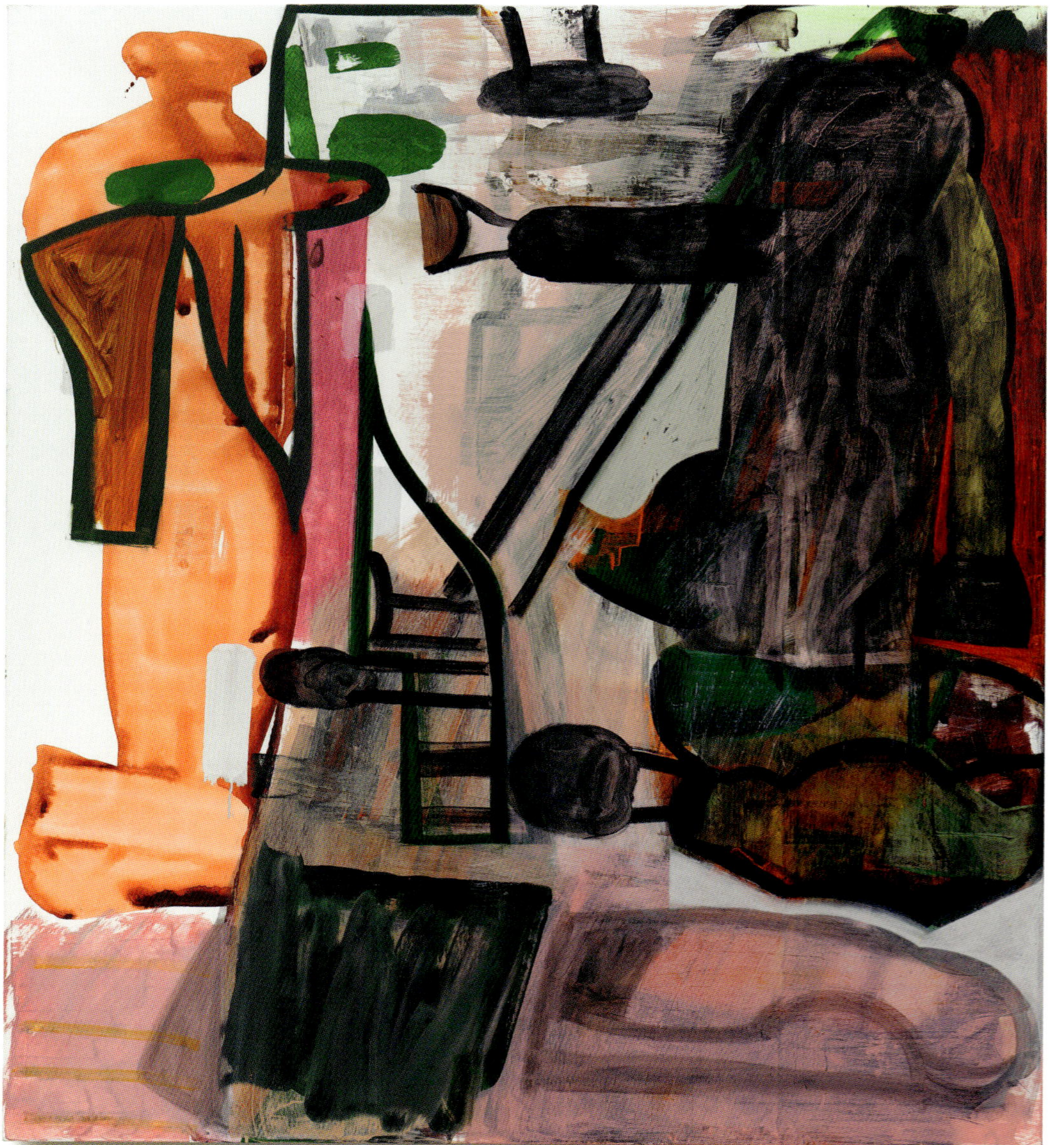

Fig.28 Amy Sillman, *Friend*, 2021, oil and acrylic on canvas, 182.9 × 165.1 cm (72 × 65 in), collection of Karim and Magda Abillama, Athens, Greece

of the body (both artist's and viewer's) in space, is also an important component of both her painting and drawing.

Her paintings explore the dichotomy between abstraction and representation, while never fully embracing one or the other. 'When I was going to school', Sillman said, 'you had to declare an allegiance to a form and an attitude towards abstraction, and from the get-go I wasn't going to declare an allegiance'.[39] It is this self-proclaimed insistence to range freely between the two that opens up the discussion of her work.

For her 2021 solo show at Capitain Petzel gallery in Berlin titled *Rock Paper Scissors*, Sillman created a set of rules. Each painting had to consist of ten layers: the first two of a body or a shape, the second two about color, the next two layers 'ruining' what she had already laid down, followed by two layers of pattern. The last two layers are 'wild cards', the thing that might differentiate, or perhaps rescue, the painting. Rock, paper, scissors is a child's game of chance, with a circular hierarchy: paper covers rock, rock crushes scissors, scissors cut paper.

Through these layers one experiences the cycle of creation, destruction and rescue that is so essential to the way Sillman works. Knowing this predetermined system also opens possibilities of other readings, interpretations. For instance, in *Friend* (2021) the washes of Pepto-Bismol pink at the bottom of the canvas and the grouping of vertical and horizontal black lines that suggests a wooden headboard and black round eyes recall Philip Guston's *Painter in Bed* (1973). In Guston's version of an artist's angst, he lies awake in bed, all eyeball and head, his subject matter of lightbulbs, hobnailed shoes and lamps floating insistently above him.

Ultimately, the subject of Sillman's work is transformation, the way that a painting changes through process – how something that was figurative becomes abstract. Failure, or the freedom to experiment to the edge of failure, is crucial to her process. If it is through the layering and obliteration of form and shape, and the insistence of the line that breaks down the one-point perspective, Sillman's irony and humor challenges the notion of the grand masterpiece, the creation of the genius offering up the triumph of the artist's struggle instead.

Though best known as an abstract painter, Suzanne McClelland began with photography, studying with feminist photographer Joanne Leonard (b.1940) at the University of Michigan before moving to New

York City in 1981. Ultimately McClelland was disappointed. While she loved capturing images out in the world, it was the alchemy that happened in the darkroom, 'the fluidity of that image emerging slowly in the red-lit water like a mystical vision',[40] that appealed to her, not a printed image on paper.

The gap between these two views of reality – a cropped version of the world seen through the lens finder and more ephemeral mutability in the processing – took McClelland to abstract painting. As she sees it, painting allows for a conflation of the two experiences.

> I'm deeply attracted to photographic imagery and even moving film. But it's always excluding something whereas in abstract paintings we are experiencing the perpetual present. Abstraction can function as a generalization or 'drawing out of' reality, a reduction, or a condensation. But I prefer to see it as linked to the structure of the world or the skeleton of real things.[41]

Over the next decade, working as a photographer documenting performances at Storefront for Art and Architecture and assisting fashion photographers, she moved further into the expansive directness of abstract painting. Exposure to Color Field artists Peter Bradley, Al Loving and the sculptor Anthony Caro, as well as critic Clement Greenberg, opened the possibilities for conflating subject and material. Jazz is inherently abstract, and she spent many nights with musicians who didn't question a gap between subject and material. This was important to the shift from a subject 'out there' to the subject within a painting.

McClelland spent time in playgrounds while raising her young daughter and noted the way the voices of children were learning to connect words to objects, places and people. Language is used in free public spaces to protest, to play, to connect, to cross boundaries and to establish them. In contrast, in politics and business it is used as a barrier. Agreements or treaties depend on languages as solid concrete walls. Jenny Holzer and Barbara Kruger used language that was feminist but graphically clean and instructional as opposed to poetic. McClelland believed that language, particularly the voice, was as important as the body as a feminist tool. Essential to the discourse, it is simultaneously abstract and real. Language, particularly the way it morphs and changes

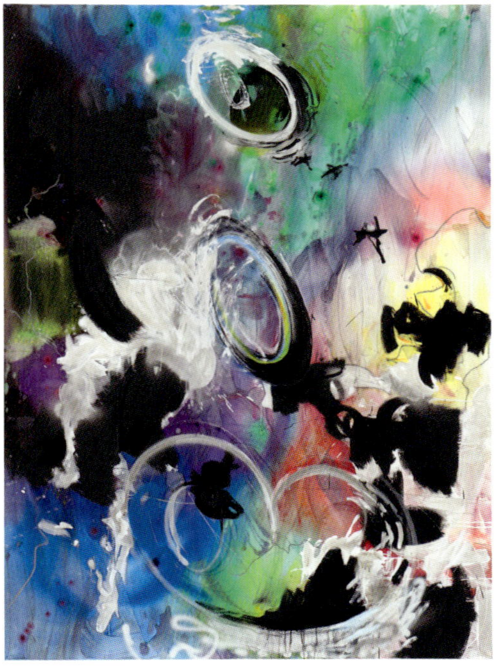

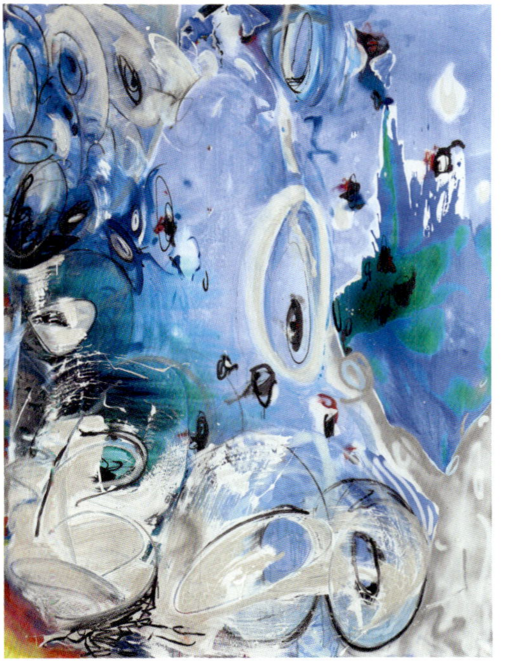

Fig.29 Suzanne McClelland, Diptych: *Falling Sky (North)*, 2022, *Falling Sky (South)*, 2022, signed, titled, dated and inscribed in ink (verso), mixed media on linen, each 259.1 × 190.5 cm (102 × 75 in), collection of Marianne Boesky Gallery, New York and Aspen

as it travels from mouth to ear, was the perfect subject/material for a painting. It can be political; it can be used to tell a story or manipulated to make a point. Importantly, McClelland notes, 'the voice is a part of the body. If they can't hear your voice, you're not in the game. You're enslaved.'[42]

As with much of McClelland's work, *Falling Skies* (2022) can be read on many levels. In a formal sense, the artist is figuring out ways of dissolving the predictable shape of a rainbow. The edge of the painting functions as the horizon line allowing gravity to be the strongest formal device. The colors are dispersed and the space trippy. In *South* the rainbow explodes across the canvas. In *North* the rainbow is squashed into the bottom left of the canvas. McClelland has long been interested in markers that orient the body in space, whether it is the name of a place in the landscape, the horizon, the stars or the moon. A rainbow is a shape in the sky, but at the same time it's ephemeral. It can't orient the viewer because where and when a rainbow emerges is unpredictable, disappearing as quixotically as it appears.

In these paintings, McClelland examines the place where fear lives, which is often between what we hear and what we see. She draws from the oral histories that exist around the world, and this story has many names. In most versions, an acorn or a coconut falls on an animal's head with a resounding thump. Believing the end is near, the animal goes on a campaign to spread the news that the sky is falling. Everyone she meets joins the hysteria, not believing what they see with their own eyes but what they hear from others. Myth congeals into fact quickly. Just as McClelland absorbed the ambient sounds of the playground, social media has become an ambient situation. With the rise of social media and cable news shows, the speed with which rumors fly can have devastating effects. The word *Boo* is both a sound and a word. It emerges, like a warning to Dorothy to turn back, in white and black cursive, floating across the skies as if it's in on the cosmic joke. The sky isn't really falling.

Post-Postmodern

'Feminism is no longer univocal', art historian Jeanne Willette notes. 'Feminism has become a movement of many voices, male and female, Western and non-Western.'[43] Today, artists of both genders making abstract work are deeply indebted to the pioneering contributions of the female abstract painters who preceded them. In a postmodern art world, 21st-century artists can draw from any number of sources, many of which came out of feminist innovations – including Performance art, Process art, a multiperspectival approach to artmaking, the use of unorthodox materials and means and reimagined craft. Unlike so many of the women painters working abstractly who had an ambivalent relationship with the pulls of pure abstraction and content, these artists use abstraction to explore the explicitly political and the deeply personal. While this reflects postmodern tendencies and styles, it is also deeply indebted to feminism for its objection to established hierarchies and rigid rules.

This is certainly true for Franklin Evans (b.1967; fig.30) who sees, in the push and pull between abstraction and representation, a way to deal with biographical issues such as queer identity, his Mexican heritage on his mother's side, his life as an artist and his background in economics and finance. 'My work has a strong relationship to the

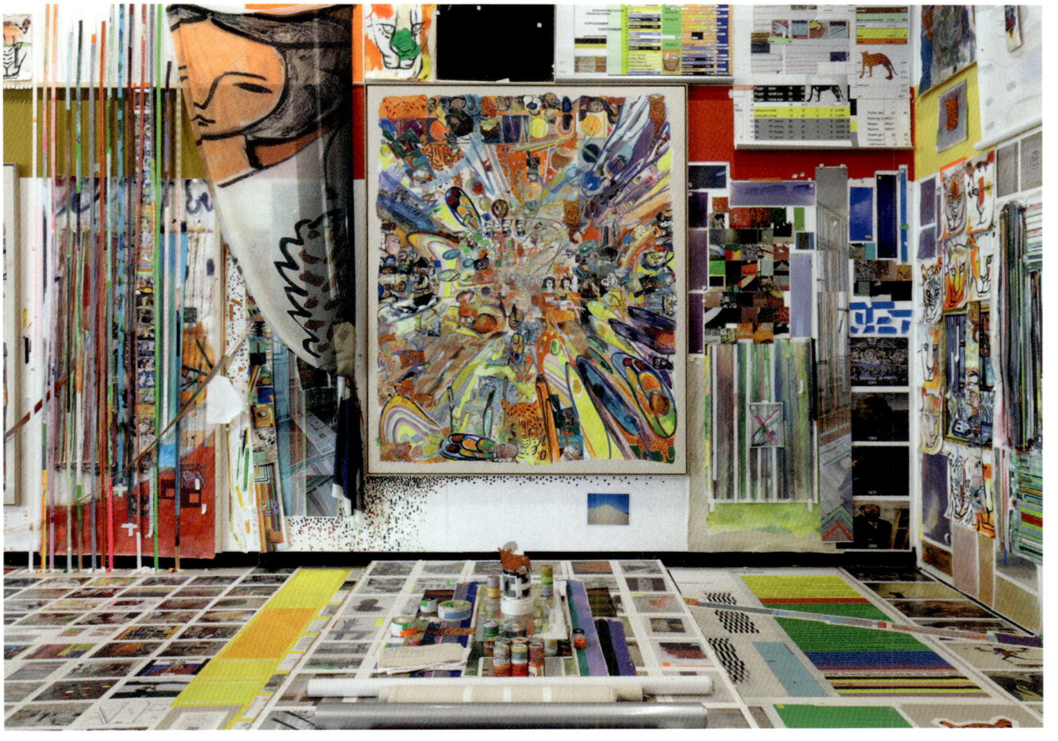

Fig.30 Franklin Evans, *perpetualstudio*, 2022, painting, collage, site-specific installation, dimensions variable, commissioned by MAXXI – National Museum of 21st Century Arts, Rome

aspect of feminism that challenges the white cisgendered heteronormative patriarchal position of modernist painting / abstraction.' Evans says, 'My work as queer and absorptive uses the powerful impulses and visual knowledge of modernism'.[44]

Each contiguous installation is an extension of his studio practice and continued exploration of what he sees as his 'brain space'. Evans is not only a cannibal of other artists but dismantles and reassembles his own work for each successive installation. The cacophony of visual images in any exhibition can include traditional paintings on canvas; floor to ceiling screens made from painter's tape; press releases from other art shows; art books; paint cans; faux Polaroids of friends or trompe l'oeil paintings of the Polaroids and homages to an entire litany of artists from Caspar David Friedrich and Henri Matisse to Donald Judd and Frank Stella. Recently, Evans has looked to the work of Pat Steir. She is, he says, 'now powering several of my paintings as I collapse her forceful drip onto my imagistic paintings – as a sort of dance among process, abstraction, and image memory'.[45] He sees in Helen Frankenthaler a connection to the way he uses the floor to make some of the work, the staining of the canvas and paper, but also in the way the floor is an important element of his installations.

Evans acknowledges his debt to feminist art practices, noting:

> The awareness that the specificity of singularity is contingent upon the forces surrounding it (history of patriarchy, colonialism – both the gains and losses of each). I tend to draw from the gains, but I also see that this lens is tied to feminism in its powerful grasp of agency. Feminism grabs the situations and negates, expands and creates from a new vantage. It is multivalent. It employs the history of otherness as a force, materially, perspectivally, imagistically, abstractly.[46]

Early on, Evans was inspired by Judy Pfaff's expansion of painting into an abstract field to realize his own paintings in the third dimension. While Pfaff's use of materials – pigment, canvas – was familiar to Evans, it was the way she pulled them apart and into an environment that he connected to, and it is the reason he now describes his own work as 'painting installations'. His environments are 'othered', a place to enter, a way to experience time and space. The paintings are worlds within worlds, psychedelic without a single-point perspective. A recent incarnation of Evans's ongoing explorations entitled *perpetualstudio* (2022) commissioned by MAXXI, the National Museum of XXI Century Arts in Rome, as part of the exhibition *What a Wonderful World* (2022) allowed him to increase the experience to even a grander scale.

It is through his lived experience that Mark Bradford (b.1961) channels the ever-widening aftershocks of feminist art, both with his choice of subject matter and materials and the way he looks at art history. As Dallas writer and poet Darryl Ratcliff writes, Bradford felt 'the most revered artists were, as he describes them, "white male cowboy macho heterosexual painters," and declar[ed] himself, as a six-foot-eight-inch skinny Black gay man, to be just as macho. "I was hiding behind the material and having a conversation with art history and who wasn't there," referring to people of color and women.'[47]

Bradford came to art in a circuitous way, working as a stylist in his mother's hair salon in South Central Los Angeles for most of his 20s, saving money to make extended visits to Europe each year. He enrolled at the California Institute of the Arts (CalArts) at the age of 30, earning a BFA in 1995 and an MFA in 1997, when the program was a hotbed for conceptual art. (Bradford hired a marching band to attend his graduation as his final undergraduate project.)

After CalArts, Bradford returned to his mother's salon, steeped in art-historical theory but still searching for his own voice, his own style. In school Bradford had glued strips of recycled posters and flyers to posters and larger pieces of paper, but he was never satisfied with the result until he began to experiment with the small permanent-wave end papers used at the salon. He flattened and burned the sides of the delicate tissues before affixing them to the canvas in an ersatz grid and then painted and sanded the subsequent layers.

Bradford uses both collage and décollage, building up the surface of the painting with cut and torn paper and paint and then cutting, tearing or sanding the original image or layer to reveal the process and materials – the history – beneath. Unorthodox, or more to the point inexpensive or free, materials define his work. Bradford has remarked that if Home Depot doesn't have it, he doesn't need it. Posters and flyers gathered from the street are free. A box of 200 end papers costs 50 cents.

The imagery recalls the delicate and luminous grids of Agnes Martin, for whom Bradford developed a huge admiration in graduate school. But rather than extending the grid to the edges, alluding to the space beyond the picture plane, Bradford textured the surface of his grid and gave it uneven edges, so it appeared to float within the space of the painting. Bradford's use of permanent-wave end papers paid homage to the Black hair salon, which Bradford calls 'the longest matriarchal engine that has existed in the US'.[48] Bradford realized that the way he made art and the way he styled women's hair were connected. 'The trick was to keep things moving – reach in, try something, and, if that didn't work, fix it and try something else, and then bring everything together at the end.'[49]

This notion of connecting life and biography to method and meaning is crucial to understanding Bradford's work, to deconstructing what he calls social abstractions. As a child Bradford had watched his neighborhood be progressively destroyed by a network of freeways that encroached into Black neighborhoods. He also focused on the urban landscape, examining the effects of redlining and rezoning on poor neighborhoods and their underground economies, on migrant communities and on appropriated abandoned spaces. Like earlier feminist artists negotiating a place between abstraction and content, between the personal and the political, Bradford found a way to combine messaging and method to make abstract art that has 'social or political context clinging to the edges'.[50]

What originality – what innovation – is still possible for a young painter who knew the history of abstraction, who understood the impact of feminism and felt her biography? When she was starting out as an artist Shoshana Dentz (b.1968) was searching for a way to make work with substantial meaning, something that was 'real' – though she herself acknowledged how slippery the word *real* could be, noting, 'You might find it real, but somebody else doesn't'.[51]

Dentz was a committed abstract painter when she enrolled in Bard College's MFA program in 2002. At Bard Dentz began a series of paintings inspired by the keffiyeh, the checked cotton headdress worn by Arab men, that she loosely based on a photograph from the cover of the *New York Times.* The image is decorative, the checks rhythmic, forming a loose grid. Yet the work is also politically charged. The keffiyeh symbolizes Palestinian nationalism, but for Dentz the image is personal. Dent was raised in an Orthodox Jewish community and his repetition of the abstracted patterning might have been a way to process her childhood fears caused by the Palestinian-Israeli conflict.

In her next series, *home lands: fences, portals & tangles* (2004–7), Dentz once again looked to abstracted imagery that referenced the real world, in this case fences, enclosures and barbed-wire barriers that lined the abandoned Williamsburg waterfront where she lived in the 2000s. The fences also recalled the tumbleweed of razor wire of a West Bank checkpoint. Dentz's discourse with historical abstraction recalls the waving, disorienting op art of Bridget Riley, the minimalist grids of Agnes Martin and even the zips of Barnett Newman. At the same time, her larger theme is containment and restriction.

In the ongoing series of paintings and drawings *Within/Without* (2009–present) Dentz continues her exploration into the way content, meaning and volume reside within abstract painting. She left behind her previously politically charged works for a calmer, more personal practice. Dentz constructed a small box from pieces of acetate taped together to form a five-sided, transparent and fragile frame. For more than a decade she has painted and drawn the box using direct and close-up observation. The box offers a place to start, just as Giorgio Morandi's small selection of vases, cups and bowls was so much more than his subject matter. 'My still life subject is a physically real object invented solely for the metaphysically contemplative space of art', Dentz has written. 'It is real but abstract, abstract but real. It actively slips between both experiential dimensions.'[52]

As Dentz sees it, content can be defined as that which is contained. For her *Within/Without* is a 'practice of repetition, renewal and persistence; a means and space for sustained devotion'.[53] Dentz finds inspiration through the repetition of the same but changing imagery, maybe not so unlike the way Hilma af Klint found inspiration by channeling her astral guides.

Conclusion

There are any number of artists who could have been included in this essay, which is not meant as a history of abstraction but a discussion of the challenges so many women artists have faced and continue to face when attempting not only to enter the male-dominated arena of painting but to challenge tradition. The situations are different because these artists speak for the struggles, opportunities and challenges they faced or face in their time. As modernism gave way to postmodernism a singular, purely formalist critical viewpoint was replaced by pluralistic viewpoints, diffusing the power of a patriarchal critical tradition. Women contributed significantly to that pluralism, helping to push beyond the universalizing concepts of formal abstraction favored by Greenberg and other midcentury theorists. Conversations of abstraction and how it developed in the early years of the 20th century to the present cannot and should not be limited to gender. And yet there is a compelling argument that overcoming the exclusions based on gender led to the groundbreaking work that changed the course and nature of abstraction.

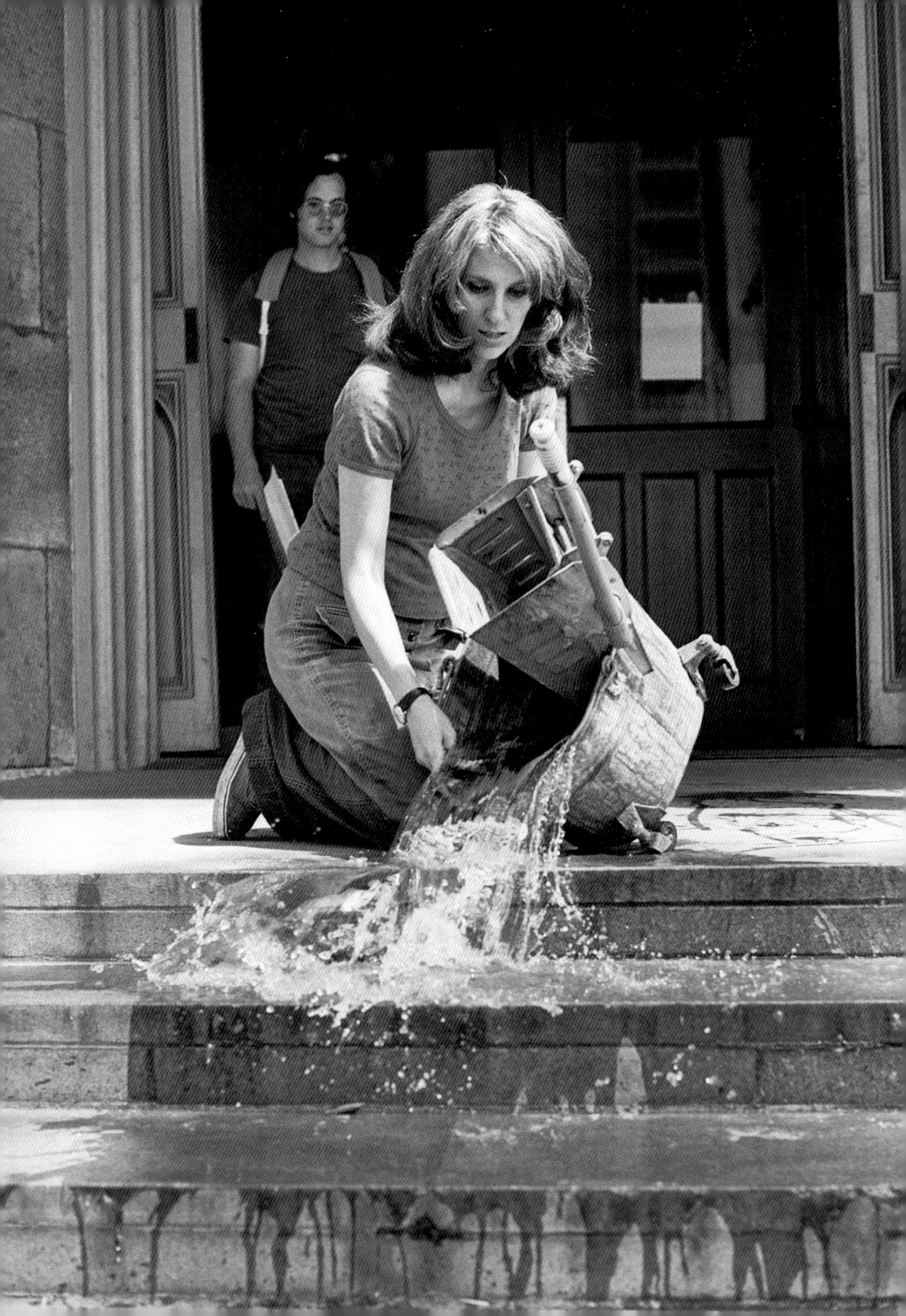

CHALLENGING DOMINIONISM

HOW WOMEN REWROTE THE ROLE OF HUMANS IN NATURE

Eleanor Heartney

> *Narratives form our reality. We become their vessels. Stories find, capture and hold us . . . From stories we absorb our goals in life, our morals, and our patterns of behavior.*[1]
>
> —Carolyn Merchant

Western culture has long been dominated by a narrative that stresses individuality, progress and human supremacy over nature. This is a narrative that was born in Genesis 1:26 with God's declaration that man should have dominion over all the creatures of sea, air and earth.[2] The idea of nature as man's tool began to be secularized and amplified in the 17th century with the scientific discoveries that led to the industrial revolution and the technological advances that have reshaped humanity's relationship with its environment and its fellow creatures. It is a narrative that emphasizes exploitation and force and is couched in a language replete with images of domination and mastery, whether over nature, colonized nations or the female sex. And in fact, this narrative makes little distinction between these entities, seeing them all as materials ripe for manipulation and conquest. Consider, for example, the following statement by philosopher Francis Bacon, quoted in Carolyn Merchant's 1980 book *The Death of Nature*. Bacon seems to elide the difference between the extraction of resources from the earth and the violent subjugation of a woman or slave when he remarks,

Fig.31 Mierle Laderman Ukeles, *Washing/Tracks/Maintenance: Outside*, 1973, part of Maintenance Art Performance Series, 1973–4, performance at Wadsworth Atheneum, Hartford, CT

'We have no right to expect nature to come to us . . . Nature must be taken by the forelock, being bald behind'.[3] Merchant also quotes the even harsher advice of 17th-century clergyman William Derham: 'We can, if need be, ransack the whole globe, penetrate into the bowels of the earth, descend to the bottom of the deep, travel to the farthest regions this world, to acquire wealth, to increase our knowledge, or even to please our eye and fancy'.[4]

From a scientific point of view, the Dominionist narrative has led to remarkable achievements – to wonders like electricity, the internal combustion engine, modern medicine, the mapping of the genome, the conquest of space and the World Wide Web. But it has also brought us to the edge of disaster as human-driven climate change threatens to make our planet uninhabitable.

In the face of these dire circumstances, a counternarrative is gaining force. This narrative also has deep roots in human history, and like Dominionism, it also provides a map for our interactions with nature. But unlike Dominionism it offers a vision of the earth as a kind of organism whose interconnected parts cannot be separated without disrupting the whole. In this telling, humankind is only one of those parts, and not even the most important one. This narrative has been given a variety of names, one of the most controversial of which is Gaianism. According to the Greek poet Hesiod, Gaia was the child of Chaos. As a primal force she produced numerous offspring that brought our world into being, which included Pontus (the Sea), Ourea (the Mountains) and Uranus (the Sky). Hesiod's Gaia was destructive and mercurial – she mated with her sons Uranus and Pontus to produce such fearsome races as the Titans, Giants and Cyclopes and persuaded her son Chronos to castrate his father. But she is also hailed as the great Mother, the origin of life and the personification of the Earth.

In the 1970s the idea of Gaia was taken up by feminists seeking an alternative to patriarchal genealogies of humankind. The Goddess Movement celebrated Gaia in a variety of guises: she served as emblem of fertility, as the embodiment of Nature, as a metaphor for the origin of society and as the locus of pre-Christian spirituality. Positing the existence of primordial matriarchal societies, some feminists drew on the idea of a Mother Earth goddess to envision new, radically non-hierarchical forms of social organization.

More recently, the Gaian narrative has been distanced from its pagan origins by a group of scientists and philosophers who employ Gaia as a metaphor for a world that is entangled, interconnected and interdependent. As developed by chemist James Lovelock and microbiologist Lynn Margulis, Gaia Theory addresses key aspects of the Dominionist narrative that have shaped our picture of science. It conceives of our planet as a self-regulating system in which living organisms coevolve with their inorganic surroundings to produce and maintain the conditions for the continuation of life. It challenges the conventional Darwinian narrative, replacing the struggle for survival of the individual organism or species with the mutualistic relations of the holobiont, an entity that encompasses the host and its surrounding species. Gaia Theory undermines the progress narrative with an acknowledgment of the living world's precarity and rejects human supremacy over nature for an ethic of interspecies cooperation. In doing so, Gaianism pushes our species off its pedestal. In the words of Bruno Latour, one of the chief theoreticians of this narrative, 'There is no living or animated thing that obeys an order superior to itself, and that dominates it, or that it just has to adapt itself to, and this is true for bacteria as much as lions or human societies'.[5] This narrative is in keeping with new developments in biology, evolutionary theory and genetics that have upended classical science. These include acceptance of the idea that trauma and environmental influences can be passed on genetically, that trees and other flora exist in symbiotic relationships and that human life is a function of the teeming mass of hundreds of trillions of microorganisms that make up the gut microbiome.

Even in the 1970s the feminist embrace of the Goddess Gaia was not universal. For many feminists the Goddess movement smacked of essentialism, ahistoricism and cultural appropriation, and came dangerously close to confirming the long-standing Western misogyny that assigned women to the realm of nature and men to the realm of culture. But from a wider perspective, feminists applauded Gaia's role as a disruptor of supposedly settled truths. During the heady period of the 1960s and 1970s, disruption spread across many fields, transforming discussions about gender, race, capitalism, colonialism and science. It is no coincidence that feminism and the modern environmental movement emerged simultaneously in a world seeking new social and economic models. The overlap between the two produced a burst of new scholarship. Historians like Carolyn Merchant investigated the ways that the Enlightenment and the Industrial Revolution had stamped out earlier, more organic and cooperative approaches to nature, gender relations and society. In a similar vein, Charlene Spretnak critiqued patriarchal assumptions behind the mechanistic orientation of modernity in books like *Green Politics* and *The Spiritual Dimension of Green Politics,* with the latter acting as a major catalyst for the formation of the US Green Party movement.

Ecofeminism emerged as the term for this merger of environmental and feminist concerns. Ecofeminists like those mentioned above pressed for a new understanding of the Earth as a living thing and for an environmental and social ethic that stressed relational thinking, interspecies responsibility and a reordering of human priorities along cooperative, egalitarian, and less nakedly competitive lines. Ecofeminism pairs the liberation of women and the struggle for racial equality with the restoration of the balance of nature. As such, it stands in sharp contrast to the developed world's worship of growth, the tepid economics-based policies that produce feeble but 'politically possible' answers to the climate crisis and the delusion that technology can save us. Once derided as the province of tree huggers, 'eco-crazies' and goddess worshipers, ecofeminism has emerged as an urgently needed corrective to the social calculus that brings us rising seas, devastating droughts, raging wildfires and worldwide pandemics.

Politically, the United States has lagged behind Europe in environmental consciousness. Beginning in the 1970s representatives of the Green Party began to take part in coalition governments, first in Belgium and Germany and then throughout the EU and eventually Canada. They were able to push for increased reliance on renewable energy, sustainable agriculture and policies promoting environmental justice. The American two-party system made such participation much more difficult. Only in the 21st century has climate change become a topic of conversation in American political debates.

But artistically, the US has been a pioneer in the creation of environmentally conscious art. Spurred in part by its association with the feminist movement, eco-art first gained traction in the United States. The 1970s saw the emergence of numerous art projects that blended feminist concerns and environmental activism. Mierle Laderman Ukeles (b.1939), for instance, was lured into environmentalism by way of her role as an artist and mother. She suggested that the practice of 'maintenance' more commonly associated with domesticity and 'women's work' might serve as a constructive model for the larger social, economic and political systems that sustain contemporary life. Agnes Denes (b.1931) adapted the often arcane and abstract principles of conceptual art to a 'visual philosophy' that champions sustainability and environmental responsibility. One outcome of this was the creation of some of the earliest eco-restoration art projects. Helen Mayer Harrison (1927–2018) began her career as a feminist and peace activist. She incorporated these ideals when she joined forces with her husband Newton Harrison (1932–2022) to create an influential new paradigm for interdisciplinary water and land use projects. From an early focus on feminist performance art, Betsy Damon (b.1940) moved on to envision water as a living thing, leading her to found the nonprofit organization Keepers of the Waters that works internationally to educate the public about the nature and restoration of living water systems.

These and other ecofeminist artists have provided important models for younger eco-artists. This is a field that has exploded over the past five decades, as eco-art has become a worldwide phenomenon. Artists from every continent are exploring myriad ways to use art to inform the public about environmental issues and to actively mitigate the effects of climate change. While eco-art often flies under the radar of conventional criticism, it has evolved its own rich network of artists, critics, curators, platforms and exhibition spaces. As an international movement, its practitioners encompass all genders, ethnicities and nationalities. And it is rapidly becoming mainstream. In 2019, Tate in London declared a 'climate emergency' and pledged to transform itself along 'green museum principles'.[6] In 2020 the Museum of Modern Art in New York announced the establishment of a research institute dedicated to understanding the interactions between architecture and ecology. The same year MOCA in Los Angeles began what has since become a trend with the creation of an Environmental Council charged with a focus on climate, conservation and environmental justice. In 2022 the funding agency Anonymous Was A Woman initiated a new grant focused on female-identifying artists from across the United States whose work engages with ecological concerns. Meanwhile, art museums around the world are presenting exhibitions that explore everything from melting arctic ice to industrial design utilizing fungi.

What follows is an exploration of the ways pioneering ecofeminist artists and writers set the stage for today's burgeoning environmental art movement. Much like the Gaianist vision of an entangled nature, the lines of transmission that connect ecofeminist artists and ideas are anything but straightforward and linear. Ideas mutate, cross-pollinate, recede and advance in complex and often serendipitous ways. So this narrative will also weave back and forth chronologically and thematically, continually returning to the original ecofeminist embrace of connection, entanglement and mutuality.

Envisioning Entanglement

> *As if the décor had gotten up on the stage to share the drama with the actors.*[7]
>
> —Bruno Latour

What does this entanglement look like? As Latour suggests in the observation above, entanglement requires a reorienting of perspective. The Dominionist narrative posited a passive earth, a mechanical nature driven by the process of natural selection and a human race whose superior intelligence allows it to rise above and direct these forces. The Gaianist/ecofeminist narrative suggests that the earth is, if not an actual living thing, at the very least a self-regulating system in which, in another of Latour's felicitous phrases, 'living things are engineers as blind as termites'.[8] In this narrative, humans are no longer the winners of an evolutionary struggle that plunges individuals and species into a zero-sum battle for survival. Instead, all living things are conceived as parts of an interdependent and interrelated system that has no single driver. It is blind in the sense that change emerges from the interactions of all the parts coevolving in an environment that is itself constantly responding to these changes.

To grasp this scenario, as Latour suggests, is to pay attention to the larger matrix in which change occurs. Helen Mayer Harrison and Newton Harrison grasped this idea from the beginning of their work together on environmental projects. They invoked the aesthetic concept of figure-ground, noting, 'A new reversal of ground comes into being where human activity becomes a figure within an ecological field as simultaneously the ecology ceases being an ever shrinking figure within the field of human activity'.[9] Agnes Denes, in her 1993 article 'Notes on Eco-Logic', puts it in a different way. She writes, 'Meanwhile, for the first time in human history, the whole earth is becoming one interdependent society with our interests, needs and problems intertwined and interfering. The threads of existence have become so tightly interwoven that one pull in any direction can distort the whole fabric, affecting millions of threads'.[10]

Writers have also grappled with ways to explain this more complex vision of the natural world. Often, like Denes and the Harrisons, they resort to metaphor. In the provocatively titled *The Mushroom at the End of the World* Anna Lowenhaupt Tsing uses the biology, harvesting and distribution of the matsutake mushroom as a basis for understanding, as she puts it in her subtitle the, 'Possibility of Life in Capitalist Ruins'. Mushrooms are a perfect figure for an entangled world. What we call mushrooms are, in fact, only the fruiting bodies of a vast underground network of tubular cells known as mycelium that branch, fuse and merge, forming a kind of highway through which nutrients and bacteria circulate between fungi and other organisms. In some cases, fungi create the conditions for their host's growth and sustenance. In others, they break down dead matter into usable soil that incubates future life. Mycologists argue that fungi, those models of interdependence, represent the principle of life.

The matsutake mushroom only emerges from damaged landscapes, making it an even more potent metaphor for our current state of existence. Trade in matsutakes operates outside the supply-and-demand paradigm of conventional economics, because they can't be cultivated. In a book that winds around ideas like an ever-expanding rhizome, Tsing investigates the systems that have evolved to find and distribute this highly prized fungus. In the course of her discussion, Tsing provides anthropological descriptions of the various ethnic groups involved in the mushroom trade, traces the symbiotic relationship between matsutake and pine forests, provides a critique of the overly restrictive scientific categories that inhibit our understanding of fungi, and points out the fallacies of 'scientific forestry'. Ultimately, the book also becomes a critique of our reliance on capitalism as a means of organizing the economy, reinforcing ideas expressed equally passionately by Carolyn Merchant in *The Death of Nature*.

These ideas find their echo in other recent books. Philosopher Donna Haraway turns to the metaphor of string figures to explain entanglement. Her *Staying with the Trouble: Making Kin in the Chthulucene* evokes the simple childhood game of cat's cradle in which patterns made with strings looped around the fingers are passed between players. The game is a model of constantly changing interconnections. Haraway urges us to imagine our existence as an equally entangled web of connections with other 'critters'. This is her designation for the totality of human and nonhuman beings, all of whom she urges us to consider as kin. She also ruminates on the nature of Gaia. She says, 'Earth / Gaia is maker and destroyer, not resource to be exploited or ward to be protected or nursing mother promising nourishment. Gaia is not a person but complex systemic phenomena that compose a living planet'.[11]

This is also the Gaia of James Lovelock and Lynn Margulis who gave the name to Gaia Theory. And it is the Gaia celebrated by the late Bruno Latour, Emeritus Professor at the Paris Institute of Political Studies referenced above. In a series of lectures reworked as a 2017 book titled *Facing Gaia: Eight Lectures on the New Climatic Regime*, Latour stresses that Gaia shouldn't be seen as a superior force or even a preordained system. He says, 'With the Gaia theory one can grasp the "power to act" of all the jumbled-up organisms without immediately integrating them into a unity that is superior to them and which they obey'.[12] This being the case, he advocates the establishment of a 'New Climate Regime' that would erase the distance between foreground and what had previously been considered background – landscape, nature and, most vitally, an 'Earth that seems to react to our actions'.[13] Nothing could be further from the Dominionist conception of a passive, exploited and easily dominated planet.

Toward a More Perfect World

> *The Death Instinct: separation, individuality, Avant-Garde par excellence; to follow one's own path to death – do your own thing, dynamic change.*
> *The Life Instinct: unification, the eternal return, the perpetuation and MAINTENANCE of the species, survival systems and operations, equilibrium.*[14]
>
> —Mierle Laderman Ukeles

Ideas like Gaianism, entanglement and reversal of figure and ground provided the compost out of which pioneering ecofeminists were able to create a revolutionary new kind of art. As Ukeles's definitions above suggest, artists struggled to find a language to describe this reordering of social and aesthetic values. Ukeles's Maintenance Art was born of her desire to heal the rift between her life as an artist and her life as a wife and mother. Her Manifesto, which opens with the statements above, contains the immortal question, 'After the revolution, who's going to pick up the garbage on Monday morning?' And it presents her battle cry in a fight for a new definition of art: 'I am an artist. I am a woman. I am a wife. I am a mother. (Random order.) I do a hell of a lot of washing, cleaning, cooking, renewing, supporting, preserving, etc. Also, (up to now separately) I "do" Art. Now I will simply do these maintenance everyday things, and flush them up to consciousness, exhibit them, as Art.'

From this manifesto was to flow a series of performances and projects that emphasize the web of often invisible tasks and systems that sustain families, communities and, ultimately, cities. Early performances involved such actions as washing the steps in front of a museum or asking all members of a corporation's maintenance staff to envision their work as art (fig.31). Ukeles then raised the stakes by convincing the New York Department of Sanitation to take her on as its official, unsalaried artist-in-residence. She has held this position since 1976 and uses it as a platform to educate the public about the disposal of their waste, to elevate the invisible workers who do the uncelebrated yet essential work that keeps the city running and to explore ways that art can actively participate in cleaning up the environment. These activities have taken various forms – ranging from the orchestration of garbage trucks as performers in street ballets to the designing of parks that transform capped landfills into public amenities. One of her longest ongoing projects is the creation of a park at the site of the Fresh Kills Landfill in Staten Island, New York. Titled *Landing*, it comprises a cantilevered overlook from which visitors can view two earthworks and experience the land below both as it is evolving today and as it originally existed as a wetland and tidal inlet. Underlying all her work is a systemic approach to the urban environment. Ukeles envisions the city as an organism, sustained – like the human body – by a series of systems: transportation as its circulatory system, architecture as its skeletal system and sanitation as its digestive system.

While one can trace aspects of Ukeles's work to currents in the art world during her formative years as an artist – among them conceptualism, land art, performance and process art – one essential element is her identity as an Orthodox Jew. This has inspired her to counter the Dominionist vision of the world with a philosophy that grows out of the Jewish idea of Tikkun Olam. Interpreted as 'Repairing the World', Tikkun Olam is linked to a Kabbalistic creation story in which seven vessels symbolizing the harmony of the universe are shattered under the impact of divine light, thereby casting the world into chaos and disharmony. Tikkun Olam puts the onus on humankind to repair this breach. As Ukeles says, 'And it's our job in the world to bring the vessels back to wholeness, to perfection again. But it's us, not the Divine – out of our power to recreate, to reinvent, to restore, to heal – we can bring those vessels back to wholeness again'.[15]

Ukeles has used Tikkun Olam as the basis for a number of works and performances, including an eponymous one in which she invites audience members to provide a written pledge to do something that will contribute to the ongoing work of Tikkun Olam. This belief in the healing power of art underlies all her work. In a field that is rife with pessimism and apocalypticism, she presents a model for environmental art that restores a natural balance through the combined efforts of the whole community.

Tikkun Olam suggests that Jews are obliged to work for a more perfect world. It hardly seems a coincidence that so many of the most important pioneers of eco-art come from Jewish backgrounds. One could also mention Alan Sonfist and Helène Aylon, along with younger eco-activists like Jackie Brookner, Aviva Rahmani, Amy Lipton and Linda Weintraub. One can see this directive at work in the art of Helen Mayer Harrison and Newton Harrison who, like Ukeles, created an influential model for artists pursuing environmental concerns. The Harrisons worked together as a husband-and-wife team from 1970 until Helen's death in 2018. Newton continued carried on with their work until his death in 2022. Their work comprises small- and large-scale environmental blueprints for system-wide approaches to specific ecological situations. Working with planners, ecologists, botanists and foresters, the Harrisons used their position as informed outsiders to influence policy discussions about land and water use here and abroad. The conventionally 'artistic' aspect of their work involved gallery installations made up of documentation, charts,

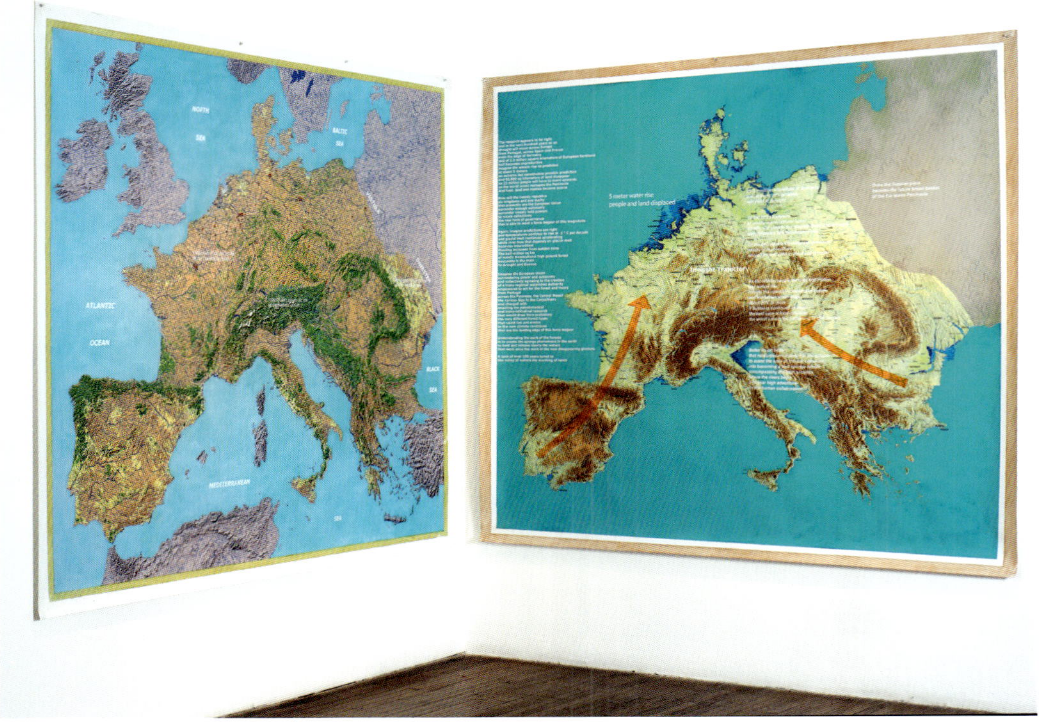

Fig.32 Helen Mayer Harrison and Newton Harrison, *Peninsula Europe*, 2007, installation at Ronald Feldman Gallery, New York, dimensions variable, collection of the Harrison studio

maps, sketches and aerial photographs accompanied by factual descriptions of problems and strategies, and poetic dialogues that blend the artists' voices with those of the experts and stakeholders with whom they have explored the situation. But in a deeper sense, the art in their work was the creation of dialogue and the insertion of new ideas and approaches into actual policy decisions.

A key element in their work was the erasure of barriers erected by local politics, short-term economic thinking, and national and regional borders. Instead, their plans pieced together formerly separated watersheds, mountains and land masses to form coherent ecological wholes. Over the years, they presented proposals that ranged in scale from their 1977 *Sacramento Meditations*, which critiqued the wasteful irrigation policies of the Sacramento-San Joaquin watershed in Northern California, to *Peninsula Europe* (2001–04), which redrew the map of the continent to present transnational strategies that would establish green farming, restore biodiversity and redirect irrigation systems (fig.32).

Around 2007 they began to rethink some of the premises of their work in light of the mounting impact of climate change. They dubbed their new approach the *Force Majeure* after the term for extraordinary circumstances that can nullify a legal agreement. Sometimes described as 'acts of God', such conditions are considered beyond the control of the parties involved. For the Harrisons, the *Force Majeure* highlighted the dire environmental consequences of human (in)action that are spiraling out of control. In the face of rising waters, storm surges, shrinking coastlines, searing heat waves, country-wide droughts and mass extinctions, they maintained that environmental problems must be addressed on a planetary scale. The *Force Majeure* comprises a set of prescriptions that demand the drastic reordering of human society and the physical landscape along lines that embrace the agency of nature. These include such 'counterextinction' measures as the relocation of whole ecosystems, the creation of fully self-sustaining 'green cities', cooperative ownership of agricultural commons and the implementation of systems that reverse the entropic loss of carbon dioxide from soil, as well as radical limits on growth, development and population.

In *Sensorium*, the Harrisons' last project, Newton took on the voice of the ocean. Using maps that view the seas as a single entity with 'dead spots' – mostly along urban coastlines – and 'safe spots' where marine life still thrives, he argued for a transoceanic approach. Measures to save this vital resource include purification of swamps, global reestablishment of wetlands, curtailing pollution and creating more sanctuaries and safe spots. In a video explaining this project, he says, 'We've lost our ability to scan – this is what artists can do'.[16]

Rethinking Capitalism

> *Our economic system and our planetary system are now at war.*[17]
>
> —Naomi Klein

Implicit in the Harrisons' approach was a critique of the capitalist system, something they shared not only with other ecofeminist artists but also with the major theoreticians of the movement. Carolyn Merchant has detailed the ecological and social devastation produced by the extractive paradigm of mechanistic science and 19th-century capitalism. Charlene Spretnak describes how global capitalism's single-minded focus on profit created a race to the bottom that has been devastating to the environment. And as a reminder that Dominionism is not the only way to interpret the Bible, Pope Francis's 2015 encyclical *Laudato si'* described man's destruction of the environment as a sin. In related remarks in an October 2014 address to participants in the World Meeting of Popular Movements, the Pontiff pointed his finger at the capitalist system: 'An economic system centered on the god of money also needs to plunder nature to sustain the frenetic pace of consumption inherent in it.'[18]

Ecofeminist artists have incorporated this critique into their works. One sees this in Ukeles's focus on collectivist action, in her efforts to redefine work and in her emphasis on empowering labor. The Harrisons stressed the failure of capitalism's growth paradigm and neoliberal economists' unwillingness to acknowledge the actual costs of environmental degradation. As they said, 'Physicists very well know that from an energy point of view there is "no free lunch". To push the metaphor a little bit, market forces perceive nature itself and all its productivity as a free lunch'.[19]

In 1982 Agnes Denes created a now-iconic work that dramatized the clash between agrarian and late-capitalist modes of production. For *Wheatfield – A Confrontation*, she planted wheat on two acres of soil that had been excavated to build the World Trade Center. The iconic photographs of this project, with yellow wheat swaying beneath Manhattan skyscrapers, serve as a reminder that even the mightiest urban system cannot survive without the ancient art of agriculture. The work offered two views of value – the real-world food value of the harvested wheat versus the transformation of the land from which it grew into an abstract financial vehicle under the aegis of Manhattan's soaring real-estate market.

Denes described the work thus: '*Wheatfield* was a symbol, a universal concept. It represented food, energy, commerce, world trade, economics. It referred to mismanagement, waste, world hunger and ecological concerns. It was an intrusion into the Citadel, a confrontation of High Civilization. Then again, it was also Shangri-La, a small paradise, one's childhood, a hot summer afternoon in the country, peace, forgotten values, simple pleasures.'[20]

Over the past 55 years, Denes has created a diverse and interdisciplinary body of work whose richness makes it hard to characterize.

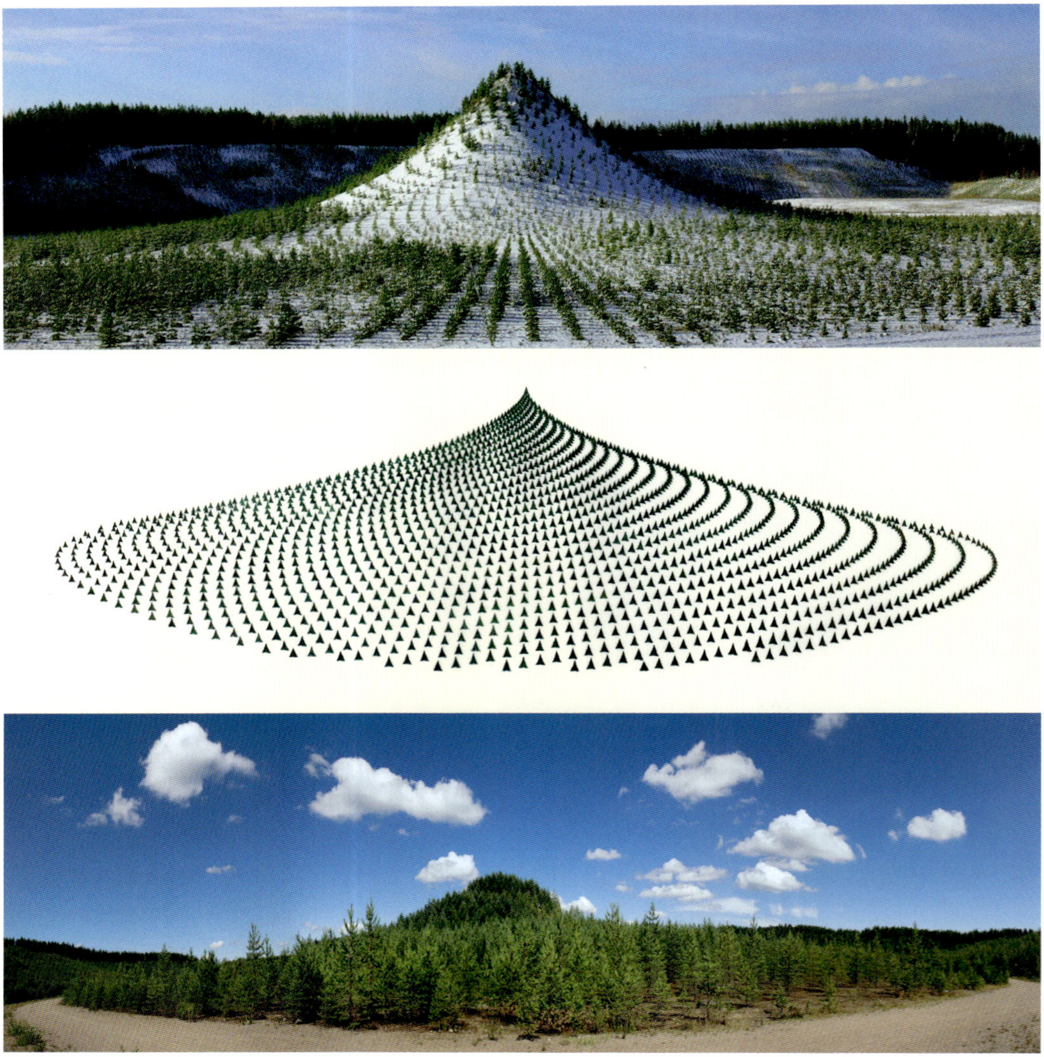

She describes her work as 'visual philosophy' devoted to an analysis of the human condition. This condition, she suggests, is one of interconnection: between disciplines; between humans and nonhumans; between nature and culture; between past, present and future. One extended series of drawings involves permutations of the pyramid form. As a mathematical figure comprised of individual units that form an interlocking whole, Denes's pyramids become a metaphor for myriad social, political and cultural concerns. Whether they stretch, coil, collapse, or take on the aspect of flying birds, these pyramids provide a metaphor for aspects of the human predicament in which

Fig.33 Agnes Denes, *Tree Mountain – A Living Time Capsule – 11,000 Trees, 11,000 People, 400 Years, 1992–96*, 1992/2013, manmade mountain in Ylöjärvi, Finland, 420 m long × 270 m wide × 38 m high (13778 feet long × 885.8 feet wide × 124.7 feet high

each of us is an individual convinced of our freedom while being inextricably enmeshed within a social system from which we cannot escape.

Between 1992 and 1996 Denes realized one of her pyramids as an artwork that, like *Wheatfield*, has also achieved iconic status. *Tree Mountain – A Living Time Capsule – 11,000 trees, 11000 People, 400 Years, 1992–96* (fig.33) is just that: a communally planted forest whose individual trees are arranged in a spiral on a mountain according to a mathematical formula derived from a combination of the golden section and the systems of the pineapple and the sunflower. Set in Finland on the site of a former gravel pit, the work again challenges the logic of capitalism: restorative rather than extractive, it reverses the damage produced by the industry while exemplifying the communal values of ecofeminism. As Denes notes, 'If our civilization as we know it ends or changes, there will be a reminder in the form of a strange forest for our descendants to ponder. They may reflect on an undertaking that did not serve personal needs but the common good and the highest ideals of humanity and its environment while benefiting future generations'.[21]

Such ideas have taken hold among a cohort of younger artists who use a variety of strategies to advance an ecofeminist critique of capitalism. One approach is to use the mechanisms of the free market against itself in order to challenge capitalism's tendency to privatize profit and socialize risk. Aviva Rahmani (b.1945) offers a particularly intriguing example of this. Her *Blued Trees Symphony* (begun in 2015; fig.34) is a performance work made within a forest by painting a musical score on the trees. The project poses the question, Can the American copyright law that protects art be used to protect land in danger of seizure under the rule of eminent domain? (This is the principle, too often abused by private interests, whereby private land can be seized by the government for purposes that serve the public good.) Rahmani pits the principle of eminent domain against the Visual Artists Rights Act of 1990. That piece of legislation protects the moral rights of artists, notably by preventing the destruction or alteration of a work of art by its owner. The various iterations of *Blued Trees Symphony* are designed to slow the construction of oil and natural gas pipelines across the country by designating pieces of land in their way as works of art.

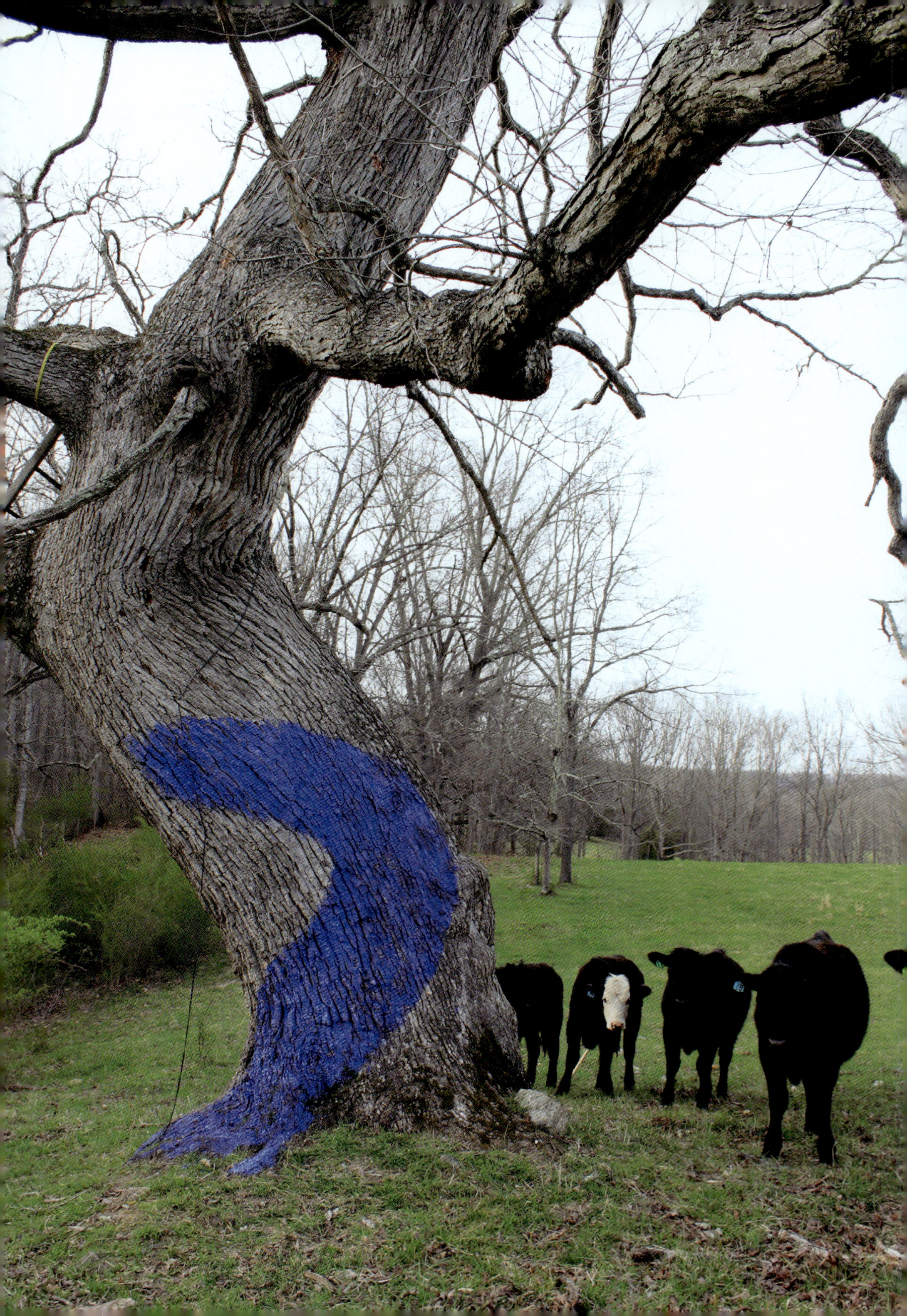

Fig.35 Amy Balkin, *Public Smog*, 2009, billboard in Douala, Cameroon

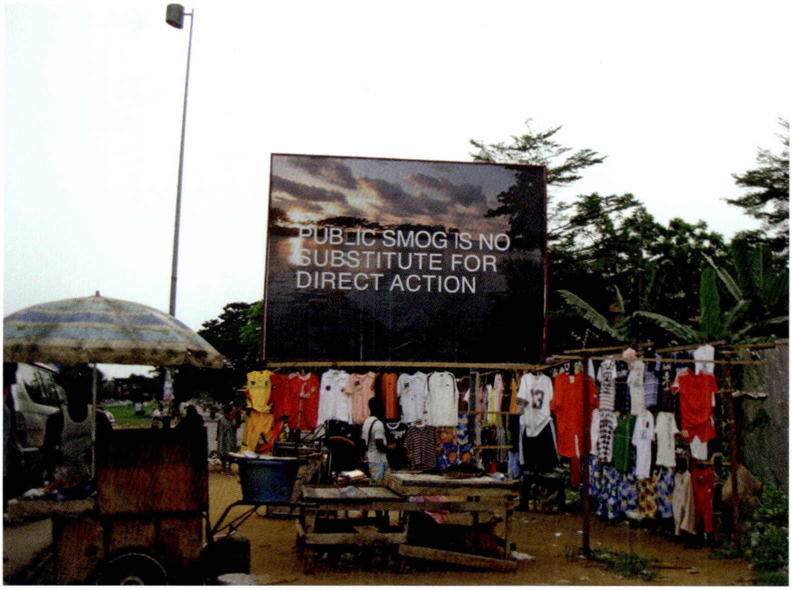

Fig.34 (left) Aviva Rahmani, *Blued Trees with Cows*, 2016, photographic documentation of one tree-note in an aerial score composed of ⅓-mile-long measures, painted with a casein of buttermilk and ultramarine blue pigment, located on Brush Mountain, VA, site of the proposed Mountain Valley Pipeline

Rahmani has composed a 'symphony' whose score is literally written on trees growing on properties in danger of being appropriated for a pipeline. She works with landowners and teams of volunteers to mark trees with sine waves in nontoxic blue paint. Each tree represents a note and each cluster of trees a chord. Each third of a mile constitutes a musical measure. The symphony can be imagined by visitors wandering through the forest. Or it can be performed on-site by musicians and singers who execute the painted score as they move through the forest. The work can also be realized digitally by feeding aerial GPS images from Google Earth into MuseScore software. Transformed into art, Rahmani argues that the forest is legally protected from destruction.

Amy Balkin (b.1967) also appropriates legal procedures for her own purposes. She exposes the absurdity of the idea, embodied in the concept of carbon tradeoffs, that the air we breathe can be bought and sold on the free market. Her *Public Smog* (2004 and after; fig.35) is a public park of shifting dimensions located in the sky. It has been created by collecting carbon offsets – credits that can be purchased by individuals, institutions or corporations from companies and programs that plant trees, fund renewable energy projects or otherwise reduce the carbon emissions into the atmosphere. In return, the buyers are allowed to exceed carbon emission standards elsewhere. The dubious premise is that this will create a net-zero increase in their carbon footprint.

By buying offsets, Balkin removes them from the open market where they could be used to justify higher levels of pollution elsewhere. *Public Smog* is thus a public commons composed of breathable air. Balkin has created several such parks in the United States and Europe. While currently they fluctuate in size according to the terms of the offsets, she is working toward getting the atmosphere designated as a World Heritage Site by UNESCO (the United Nations Educational, Scientific and Cultural Organization), which will make her reductions permanent.

In a similar spirit *All the Way to Hell* (begun 2020) by Eliza Evans (b.1967) uses the mechanisms of the capitalist system to forestall the practice of fracking near the three acres of land she inherited in Creek County, Oklahoma. Fracking is a controversial process whereby oil or gas is extracted from deep underground by injecting liquid at high pressure into fuel deposits in subterranean shale. Fracking can be highly profitable, leading drilling companies to offer landowners large sums for the mineral rights to their property. However, environmentalists decry the practice. Not only does it waste huge amounts of water, they argue, but it can set off earth tremors and lead to the contamination of the groundwater throughout the surrounding area. This impacts not just the mineral-rights holders but their neighbors as well. Current property law in some states maintains that a holdout's property can be fracked without the owner's consent if the surrounding neighbors have reached an agreement with the company.

Evans's project places what she hopes are insurmountable obstacles to drilling companies attempting to purchase mineral rights. She is selling the mineral rights to her three acres to 1,000 people – forcing any company to negotiate individually with each of these owners in any effort to obtain fracking rights. And she points out that this project has much larger implications. '*All the Way to Hell* is about the cultural constitution of space, even that space thousands of feet underground', she says. 'White people have continuously used property ownership regimes to forcibly divest BIPOC and women of their property throughout US history.'[22] Her project exploits the system to suggest a means of resistance.

Evans is not alone in pointing out the disproportionate impact that corporate policies and industrial practices have on disadvantaged groups. LaToya Ruby Frazier (b.1982) has made a case study of her hometown of Braddock, Pennsylvania. She uses photography to document the economic and social devastation visited on her family, friends and neighbors following the demise of the steel industry there in the 1960s and 1970s. Her family first arrived in Braddock four generations ago as part of the Great Migration of African Americans from the South. Although her grandmother could still remember when Braddock was a thriving community, by Frazier's childhood financial collapse had turned the neighborhood into a ghost town, while redlining (the denial of loans by banks and insurance companies to neighborhoods deemed poor risks for investment) had made it difficult for her relatives to leave. *The Notion of Family* is a kind of family album that reveals the impact of economic insecurity, disappearances of services and the mills' health-destroying pollution on her close relatives. Frazier reveals her subjects' dignity and stoicism in the face of devastating circumstances.

In a subsequent project Frazier turned her attention to another community devastated by corporate and government malfeasance. The city of Flint, in Michigan, former headquarters of General Motors, has become a poster child for ecological injustice. Following a cost-cutting move by the city manager in 2014, this low-income, predominantly Black community began to get its water directly from the Flint River, which had been polluted by raw sewage and industrial waste for decades. Almost immediately residents began to fall sick, and children's lead levels began to double. No action was taken for two years, until residents sued the city and state and brought the situation to national attention. Over a five-year period, Frazier worked with two mothers and their families to document the personal and community-wide impact of this crisis. The result was *Flint is Family* (fig.36), a book that presents their stories through photos and text and provides a toolkit for others facing similar situations.

The economic injustice surrounding lead pollution is also at the heart of an ongoing project by artist Mel Chin (b.1951). He first became involved in the issue when he visited New Orleans following Hurricane Katrina. Community groups alerted him to the high levels of lead in the soil of some of the most devastated neighborhoods. It turned out this problem predated Katrina and was the result of years of airborne lead dust from gasoline, paint and other industrial emissions.

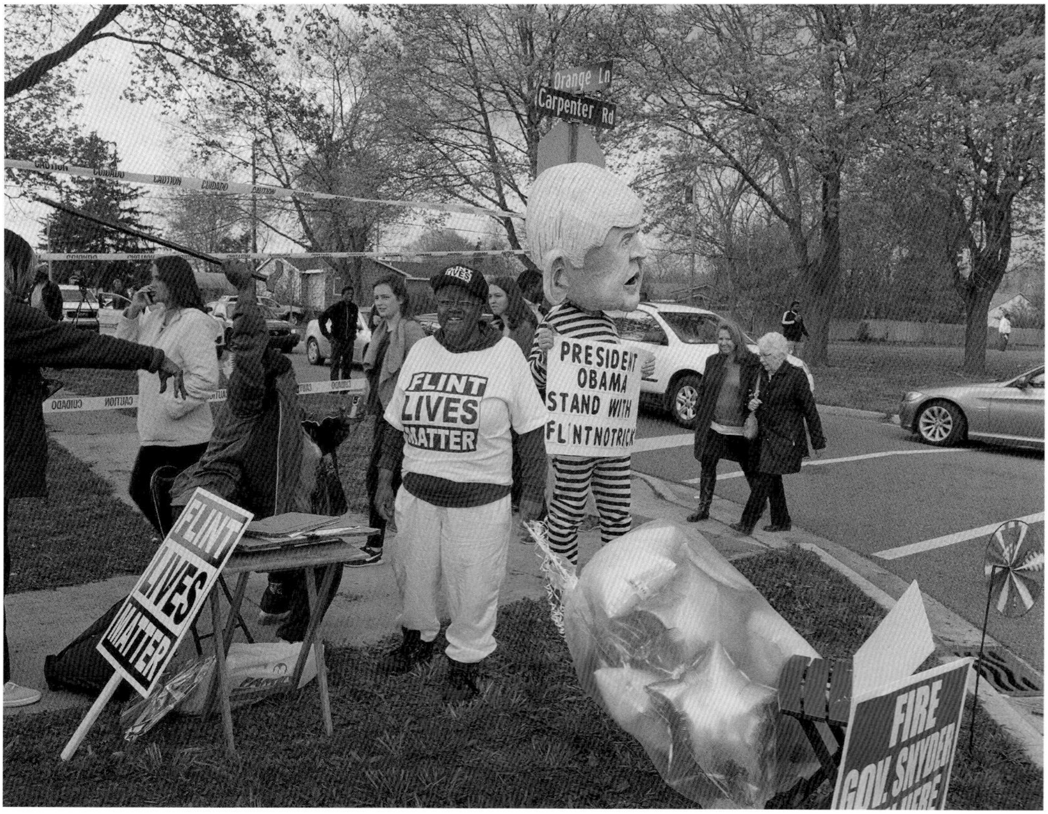

Fig.36 LaToya Ruby Frazier, *Flint Students and Community Members Outside Northwestern High School (Est.1964) Awaiting the Arrival of President Barack Obama, May 4, 2016, Flint, Michigan, III*, 2016–17, gelatin silver print, 50.8 × 61 cm (20 × 24 in)

Further investigation revealed that this was a nationwide issue and that high concentrations of lead tend to be located in underprivileged neighborhoods.

Chin reached out to scientists for a technological solution to the problem. But he also realized that a bigger problem involved the residents' lack of visibility and clout. This led to the birth of *Fundred* (fig.37) – an ongoing work of art that was also an initiative designed to bring the voices of vulnerable children to the attention of the lawmakers who might be able to actually do something about lead levels. Chin proposed to counter the vast amount of money spent by lobbyists for corporate polluters with millions of 'fundreds'. A contraction of *fun* and *hundred*, 'fundreds' are 100-dollar bills hand drawn from a template by children in neighborhoods affected by lead pollution. Chin worked with local community groups and institutions to help collect and deliver stashes of this symbolic cash to members of Congress.

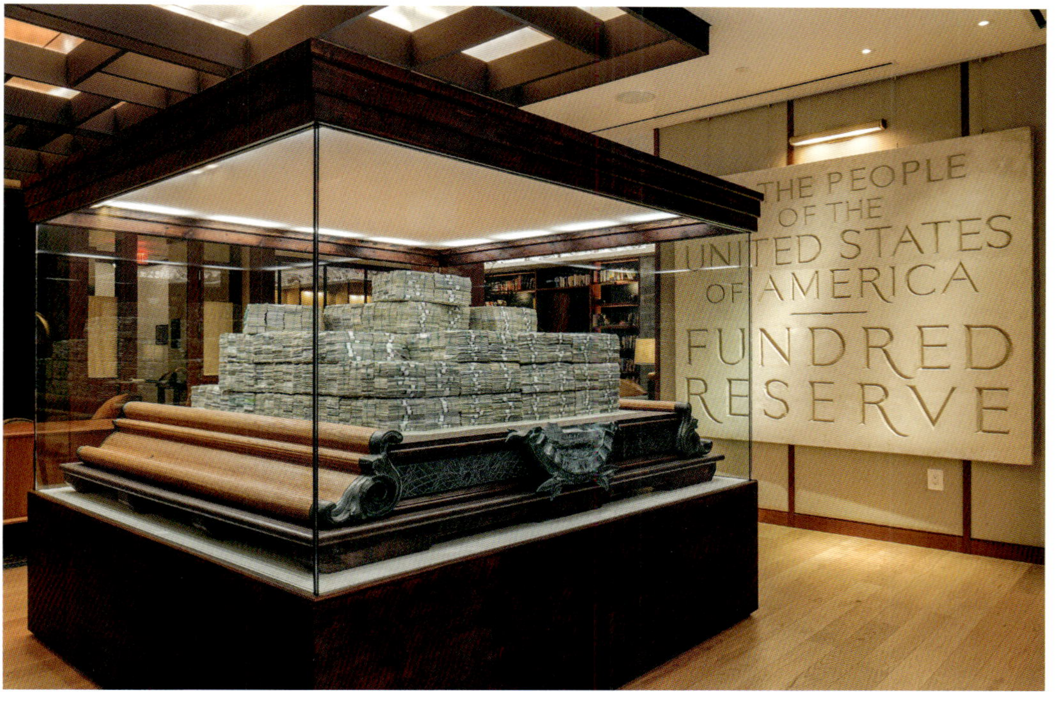

Fig.37 Mel Chin, *Pallet and Sign*, Eaton Workshop, Washington, DC, 2019, part of Operation Paydirt/Fundred Dollar Bill Project, 2006 – ongoing.

Chin's innovative approach has evolved over time. Where he originally envisioned the project as an exchange of symbolic dollars for real dollars, he came to realize that the project's real value was as an organizing tool. *Fundred* brought together groups and individuals working toward the goal of lead mitigation. It also exploited the ensuing media attention to help encourage political leaders to take action on an issue vital to the lives of their noncorporate constituents. Eventually the project took on its own life. Following the delivery of half a million fundreds to policymakers in Washington, DC, in 2020, today *Fundred* continues as a set of practices to help communities bring attention to numerous local issues.

Another way artists challenge corporate domination is by envisioning forms of social order that alter the prevailing paradigms of consumption and unchecked growth. This is the visionary approach taken by Mary Mattingly (b.1978). In 2013 she examined her own materialism by gathering all her possessions into a twine-wrapped ball and dragging it across the Bayonne Bridge, which stretches between Bayonne, New Jersey, and Staten Island, New York.

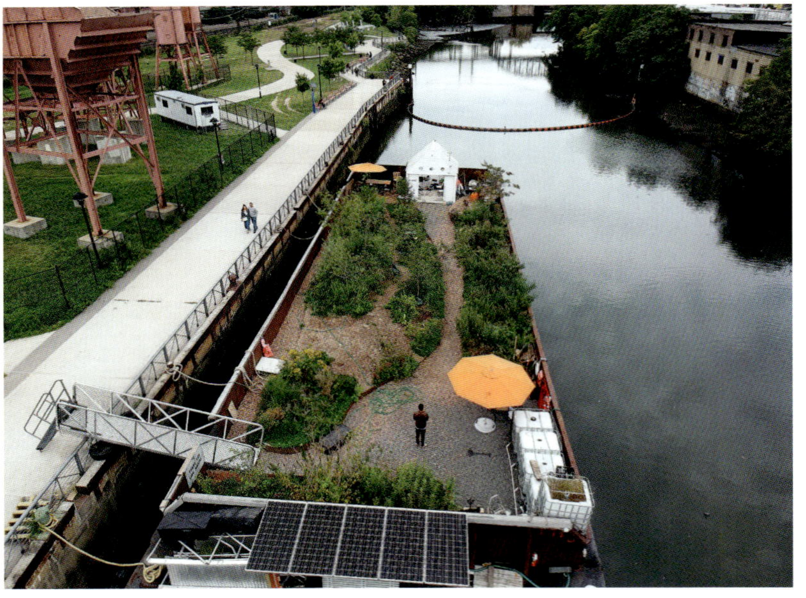

Fig.38 Mary Mattingly, *Swale*, 2017, floating food forest barge at Concrete Plant Park, New York

This action was accompanied by experiments in alternate living practices that challenge the urban paradigm of consumption and materialism. Mattingly specializes in self-sustaining environments that she places in or around New York City. Her 2009 *Waterpod Project* took place in the City's East River. It was an amphibious home built atop a 30-by-100-foot barge – complete with living quarters, a greenhouse, a windmill and a chicken coop on which she, three crew members and various guests lived for five months. Her mobile *Flock Houses* (begun 2011) are modular units designed to hitch to vehicles for easy transport around the city. They comprise geodesic domes covered with tarps made from reclaimed materials and are equipped with systems for rainwater capture, inner-city agriculture, and solar and human-powered energy. Such structures suggest how little is actually needed to live even in one of the world's most expensive cities. Implicit in such works is a critique of the city's failure to provide for its neediest residents who languish in the shadow of the private sector's almost obscene prosperity. Similarly, Mattingly's *Swale* (fig.38) is an ongoing project that challenges New York City's prohibition against growing or foraging food on public lands. It takes advantage of marine common law to create a floating public park and vegetable and herb garden on a barge moored on the East River. Until it was shuttered by COVID-19, its produce was freely available to any and all comers.

Performing Ecofeminism

We are storytellers. Our art is about direct engagement.[23]

—Newton Harrison

What can art do that science can't? Certainly one answer is that art can dramatize otherwise abstract concepts through performance. Visions of Mattingly struggling across the Bayonne Bridge with all her possessions on her back, of Ukeles washing the front steps of a museum and of Rahmani orchestrating a forest symphony offer audiences a visceral way to engage with environmental issues.

And these are only a fraction of the performative eco-works that have taken place. During the 1960s and 1970s, civil rights demonstrations and antiwar protests engulfed the United States. Against this background, performance helped artists collapse the boundaries between art, politics, environmentalism and science. Performance presented a vehicle for ideas that had no place in the commercial gallery world. And for women, in particular, performance provided a way to tie the oppressions of patriarchal society and the destructive ethos of capitalism directly to their impact on human bodies.

It is striking how many pioneering ecofeminist artists explored this medium. Curator Monika Fabijanska argues that performance is an integral aspect of ecofeminist art. She notes, 'Whether actions and performances, projects of ecological Land Art, or turning towards what could be considered urban planning, [ecofeminist projects] almost always include the element of ritual. Secretive and intimate, or public, ecofeminist rituals signify purification and pay respect to the cycle of life, where birth, growth, change and decay are its natural stages.'[24] This is evident in many early performances by the Denes, Rahmani and Harrisons, as well as eco-pioneers like Betsy Damon and Bonnie Ora Sherk.

Not all such works took place in front of audiences. Some were more strictly speaking performative, involving private rituals designed to put the artist in closer communion with natural forces. One such iconic work was Denes's 1968 *Rice/Tree/Burial*. The work had three elements: Denes planted a rice field in rural Sullivan County, New York, chained a group of trees and buried her own poetry in the earth. It thus represented a melding of creation, destruction and fusion with the earth. Similarly, the *Siluetas* of Ana Mendieta (1948–85), a performance in which the Cuban-born artist lay in a shallow grave-like space covered with flowers, addressed a sense of body and earth as one and of birth and death as part of an endless cycle of renewal.

Earth Ambulance by Helène Aylon (1931–2020) was more overtly political. This 1982 work pointed to the ties between Cold War militarism and human-induced environmental threat. *Earth Ambulance* was a truck emblazoned with a Red Cross logo that carried pillowcases filled with earth from 14 selected SAC (Strategic Air Command) military bases across the United States to a mass demonstration during SALT (Strategic Arms Limitation Talks) disarmament talks at the United Nations. Explaining the genesis of the idea, Aylon remarked, 'It was not long after hearing Dr Helen Caldicott speaking at the university about the drastic need for disarmament and critical need to end the Cold War. Looking at news photos of refugees, there are always images of women fleeing with a "sac" of precious belongings in one hand, a child clasping the other hand. We, too, would take our most precious belonging – i.e. the Earth itself, in all its variety, in our "sac", and carry it to safety.'[25]

In a quieter mode, *The Great Cleansing of the Rio Grande* (1987–94) by Dominique Mazeaud (b.1941) provided a nonurban counterpart to Ukeles's Maintenance Art. For this seven-year-long project, Mazeaud walked along the banks of the river monthly, collecting found objects, which she has referred to as gifts from the river. The eco-performance works of Cecilia Vicuña (b.1948) are equally low-key. Since the 1960s she has used her art to express concern about the fragility of the ecosystem and the need to reconnect with older indigenous ways of thinking. Among her best-known works are those that adapt the *quipu*, a form of communication from precolonized Andean cultures that used knotted cords to create intricate webs. Vicuña has woven these 'cloud nets' in to performances and presented them in installations that speak to the interconnectedness of nature and the threats to this unity posed by climate change.

Finding Solutions

We're in trouble if all artists can do is activate our fears.[26]

—Lucy Lippard

Performance was not the only way artists exited the gallery in the 1970s. Many moved into the landscape under the aegis of land art. This movement involved the creation of 'earthworks', the name given to interventions in remote, nonurban settings using natural materials found on site. Land art projects were variable in their degree of invasiveness – they ranged from Michael Heizer's 1969 *Double Negative* which consisted of a huge trench dug in the Nevada Desert to Dennis Oppenheim's 1968 *Annual Rings*, an ephemeral work created by cutting a series of rings in the snow covering the waterway that divides the United States and Canada. What united works by this mostly male group of artists was a tendency to aestheticize nature by regarding the land itself as a kind of canvas. At the same time, however, a countermovement, some of whose practitioners we have already met, were thinking more holistically. They were considering the environment as an ecological system and thinking about how to transform degraded sites into viable living spaces in which plants, animals and humans could flourish together.

In 1992 Barbara Matilsky, then curator at the Queens Museum of Art in New York City, gathered a group of these artists in an exhibition titled *Fragile Ecologies: Contemporary Artists' Interpretations and Solutions*.[27] Reviewing the catalogue from the perspective of the 2020s, it is clear that Matilsky was remarkably prescient. As her subtitle suggests, the show presented artists whose work aimed to restore, reclaim or remediate the damage wrought by urbanization, industrialization and commercial exploitation of the land.

Fragile Ecologies was the first major exhibition of this kind of art. In the catalogue, Matilsky sought to distinguish her artists from the apolitical land artists. She quoted from a 1979 symposium on earthworks in which artist Robert Morris pointed out the contradictions inherent in projects that merely aestheticize devastated landscapes without addressing the larger issues that created the problem: 'The most significant implication of art as land reclamation is that art can and should be used to wipe away technological guilt ... Will it be a little easier in the future to rip up the landscape for one last shovelful of non-renewable energy source if an artist can be found (cheap, mind you) to transform the devastation into an inspiring and modern work of art? Or anyway, into a fun place to be? Well, at the very least, into a tidy, mugger-free park?'[28]

Today similar charges of unwitting complicity are sometimes levied against the artists Matilksy championed. Critics like T.J. Demos suggest the participants in *Fragile Ecologies* didn't go far enough in their critique of the extractivist paradigm of the capitalist system. He also charges that in their failure to address 'inequality between post-industrial nations and the global South', they were insufficiently 'woke'.[29] But this criticism obscures the truly revolutionary aspect of the work of these pioneers. By using the processes of nature to heal the damage done by human interventions they were inventing a new model for activist art.

Matilsky presented documentation of early works by the Harrisons and Mierle Laderman Ukeles and included Mel Chin's first foray into environmental action. His *Revival Field*, begun in 1990, now serves as a prototype for 'green remediation'. Working with Dr Rufus Chaney, a senior research agronomist at the USDA (United States Department of Agriculture), Chin planted 'hyperaccumulater' plants in a field that had been contaminated with heavy metals. Chin and Chaney wanted to see if these plants could cleanse the soil by sucking out the metals, thereby providing a low-tech and low-impact alternative to more costly and unsatisfactory remediation methods. The three-year project identified the plant most adept at absorbing the toxins, opening the door to a new way of thinking about land restoration.

Fragile Ecologies included other groundbreaking works. For *Time Landscape* (mid-1960s to present), Alan Sonfist (b.1946) planted half a city block of downtown Manhattan with native plants, restoring the site to a semblance of its precolonial state. Surrounded by a fence and planted in the midst of an actively developing urban neighborhood, *Time Landscape* remains to this day as a kind of time capsule memorializing a world that has been lost. Matilsky cites Patricia Johanson (b.1940), whose first project dates to 1969, as the first artist to propose the reclamation of a landfill as art, now a fairly common artistic enterprise. *Fragile Ecologies* documented several of her habitat gardens that allow nature, in all its biodiversity, to reestablish itself in urban areas on damaged and degraded sites. By placing these gardens in dense urban areas, Johanson solves specific environmental problems like erosion, sewage overruns and decimation of local flora and fauna, while providing the public with an opportunity to experience a fully functioning ecosystem. Betty Beaumont (b.1946) was represented in *Fragile Ecologies* by her *Ocean Landmark Project* (completed 1980). This was an artificial reef created from recycled coal ash in an area depleted by overfishing and waste disposal. Transformed into a fish haven and lush underwater garden, it created a prototype for a new industry.

While she included men and women and did not frame her ideas explicitly in terms of ecofeminism, Matilsky chose the works in *Fragile Ecologies* for their conception of nature as a life-generating and potentially self-sustaining entity. Underscoring her belief in an entangled nature, she chose as an epigram for her introduction a quotation from the artist Rachel Rosenthal: 'Why is it that all of Gaia dances in harmony while we humans are the only ones out of step?'[30]

Though not included in the exhibition, Betsy Damon was also thinking along these lines in 1991 when she founded Keepers of the Waters, a nonprofit organization that serves as the umbrella for diverse activities designed to educate the public about the nature of what she calls 'living water systems'. Damon defines her 'living water systems' as water derived from natural sources that flows exclusively through streams and rivers fashioned by nature. This project evolved from her earlier work as a feminist performance artist practicing healing rituals, a concept that grew to encompass the health of the ecosystem.

One recurring theme in her projects is water's ability to cleanse itself when unimpeded by development and industry. Much of her current work evolved from a 1995 project in Chengdu, China, that involved a two-week residency with a group of local artists. Together they produced temporary public artworks and performances that dramatized the history and consequences of the industrialization of the Funan River. This in turn led to a return invitation, this time to create a city park that she dubbed the *Living Water Garden* (fig.39). The six-acre site, which opened in 1998, includes a natural wetland that acts as a water-cleaning system, an environmental education center and an amphitheater and interactive water sculptures, including a giant fish that symbolizes regeneration. The *Living Water Garden*'s purpose is to demonstrate the

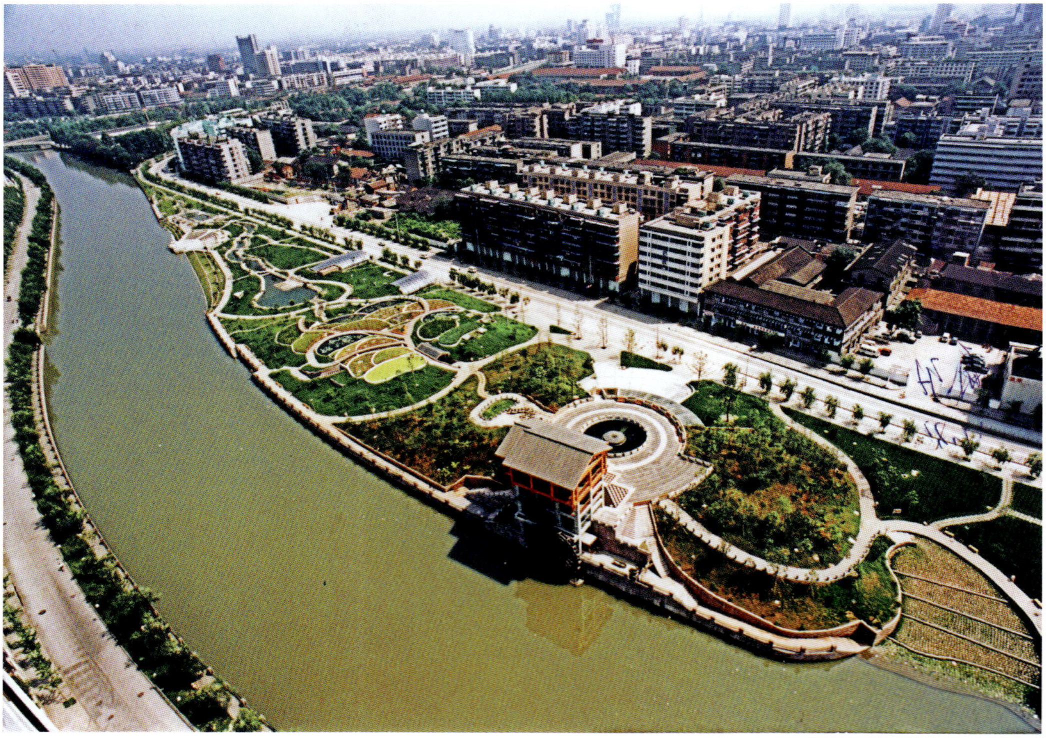

Fig.39 Betsy Damon, *Living Water Garden*, 1998, aerial view, 23,876.5 m² (5.9-acre) urban park in Chengdu, China

use of natural processes to cleanse water. As with the earlier festival, it was the product of extensive community meetings and discussions about local water conditions.

Damon has taken this model to other locations including across the United States as well as to China and Tibet. She characterizes Keepers of the Waters as a catalyst: her organization brings together community leaders and experts and helps them brainstorm solutions to environmental problems, while leaving control in local hands. It also involves a wide-ranging educational effort, through a website, blog, memoir and newsletter, that details the latest news from scientists, artists and other activists on issues ranging from the toxicity of tap water throughout the United States to green solutions like reforestation and eco-friendly lawns.

Like other ecofeminist artists, Damon has looked to indigenous land use practices as inspiration for her work. In 1981 the feminist publication *HERESIES* put out an issue titled 'Feminism and Ecology'.[31] Even in those early days, before the term 'intersectionality' had entered the feminist vocabulary, the editors sought to be as inclusive as possible and included several articles from Native women active in the environmental movement. These included Rocky Olguin, a member of the Red Power Movement, Lois Red Elk, participant in a 1980 Survival Gathering in the Black Hills of South Dakota and Madonna Thunder Hawk, founder of WARN (Women of all Red Nations). These writers discussed their work to protect tribal lands and the protests organized to publicize the impact of irresponsible mining practices on Native communities.

More recently indigenous artists have been in the forefront of efforts to stop the now cancelled Keystone XL Pipeline and the still functional Dakota Access Pipeline, pointing out the risks they pose to crucial water supplies, the dangers of heightened global warming from their release of greenhouse gases, the destruction of habitats of wildlife and migratory birds, and the despoliation of various sacred sites. One of the standout works of the 2022 Whitney Biennial was a 2016 work titled *Silent Choir*, created by Navajo artist Raven Chacon (b.1977). This audio-field recording documents a moment of silent resistance when hundreds of activists faced off against state police and pipeline security forces, who were guarding access to the drilling grounds of the Dakota Pipeline. As described by the *New York Times* critic Holland Cotter, 'With only the sound of rustling and breathing and the occasional whir of surveillance helicopters breaking the silence, it's a deeply moving piece of history-almost-not-there'.[32]

Other indigenous artists have created works that highlight the environmental efficacy of native practices. One example of this is *Midden* (2021) by Mohawk artist Alan Michelson (b.1953). It comprises video images of Newtown Creek in Queens, New York, and the Gowanus Canal in Brooklyn, New York, projected over three tons of oyster shells positioned such that they resemble a shoreline. The work's title refers to the enormous mounds of oyster shells that lined Manhattan's precolonial shoreline when it was home to the indigenous Lenape peoples. Such oyster reefs served multiple purposes in their lives. Not only were oysters a major food source but their shells were used to decorate the wampum belts used for diplomacy and trade. Oysters also had ecological functions. They filtered and cleaned the waters and created habitats for hundreds of other species, while the middens protected the shorelines.

When the Dutch arrived, colonists took advantage of the abundance of oysters to create a thriving industry. Oysters were devoured by rich and poor alike, and their discarded shells were used to fertilize crops, create mortar for new construction and pave streets. Eventually overharvesting and industrial pollution led to the disappearance of the oyster population along with the environmental benefits they bestowed. Today the former oyster beds of Newtown Creek and the Gowanus Canal are among the nation's most polluted waterways. To gather the shells for his installation, Michelson worked with the Billion Oyster Project, a nonprofit group that aims to restore the New York Harbor by recreating an oyster habitat through the distribution of discarded oyster shells from local restaurants. Drawing attention to these efforts, Michelson's work revives a lost history, while pointing to a possible solution to problems posed by pollution, rising waters and erosion due to climate change.

Oysters of another sort feature in a remediation project by Jan Mun (b.1971). Her subject is also the toxic Newtown Creek, but she is working with oyster mushrooms. These remarkable fungi are able to neutralize hydrocarbons present in petroleum products such as oil, pesticides and herbicides. And like Mel Chin's hyperaccumulator plants, oyster mushrooms can absorb heavy metals. Since 2013 Mun has collaborated with ExxonMobil to create *The Fairy Rings @ ExxonMobil Greenpoint Petroleum Remediation Site*. Newton Creek is a Superfund site. It was contaminated by an oil spill in 1950 that was not discovered until 1978, by which time it had polluted the groundwater for decades. Mun's project aimed at restoring the quality of the site's contaminated soil by wrapping oyster mushroom mycelium around monitoring wells. Tests demonstrated the mushroom's ability to decompose the pollutants. Mun continues to explore the possibilities of myco-remediation in ongoing collaborations with scientists, corporate partners and community groups.

These examples represent only a tiny fraction of the remediating work being done by artists today. Other important practitioners include Harriet Feigenbaum, Buster Simpson, Lillian Ball, Jackie Brookner, Frances Whitehead and Lauren Bon. Their works illustrate the potential of natural processes to restore the damage done by human intervention. This conception of environmental art is a practical expression of the Gaian vision of the earth as a potentially self-regulating system.

Breaking the Human-centric Vision

> *Recuperation is still possible, but only in multispecies alliance, across the killing divisions of nature, culture, and technology and of organism, language and machine.*[33]
>
> —Donna Haraway

Joseph Beuys (1921–86) was one of the founders of the German Green Party. He is often hailed as the ultimate Shaman artist who dissolved the boundaries between the human, animal and spirit worlds. In a famous 1974 performance work titled *I Like America and America Likes Me*, he wrapped himself in a felt blanket, carried a shepherd's crook and spent three days in a cage penned up with a live coyote. The work, it has been explained, invoked Native American understandings of nature and mythology in order to present a model for the melding of human and animal consciousness.

But before Beuys cohabited with the coyote (and with much less self-aggrandizement), Bonnie Ora Sherk (1945–2021) undertook a series of performances devoted to the comingling of humans and diverse living species. In 1970 she created three *Portable Parks* in San Francisco. These temporarily rehabilitated derelict public spaces offered drivers and passersby the astonishing sight of farm and zoo animals communing on concrete islands adjacent to a freeway off-ramp.

Sherk followed this up in 1971 with *Public Lunch*. For this work, she ate lunch in a cell at the San Francisco Zoo in the company of a caged rat while the tiger next door looked on. For *Living in the Forest: Demonstration of Atkin Logic, Balance, Compromise, Devotion, etc.* (1973) at the De Saisset Museum in Santa Clara, California, she created an entire ecosystem in a museum gallery, complete with trees and various animals, among them chickens, rabbits, doves, a rat and a pig. She allowed the constituents to interact, noting, 'I began doing work with the animals who I saw as performers as well, with me in relation to them and with them, and the animals in relation to each other and me. They were not pets, which I thought of as being "animals of compromise". I was not fully controlling their behavior.'[34] The animals followed their natural instincts, mating, nesting, giving birth, establishing territory and, in one case, dying of old age.

These efforts culminated in a seven-year project titled *The Farm* that lasted from 1974 to 1980. Located at an intersection of freeway overpasses in San Francisco, it was a more expansive, longer-term correlate to the *Portable Parks. The Farm* comprised organic gardens, an animal sanctuary, art exhibitions and performance spaces for musicians and actors.

Sherk saw these works as experiments in which she learned from animals about natural systems, ecology and art. As a scientist as well as an artist (she has degrees in engineering, neuroscience and bioengineering), Natalie Jeremijenko (b.1966) takes an even more rigorous empirical approach to her projects. She designs situations and experiments that explore unusual partnerships between humanity and nature. Her projects are developed under the auspices of Jeremijenko's Environmental Health Clinic. She notes that she wants to change the status of nonhumans by extending to them the kind of rights currently reserved for humans. Her projects are designed to provide the public with models for ecological action. Her *Feral Robotic Dogs* are remote-controlled dog-shaped toys equipped with chemical sensors so that they can sniff out environmental toxins. Her *Butterfly Bridges* encourage butterfly pollination across otherwise disconnected patches of urban nature. *Tree X Office* was a solar-powered workspace installed in the summer of 2012 at Socrates Sculpture Park in Queens, New York. It was 'owned' by the tree in which it was constructed. As landlord, the tree made US$400 a month and used the profits for its own interests, which included sending its saplings to be planted at various universities. Jeremijenko has also set up *Fish Restaurants* (begun 2010) where, as she notes, fish are fed rather than eaten. Their algae-based food binds to heavy metals they may have ingested, allowing the toxins to pass through them.

One particularly innovative project was *Mussel Choir* (fig.40). This work was created in collaboration with architects Mark Shepard and David Benjamin for the 2012 Venice Biennale and has had several other iterations since then. It relies on the fact that mussels filter water at a prodigious rate. The mollusks are outfitted with sensors that detect the opening and closing of their shells. This data is then converted into sound, allowing the bivalves to literally sing. Because mussels flap in distress when there are high levels of pollution, their songs will communicate the condition of the surrounding water.

Fig.40 Natalie Jeremijenko, Mark Shepard and David Benjamin, *Mussel Choir*, 2012, a monitoring system using live mussels as bio-sensors commissioned by the US Pavilion for the Venice Biennale, 2012

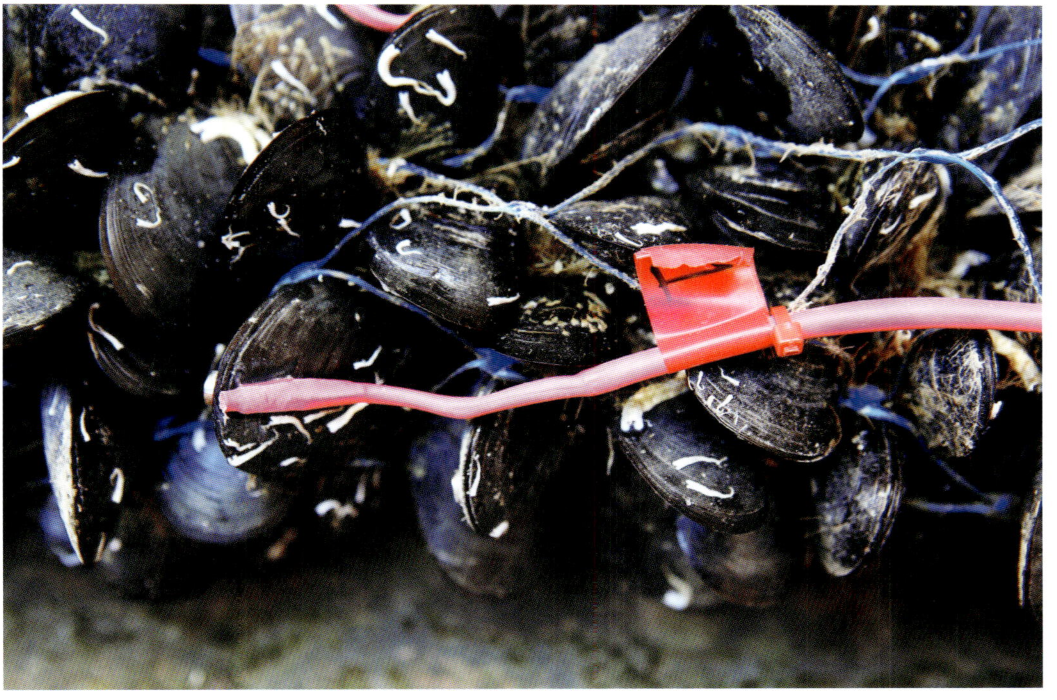

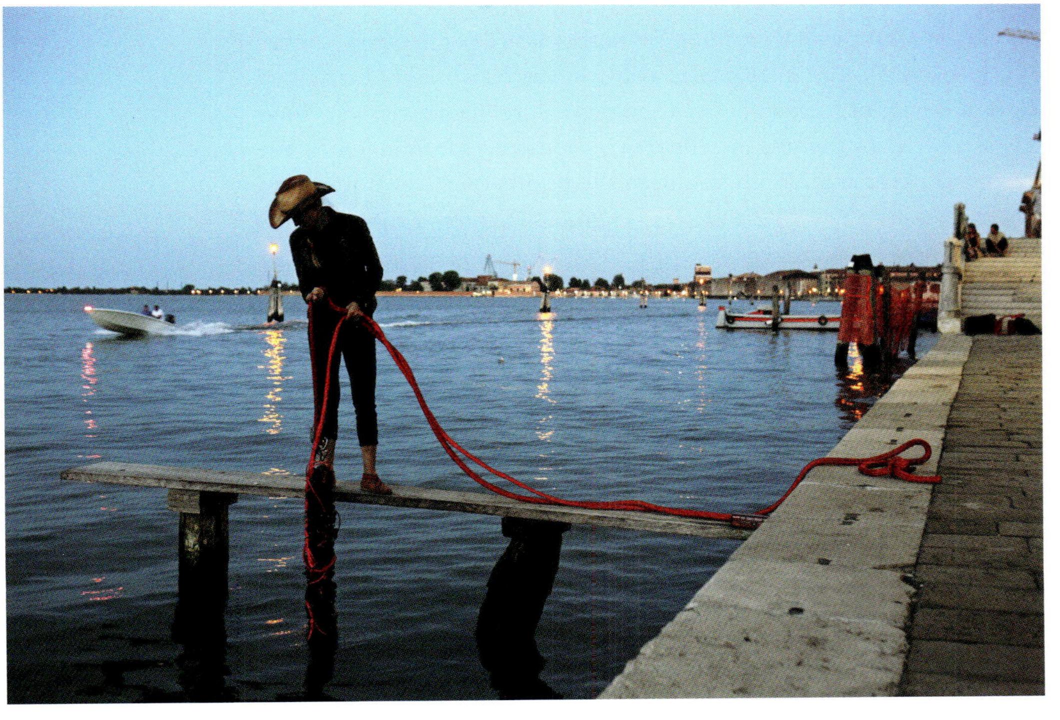

Such work underscores the benefits to humans of a more cooperative relationship with other life forms. Other artists take the idea of interspecies collaboration a step further, creating works to benefit species that have been endangered by human activity. Lynne Hull (b.1956) coined the phrase 'trans-species art' in 1985 to describe art made for animals. She creates or enhances habitats for 'clients' that include hawks, eagles, pine martens, ospreys, owls, spider monkeys, salmon, butterflies, bees, frogs, toads, newts, bats, beavers, songbirds, otters, small desert species and waterfowl. Her first work of this nature, created in 1983, consisted of spiral hydroglyphs carved into rocks to store water for desert wildlife. She has built marten havens, raptor roosts, monkey bridges, salmon-spawning pools, floating art islands for aquatic species and other works designed to protect and shelter animals from the dangers posed by urbanization and industrial development.

While Hull's work directly addresses the needs of her 'clients', it also provides human benefits through the restoration of biodiversity to our increasingly impoverished ecological environment. She notes that her works 'function in the temporal gap between the time reclamation of damaged sites begins and the time nature recovers'.[35]

Writer Donna Haraway is one of the prime proponents of the Gaian worldview. Her philosophy has been described as feminist posthumanism, meaning that it moves beyond an anthro-centric vision of nature to view all living entities as equally important. Using pigeons as a model, she illustrates what this vision of other species would look like. 'Pigeons have very old histories of becoming-with human beings', she notes, adding, 'They are treasured kin and despised pests, subjects of rescue and of invective, bearers of rights and components of the animal-machine, food and neighbor, targets of extermination and of biotechnical breeding and multiplication, companions in work and play and carriers of disease, contested subjects and objects of "modern progress" and "backward tradition"'.[36]

Haraway's point is to see pigeons and humans as partners in a long and entangled relationship. She urges us to recognize the role pigeons have played in human history and the role we have played in theirs. She suggests we imagine ways that pigeons and humans can work together for mutual benefit. For an example of this she describes the *Pigeonblog*

(2006–8), an art/science project spearheaded by artist-researcher Beatriz da Costa (b.1974). Working with artists, engineers, pigeon fanciers and the birds themselves, da Costa outfits racing pigeons with pollution-sensing devices. They are trained to use their special homing skills and flight patterns to collect and distribute information about air quality in San Jose, California. Such conditions, da Costa points out, affect humans and pigeons alike. As *Pigeonblog*'s now defunct website maintained, '*Pigeonblog* attempted to start a discussion about possible new forms of co-habitation in our changing urban ecologies and made visible an already existing world of human-pigeon interaction'.[37] Such thinking is based on the possibility of mutual flourishing for all members of the interspecies community.

Trans-species art extends to other life forms as well. Humans are often beside the point in the works included in *Symbionts: Contemporary Artists and the Biosphere,* an exhibition presented in a 2022 exhibition at the MIT List Visual Arts Center in Cambridge, Massachusetts. Curated by Caroline A. Jones, Natalie Bell and Selby Nimrod, *Symbionts* probed various forms of symbiotic entanglement through the work of an intriguing group of artists whose work cuts across such disciplines as microbiology, chemistry, mycology and entomology. Among the projects, Pierre Huyghe introduced spiders into the gallery where they were free to create webs and live without regard for human visitors. Candice Lin fertilized lion's mane mushrooms with the urine of staff volunteers, nourishing a beneficial fungus with human waste. Jenna Sutela interrogated the intelligence of bacteria by placing social amoebas into a maze that the organism must navigate to reach a supply of oats. Claire Pentecost highlighted the value of 'living soil' by pressing it into gold-leaf-covered ingots to create a form of currency. Anicka Yi suggested the kinship of living organisms and machines by creating tableaux within a wall-mounted aquarium of freshwater algae interacting with various 3D-printed elements. Taken together the works provided a celebration of Gaianistic mutualism. In her catalogue essay, Jones underscored this aspect of the exhibition by identifying the questions that drove her exhibition: 'If we are dependent on other living entities to survive, how should we acknowledge and honor that affiliation? How shall we live with responsibility and reciprocity in mind?'[38]

A Hopeful Future

> *The image of the lost paradise garden leaves one without a solid dialectic, and causes one to suffer an ecological despair.*[39]
>
> —Robert Smithson

Haraway's multispecies flourishing may seem a utopian dream in these darkly apocalyptic times. More typical now is the kind of narrative that drives the 2022 film *Don't Look Up* in which a looming asteroid serves as a metaphor for the unfolding climate crisis. In the film, a few hysterical whistleblowers are unable to rouse earth's political, corporate and media classes to prevent an entirely avoidable catastrophe. The film ends with the obliteration of the planet and everything on it. While many critics were unkind to the film, climate scientists remarked on its spot-on depiction of the difficulties they face in directing officialdom's attention to a threat that could destroy everything we hold dear.

In a time when the debate has shifted from whether we have reached a tipping point to how badly things are going to change, it is easy to succumb to inertia and ecological despair. But the lesson of ecofeminism is today, as it has been since its origins in the 1970s, that we must reshape our thinking about our place in the world. Haraway calls it 'staying with the trouble'. Anna Tsing ruminates on 'the Possibility of Life in Capitalist Ruins'. In a text poem that accompanies the *Force Majeure*, the Harrisons urge 'surrendering the idea that humankind is a special case / understanding that we are simply / even humbly, a species among species'.[40]

We cannot bring the old world back. But we can create a livable future. In a 2022 interview given when he had reached the venerable age of 102, James Lovelock remarked, 'But my fellow humans must learn to live in partnership with the Earth, otherwise the rest of creation will, as part of Gaia, unconsciously move the Earth to a new state in which humans may no longer be welcome'.[41] The artists here present blueprints for an alternative vision. In place of Dominionism, ecofeminist artists tell stories of an entangled nature, and they present strategies for acting on that vision. The rest is up to us.

EPILOGUE

Feminist art, which emerged in the 1960s with the women's movement, is the formative art of the last four decades. Scan the most innovative work, by both men and women, done during that time, and you'll find feminism's activist, expansionist, pluralistic trace. Without it identity-based art, crafts-derived art, performance art and much political art would not exist in the form it does, if it existed at all. Much of what we call postmodern art has feminist art at its source.[1]

—Holland Cotter

Mothers of Invention articulates the links that bind feminist ideas to the evolution of contemporary art. This is a project that allowed each of us to delve into ideas that have been central to our thinking for over forty years. Digging deep into four crucial practices, we were able to illuminate how the feminist revolution also sparked an artistic one. We uncovered evidence of the ways that feminist ideas like mutualism, impurity, corporality and return to the handmade shook up a calcifying art establishment and provided the nourishment for new ideas and approaches to art. And we were able to trace the continuing influence of these ideas on artists today.

Our title and the organization of this book highlight the contributions of women artists to this transformative process. We began to think about the importance of certain pioneering women in laying the groundwork for current conceptions of performance, craft, abstraction and ecofeminism. These figures are indeed mothers. The possibilities they gave birth to have gone on to shape today's art world. We pay homage to their nurturing influences by opening each chapter with a photograph of a key figure in each of our narratives. These historical images serve as a link between the feminist revolution and the art of today.

'Performance Art and Action' opens with an image of Marina Abramović's *Rhythm 0* (1974), a six-hour piece in which she invited the audience to use a range of objects on her as they desired. During this performance, benign gestures like offering a rose soon escalated into acts of violation and violence, leaving the artist half-naked and bleeding. Abramović's striking work exemplifies the central tenets of performance art – the breakdown of boundaries between art and life, artist and audience, an emphasis on knowledge gained through the body and the introduction of personal and political meaning and content through works that consistently test her physical and psychological limits. In hindsight it is clear that Abramović and her feminist peers essentially invented the radical medium known as performance, with Abramović widely hailed as its 'grandmother'. And while the visceral impact of live art focused on the body galvanized audiences when it first emerged in the late 1960s and early 1970s, the sense of disembodiment that increasingly defines the digital age has made the presence of performance even more compelling – and powerful – today.

'Handmade: Art, Craft and Feminism' is introduced by a photograph of Lenore Tawney, taken in her studio in 1958. She was soon to be acknowledged as a leader of the nascent fiber arts movement, itself an early indication that the old hierarchies determining which disciplines demanded serious scholarly and public attention (painting and sculpture) and which did not (craft) were about to be dismantled. Tawney, serene and determined, winding threads from bobbins onto a loom in a process that distinctly resembles an old-fashioned telephone operator at work, is busy weaving a new story in this picture. It would broadcast that the value of the hand, and of lived experience, would no longer be eclipsed. After 65 years, *craft* and *artisanal* are terms of luxury in the consumer marketplace; their status affirms that once again handcraft as promoted by artists is challenging established values. And now as earlier, women are in the forefront. The industrial age was dominated by men, and its processes and materials were the backstory of many in the minimalist generation. That culture's death has had colossal sociopolitical consequences. While it lingered, women were already forging ahead, seeing the importance of other forms, of fluid working conditions, of the skills of domesticity, and of admitting introspection and self-expression as important forms of intelligence. In the present moment those values are more important than ever. If heavy industry was inhospitable to women, NFTs and other algorithm-driven artworks, like AI-driven text, may prove inimical to humanity. But handmade artworks, like printed books, have been prematurely dismissed many times and are as vital now as ever.

The opening image for 'Beyond Tragic and Timeless: Women, Abstraction and Feminism' is the iconic photograph of Pat Steir flinging white paint onto an immense black canvas already alive with drips, gestures and pours. Taken in Steir's New York studio in 1990, the photographer captures Steir mid-gesture, the paint frozen in air as it travels from paintbrush to canvas. The picture reveals the culmination of Steir's explorations of art history of the previous decade – seen through both a conceptual and minimalist lens – resulting in a reimagination of painting. By adopting and adapting the drip technique of Jackson Pollock, Steir also challenged the patriarchal norms of the art world at the time. This single image conveys so much. It's performative and physical and reveals the primacy Steir and other women at the time placed on material. Here the artist creates a waterfall, not an image of a waterfall, and an alchemical transformation takes place as the paint becomes the falling water. Gravity plays a role, but so does the tempo and the choreography of the gesture. Like Hilma af Klint, an early 20th century pioneer of abstraction, Steir believes in the power of abstract art to convey a higher truth or perhaps a different truth. Not surprisingly, Steir's favorite artwork in the collection of the Metropolitan Museum of Art in New York is the 19th-century Kongo Power Figure, a collaboration between the tribal artist and the shaman that is imbued with a magical power to protect and heal the tribe. Today abstraction continues to be ripe for reinvention, for reenvisioning what truth looks like in a 21st-century world.

A photograph of Mierle Laderman Ukeles washing the steps of the Wadsworth Atheneum opens the discussion of ecofeminism. Her radical idea – announced in her 1969 'Manifesto for Maintenance Art' – was a feminist version of the collapse of art into life. She expanded the traditional female role of domestic nurture and transformed it into a form of care for society at large and ultimately for the planet itself. In the

1973 performance documented here she embraced the tasks of cleaning and maintenance that were usually consigned to a corps of low-paid workers. Meticulously scrubbing the museum steps, she underscored the reality that art institutions like the Wadsworth Atheneum do not exist in a vacuum. Instead their existence is predicated on a larger network of workers whose activities may be invisible to the artgoing public. The idea of interconnection and interdependence runs through the entire body of Ukeles's work. This makes her the ideal figure with which to introduce a discussion of ecofeminism's challenge to long-standing and destructive assumptions about the relationship between humankind and nature. Ukeles's call for an ecological consciousness that stresses collaboration, reciprocity and connection reverberates through the work of a growing group of younger eco-minded artists. Today climate change is casting an ever-longer shadow, revealing the unintended consequences of the extractive, human-centric dominionist paradigm. By refusing the logic of mastery and control, ecofeminist artists provide models for other ways of envisioning our relationship to the natural world. In the process, they restore our sense of agency in the face of what is indeed an existential threat to human existence.

As we worked on this book, we found ourselves thrown between optimism and pessimism. The narratives presented in *Mothers of Invention* are deeply inspiring. Feminism's role in shaping our cultural consciousness becomes ever clearer. But in recent years we have also become aware of the reality that many of feminism's advances on the practical and political front are eroding. This backsliding is occurring in a world that is also threatened by climate change, creeping authoritarianism and reactionary politics. This makes the project of excavating our artistic history more vital than ever. By going back to the artists and ideas that sparked the feminist revolution, we can rediscover the tools that made change possible. And we can reacquaint ourselves with the invigorating emotion of hope.

NOTES

Performance Art and Action

1 Lucy R. Lippard, quoted in Robert Nickas, 'Introduction' in, *The Art of Performance: A Critical Anthology* (Gregory Battcock and Robert Nickas, eds.), E. P. Dutton, New York, 1984, p.xiii.

2 Amelia Jones, *Body Art/Performing the Subject*, University of Minnesota Press, Minneapolis, 1998. I am greatly indebted to Professor Jones for her critical insights into body art of the 1970s.

3 Amelia Jones, 'Introduction' in, ibid., p.9.

4 Nancy Princenthal, *Unspeakable Acts: Women, Art, and Sexual Violence in the 1970s*, Thames & Hudson, London, 2019, p.34.

5 Jones, op.cit., esp. see ch.2, 'The "Pollockian Performative" and the Revision of the Modernist Subject'.

6 Victoria Horne, '"the personal clutter . . . the painterly mess . . ." Tracing a History of Carolee Schneemann's *Interior Scroll*', Wiley Online Library, September 28, 2020, https://doi.org/10.1111/1467-8365.12529.

7 Carolee Schneemann quoted in Robert C. Morgan, 'Carolee Schneemann: The Politics of Eroticism', *Art Journal*, vol.56, no.4, winter 1997, p.100.

8 Leslie Dick, 'Hannah Wilke "The Internal Scars Don't Really Show"', *X-TRA Contemporary Art Quarterly*, June 1, 2004, https://www.mutualart.com/Article/HannahWilke/32C4CF886E491516.

9 *Cut Piece*, MoMA Learning, https://www.moma.org/learn/moma_learning/yoko-ono-cut-piece-1964/.

10 *Rhythm 0*, https://en.wikipedia.org/wiki/Rhythm_0.

11 Nancy Princenthal, 'Looking for Trouble' in, Princenthal, *Unspeakable Acts*, p.46.

12 Suzanne Lacy and Moira Roth, 'Oral History Interview with Suzanne Lacy, 1990 Mar. 16–Sept. 27', *Archives of American Art*, p.8.

13 'Mary Kelly', interview by T. Maloon, *Artscribe*, no.13, 1978.

14 The title of this work comes from the title of a related gelatin silver print with oil crayon by Adrian Piper titled *The Mythic Being: I Embody Everything You Most Hate and Fear*, 1975.

15 Valerie Smith, 'Abundant Evidence: Black Women Artists of the 1960s and 1970s' in, *WACK! Art and the Feminist Revolution* (Lisa Gabrielle Mark, ed.), Museum of Contemporary Art, Los Angeles, and MIT Press, Cambridge, MA, 2007, p.412.

16 Craig Owens, 'The Discourse of Others: Feminists and Postmodernism' in, *The Anti-Aesthetic: Essays on Postmodern Culture* (Hal Foster, ed.), Bay Press, Port Townsend, WA, 1983, p.59.

17 Joan Riviere, 'Womanliness as a Masquerade', *International Journal of Psychoanalysis (IJPA)* 10, 1929.

18 'Jacques Lacan: Sexual Difference', *No Subject - Encyclopedia of Psychoanalysis*, https://nosubject.com/Jacques_Lacan:Sexual_Difference.

19 'Dara Birnbaum', *Electronic Arts Intermix*, https://www.eai.org/artists/dara-birnbaum/biography.

20 David Wojnarowicz, text from *Untitled (Hujar Dead)*, 1988–9, black-and-white photograph, acrylic, text, and collage on masonite, 99.06 × 81.28 cm (39 × 32 in).

21 Donna J. Haraway, introductory wall text for the 'The Seduction of the Cyborg' exhibition at the 59th Venice Biennale, 2022.

22 The Berkeley *Socialist Review* Collective published the essay, 'A Cyborg Manifesto', in 1985 under editor Jeff Escoffier. The essay was most widely read in Donna J. Haraway's 1991 book *Simians, Cyborgs and Women: The Reinvention of Nature*, Routledge, Oxfordshire, UK, 1990.

23 Rebecca Horn, quoted in 'The Peacock Machine: Rebecca Horn' in, *Tique: Publication on Contemporary Art*, https://www.tique.art/exhibitions/rebecca-horn-the-peacock-machine/.

24 Alexandra Schwartz, 'Chaotic Input: Art in the United States, 1989–2001' in, *Come as You Are: Art of the 1990s* (Alexandra Schwartz, ed.), Montclair Art Museum and the University of California Press, Montclair, NJ, 2015, pp 9–22. Please see Schwartz's essay for further insight into the effect of globalization on the art world of the 1990s.

25 Johannes Birringer, 'Art in America (The Dream): A Conversation with Tania Bruguera', *Performance Research*, vol.3, spring 1998, p.26.

26 Shirin Neshat, 'Shirin Neshat on telling complex stories through art', *CNN Style*, February 15, 2021, https://www.cnn.com/style/article/shirin-neshat-personal-essay-art/index.html.

27 Catherine Opie quoted in Nat Trotman, 'Self-Portraits and Dyke', *Catherine Opie: American Photographer*, Solomon R. Guggenheim Museum, New York, 2009, p.72.

28 Thessaly La Force, Zoë Lescaze, Nancy Hass and M.H. Miller, 'The 25 Most Influential Works of American Protest Art Since World War II', *New York Times Style Magazine*, October 15, 2020, https://www.nytimes.com/2020/10/15/t-magazine/most-influential-protest-art.html.

29 Documented in *Pussy Riot: A Punk Prayer*, a 2013 film

by Mike Lerner and Maxim Pozdorovkin.
30 Sebastian Smee, 'Pussy Riot Arrives in Iceland, Urinates on a Putin portrait', *Washington Post*, December 17, 2022, https://www.washingtonpost.com/arts-entertainment/2022/12/16/pussy-riot-takes-iceland/.
31 *Pussy Riot: A Punk Prayer*, 2013.
32 Editorial Board, 'Hate in America is on the rise', *Washington Post*, November 25, 2017, https://www.washingtonpost.com/opinions/hate-in-america-is-on-the-rise/2017/11/25/33808364-c94d-11e7-8321-481fd63f174d_story.html.
33 'Brown II', Johnson-Kulukundis Family Gallery, Harvard Radcliffe Institute, Cambridge, MA, https://www.radcliffe.harvard.edu/event/2021-brown-ii-exhibition.
34 Risa Puleo, 'The Linguistic Overlap of Color Theory and Racism', *Hyperallergic*, December 14, 2016, https://hyperallergic.com/345021/the-linguistic-overlap-of-color-theory-and-racism/.
35 A. Will Brown, 'Marisa Williamson: "I want to make history alive in people's worlds"', *Studio International*, March 13, 2015, https://www.studiointernational.com/marisa-williamson-interview-sally-hemings-slave-mistress-thomas-jefferson. It should be noted that Thomas Jefferson founded the University of Virginia in 1819.
36 Regarding the *spectacle,* this is a spin on 'the play's the thing', Shakespeare's famous quotation from *Hamlet*. For more on Taylor Mac's performance, see Wesley Morris, 'Normally a Star, but Today a Solar System', *New York Times*, October 11, 2016.
37 madison moore, 'You Have a Whole Stage to Fill – Why Not Fill It Up!: Machine Dazzle's Queer Maximalism', *Queer Maximalism × Machine Dazzle*, Rizzoli Electa, New York, 2022, p.97.
38 Dan Avery, 'Russian Police Detain Pussy Riot Activists for Hanging Pride Flags Around Moscow', *NBC News*, October 9, 2020, https://www.nbcnews.com/feature/nbc-out/russian-police-detain-pussy-riot-activists-hanging-pride-flags-around-n1242713.
39 ibid.

Handmade: Art, Craft and Feminism

1 The phrase 'live form' lends Jenni Sorkin's book *Live Form: Women, Ceramics, and Community* (University of Chicago Press, 2018) its title. The book explores the many ways in which ceramics engages performance and pedagogy.
2 Julia Bryan-Wilson, *Fray: Art + Textile Politics*, University of Chicago Press, Chicago, 2017.
3 Anthea Black and Nicole Burisch, 'From Craftivism to Craftwashing' in, *The New Politics of the Handmade: Craft, Art and Design*, Bloomsbury Visual Arts, London, 2021, pp 13–32.
4 David Pye, 'Is Anything Done by Hand?' in, *Craft: Documents of Contemporary Art* (Tanya Harrod, ed.) Whitechapel Gallery, London, 2018, p.30.
5 Ezra Shales, *The Shape of Craft*, Reaktion Books, London, 2017, p.17.
6 Glenn Adamson, *Thinking Through Craft*, Bloomsbury Visual Arts, London, 2018, p.4.
7 Shales, op.cit, pp 21, 25.
8 Adamson, op.cit., pp 9, 2.
9 Richard Sennett, *The Craftsman*, Yale University Press, New Haven, CT, 2008, p.22.
10 ibid., p.23.
11 ibid., pp 53–4.
12 ibid., p.73.
13 Susan Tallman, 'Knowing How', *New York Review of Books*, April 2021, https://www.nybooks.com/articles/2021/08/19/knowing-how/.
14 Adamson, op.cit., p.108.
15 Marcia Tucker, 'A Labor of Love', in, *Out of Bounds: The Collected Writings of Marcia Tucker* (Lisa Phillips, Johanna Burton and Alicia Ritson, eds.), Getty Research Institute, Los Angeles, and New Museum, New York, 2019, p.151.
16 John Dewey, *Art as Experience*, Perigee Books, New York, 1980, p.40.
17 ibid., p.81.
18 ibid., p.51.
19 Quoted in Mary Jane Jacob, *Dewey for Artists*, University of Chicago Press, Chicago, 2018, p.13.
20 Tucker, op.cit., pp 158–60. Tucker wrote further that it had 'striking parallel to what ethnographer James Clifford calls "the salvage paradigm".'
21 Of course, borrowing from – exploiting – the forms, materials and processes of colonized people in the global South was commonplace in early 20th-century European art, which Americans appropriated in turn.
22 Quoted in Adamson, op.cit., p.84.
23 Sorkin, op.cit., pp 63–4.
24 ibid., p.65.
25 Quoted in Roszika Parker, *The Subversive Stitch: Embroidery and the Making of the Feminine*, The Women's Press, London, 1984, p.190.
26 ibid., p.191.
27 ibid., p.195.

28 Quoted in ibid., p.190.
29 Adamson, op.cit., p.114.
30 Tallman, op.cit.
31 Sorkin, op.cit., p.119.
32 These schools include Haystack Mountain School of Crafts (Deer Isle, Maine, founded 1950), the Cranbrook Academy of Art (outside Detroit) and Alfred University (Alfred, New York). There are sought-after residencies in glassmaking at Pilchuck Glass School (Oregon) and in ceramics at the Kohler Arts/Industry residency program (Sheboygan, Wisconsin, established in 1974).
33 Sorkin, op.cit., p.151.
34 ibid., p.197. Karen Karnes, also founding member of Gate Hill, became a very successful potter, making casseroles and other ceramic goods for upscale shops, as a sign of cosmopolitan back-to-the-land impulse.
35 M.C. Richards, *Centering in Pottery, Poetry, and the Person*, 25th anniversary ed. with an introduction by Matthew Fox, Wesleyan University Press, Middletown, CT, 1989, p.12.
36 ibid., p.33.
37 ibid., p.24.
38 Parker, op.cit., p.204.
39 ibid., p.204.
40 Richards, op.cit., p.13.
41 Quoted in Richards, op.cit., p.21.
42 Mildred Constantine and Laurel Reuter, *Whole Cloth*, The Monacelli Press, New York, 1997, p.116.
43 Mildred Constantine and Jack Lenor Larsen, *MoMA Wall Hangings*, exh.cat., Museum of Modern Art, New York, 1969, unpaginated. Accessed on the MoMA website, spring 2023, https://www.moma.org/documents/moma_catalogue_1800_300062374.pdf.
44 Glenn Adamson, 'Experiencing the Shock of the Old, Fiber Artists Rediscover Shows Like MoMA's Pivotal 1969 "Wall Hangings"', *Art in America*, June 2020, https://www.artnews.com/art-in-america/features/wall-hangings-moma-rediscovered-fiber-art-1202692079/.
45 Rose Slivka, 'The New Ceramic Presence', *Craft Horizons,* vol.21, no.4, July/August 1961, quoted in Adamson, *Thinking through Craft*, p.43.
46 Lucy R. Lippard, 'What Is Female Imagery?' in, *From the Center*, Dutton, New York, 1976, p.86.
47 Norma Broude and Mary Garrard, 'Conversations with Judy Chicago and Miriam Schapiro' in, *The Power of Feminist Art: The American Movement of the 1970s, History and Impact* (Norma Broude and Mary Garrard, eds.), Harry N. Abrams, New York, 1984, p.74.
48 In Nancy Princenthal, 'Inspired by Harriet Tubman, an Artist Takes Glass to Extremes', *New York Times*, January 5, 2018.
49 Quoted in Tallman, op.cit.
50 Bryan-Wilson, op.cit., p.78.
51 ibid., p.72.
52 ibid., p.74.
53 Quoted in Adamson, *Thinking Through Craft*, p.28.
54 John Perreault, 'Issues in Pattern Painting', *Artforum*, November 1977 in, Perreault, 'Deluxe Redux: Legacies of the Pattern and Decoration Movement' in, *Pattern and Decoration: An Ideal Vision in American Art, 1975–1985* (Anne Swartz, ed.), Hudson River Museum, Yonkers, NY, 2007, p.55.
55 ibid., p.52.
56 Quoted in ibid., p.51.
57 Nancy Princenthal and Phillip Earenfight, *Joyce Kozloff: Co+ordinates*, Trout Gallery, Dickinson College, Carlisle, PA, 2008, p.47.
58 Arthur Danto, 'Pattern and Decoration as a Late Modernist Movement' in, *Pattern and Decoration* (Anne Swartz, ed.), p.10.
59 ibid.
60 Perreault, op.cit., pp 50–51.
61 At the Hessel Museum of Art, Bard College, Annandale-on-Hudson, NY.
62 Parker, op.cit., pp 210–11.
63 Tucker, op.cit., p.161.
64 ibid., p.145.
65 Shales, op.cit., p.12.
66 Ingrid Schaffner, 'On Dirt' in, Ingrid Schaffner, Jenelle Porter and Glenn Adamson, *Dirt on Delight: Impulses That Form Clay*, Institute for Contemporary Art, University of Pennsylvania, Philadelphia, 2009, pp 25–31, https://ingridschaffner.com/2009/01/on-dirt/.
67 Hamilton's installation at the pier was presented in connection with a survey exhibition of her work at the Fabric Workshop in Philadelphia, which was established by Marion Boulton Stroud and is a landmark in the integration of craft and art.
68 Ann Hamilton's website: www.annhamiltonstudio.com.
69 It traveled to the Museum of Arts and Design, New York, in 2022.

Beyond Tragic and Timeless: Women, Abstraction and Feminism

1 Harmony Hammond, 'Feminist Abstract Art –

A Political Viewpoint', *HERESIES: A Feminist Publication on Art and Politics*, vol.1, no.1, 1977, p.66.
2 ibid.
3 Smithsonian Institution, 'Then: 1977 Exhibition', Archives of American Art, https://www.aaa.si.edu/exhibitions/what-is-feminist-art/what-is-feminist-art-1976.
4 This is from a public, unauthored statement from the Museum of Modern Art's website. 'Feminist Art', MoMA, 2022, https://www.moma.org/collection/terms/feminist-art.
5 Griselda Pollock, 'Women, Art, and Ideology: Questions for Feminist Art Historians'. *Women's Studies Quarterly*, vol.15, no.1/2, 1987, p.3.
6 Oral history interview with Hedda Sterne by Phyllis Tuchman, Archives of American Art, Smithsonian Institution, Washington, DC, December 17, 1981, https://www.aaa.si.edu/collections/interviews/oral-history-interview-hedda-sterne-13262.
7 Hilton Kramer, 'On the Spiritual Art in Los Angeles', *New Criterion*, vol.5, no.8, April 1987, p.1.
8 Helen Molesworth, 'Art for Another Future: Learning from Hilma af Klint' in *Hilma af Klint Paintings for the Future* (Tracey Bashkoff, ed.), Solomon R. Guggenheim Museum, New York, 2018, p.36.
9 ibid., p.37.
10 Julie Voss, *Hilma Af Klint: A Biography*, University of Chicago Press, Chicago, 2022, p.135.
11 Margaret Rossiter, 'The Matthew Matilda Effect in Science', *Social Studies of Science*, vol.23, 1993, pp 325–41.
12 Matilda Joslyn Gage, 'Woman as an Inventor', *North American Review*, vol.136, May 1, 1883, p.488. A digitized version of this source is available on the Internet Archive, https://archive.org/details/jstor-25118273/page/n11/mode/2up.
13 Daniel Belasco, 'The Best of Everything: Women in the New York School' in *'The Heroine Paint': After Frankenthaler* (Katy Siegel, ed.), Gagosian Gallery, New York, 2015, p.98.
14 Henry Geldzahler, 'An Interview with Helen Frankenthaler', *Artforum*, October 1965, https://www.artforum.com/print/196508/an-interview-with-helen-frankenthaler-36915.
15 Katy Siegel, 'Contextually Boundless' in '*The heroine Paint': After Frankenthaler,* Katy Siegel, ed., New York: Gagosian Gallery, 2015 p. 17.
16 John Elderfield, 'On Frankenthaler's Decisions' in, Siegel, '*The Heroine Paint',* pp 55–7.
17 Ibid, p.56.
18 Barbara Cold, *Alma W. Thomas: A Retrospective of the Paintings,* exh.cat., Fort Wayne Museum of Art, Pomegranate, San Francisco, 1998, p.40.
19 Donald Judd, 'In the Galleries: Anne Truitt', *Art Magazine*, April 1963, p.61.
20 James Meyer, interview with Anne Truitt in, *Minimalism Art and Polemics in the Sixties,* Yale University Press, New Haven, CT, 2001, p.74.
21 Anne Truitt, *Daybook: The Journal of an Artist*, Penguin, New York, 1984, p.164.
22 Meyer, op.cit., p.74.
23 Clement Greenberg, 'Anne Truitt, An American Artist', *Vogue*, May 1968, pp 212–13, reprinted in Clement Greenberg, *The Collected Essays and Criticism*, vol.4, University of Chicago Press, Chicago, p.290.
24 Helen Molesworth, 'Painting with Ambivalence', *WACK! Art and the Feminist Revolution*, exh.cat. Museum of Contemporary Art, Los Angeles, and MIT Press, Cambridge, MA, 2007, p.429.
25 Rosalind Krauss, 'Grids', *October*, vol.9, summer 1979, p.54.
26 Charlotte Jansen, '5 Questions with Joan Snyder', *Elephant*, August 28, 2017, https://elephant.art/5-questions-joan-snyder/.
27 Lucy Lippard, 'What Is Female Imagery?' in, *From the Center: Feminist Essays on Women's Art*, E.P. Dutton, New York, 1976, p.86.
28 Ken Johnson, 'From a Minimalist Approach, Maximum Impact', *Boston Globe*, October 13, 2006, http://archive.boston.com/ae/theater_arts/articles/2006/10/13/from_a_minimalist_approach_maximum_impact/.
29 Roberta Smith, 'Jennifer Bartlett, Conceptual Painter on Vast Scale, is Dead at 81', *New York Times*, August 4, 2022, https://www.nytimes.com/2022/08/04/arts/jennifer-bartlett-dead.html.
30 Amy Sherlock, 'Surfing on Acid', *Frieze*, June 8, 2016, https://www.frieze.com/article/surfing-acid.
31 John Yau, 'Mary Heilmann Invites Us to Join Her in Arcadia', *Hyperallergic*, September 29, 2015, https://www.frieze.com/article/surfing-acid.
32 Lilly Wei, 'Pat Steir – Interview', *Studio International*, August 15, 2020, https://www.studiointernational.com/pat-steir-interview.
33 ibid.
34 Harmony Hammond, 'Feminist Abstract Art – A Political Viewpoint', *HERESIES: A Feminist Publication on Art and Politics*, 1977, pp.60–66.
35 Polly Apfelbaum, artist's statement, 'Polly

Apfelbaum' in Buffalo AKG Art Museum, April 2016, https://buffaloakg.org/artworks/200423-reckless-series-fallen-paintings.
36 Polly Apfelbaum, artist's talk, New York Studio School, March 7, 2017, https://nyss.org/polly-apfelbaum-fallen-paintings/.
37 Linda Nochlin, *Women, Art, and Power and Other Essays*, Harper and Row, New York, 1988, p.158.
38 There are many artists who deserve more than a mention here, but space is limited. Among those I would love to have discussed in fuller detail Lydia Dona (b.1955), Charline von Heyl (b.1960), Jacqueline Humphries (b.1960), Joanne Greenbaum (b.1953) and Carrie Moyer (b.1960).
39 Andrew Goldstein, 'Amy Sillman on Painting, Stand-Up Comedy, and Making "Inappropriate" Art', *Artspace*, March 5, 2014.
40 Suzanne McClelland, email correspondence and conversation with the author, February 10, 2023.
41 ibid.
42 ibid.
43 Jean Willette, 'The Influence of Feminism on Art', Art History Unstuffed, June 29, 2012, https://arthistoryunstuffed.com/the-influence-of-feminism-in-art/.
44 Email correspondence with the author, January 10, 2023.
45 ibid.
46 ibid.
47 Darryl Ratcliff, 'A New Kind of Content', *Patron Magazine,* April 2020, p.70, https://issuu.com/patronmagazine/docs/april-issue-2020-small.
48 ibid.
49 Calvin Tompkins, '"What Else Can Art Do?" The Many Layers of Mark Bradford's Work', *New Yorker*, June 22, 2015, https://www.newyorker.com/magazine/2015/06/22/what-else-can-art-do.
50 ibid.
51 Shoshana Dentz in conversation with the author, April 25, 2018.
52 Shoshana Dentz, unpublished artist's statement, emailed to the author, May 7, 2018.
53 Shoshana Dentz in conversation with the author, April 25, 2018.

Challenging Dominionism: How Women Rewrote the Role of Humans in Nature

1 Carolyn Merchant, *Reinventing Eden: The Fate of Nature in Western Culture*, Routledge, New York, 2004, p.3.
2 Genesis 1:26: 'Let us make humankind in our image, according to our likeness; and let them have dominion over the fish of the sea, and over the birds of the air, and over the cattle, and over all the wild animals of the earth, and over every creeping thing that creeps upon the earth'.
3 Carolyn Merchant, *The Death of Nature: Women, Ecology and the Scientific Revolution*, Harper, San Francisco, 1980, p.170.
4 ibid., p.249.
5 Bruno Latour, 'Bruno Latour Tracks Down Gaia', *Los Angeles Review of Books*, July 3, 2018, https://www.lareviewofbooks.org/article/bruno-latour-tracks-down-gaia/.
6 Press Release, Tate, 'Tate Directors declare climate emergency', 17 July, 2019, https://www.tate.org.uk/press/press-releases/tate-directors-declare-climate-emergency
7 Bruno Latour and Catherine Porter, trans., *Facing Gaia: Eight Lectures on the New Climatic Regime*, Polity, Cambridge, UK, 2017, p.3.
8 Latour, 'Bruno Latour Tracks Down Gaia'.
9 Eleanor Heartney, 'Ecopolitics/Ecopoetry, Helen and Newton Harrison's Environmental Talking Cure' in, *But is it Art? The Spirit of Art as Activism* (Nina Felshin, ed.), Bay Press, Seattle, 1995, p.144.
10 Agnes Denes, 'Notes on Eco-Logic: Environmental Artwork, Visual Philosophy and Global Perspetive' in, 'Leonardo', special issue, *Art and Social Consciousness*, vol.26, no.5, 1993, p.387, https://www.jstor.org/stable/1576033.
11 Haraway, op.cit., p.43.
12 Latour, 'Bruno Latour Tracks Down Gaia'.
13 Latour, *Facing Gaia*, p.3.
14 Mierle Laderman Ukeles, 'Manifesto for Maintenance Art', 1969, unpublished document, later published on the Queens Museum website, https://queensmuseum.org/wp-content/uploads/2016/04/Ukeles-Manifesto-for-Maintenance-Art-1969.pdf.
15 Natalie Hegert, 'Interview with Mierle Laderman Ukeles', *Artslant*, May 2008, https://nataliehegert.com/post/162955614388/interview-with-mierle-laderman-ukeles-artslant/amp.
16 Harrison Studio, 'Sensorium for the World Ocean', YouTube video, uploaded September 12, 2021, https://www.youtube.com/watch?v=KFEj4VBWdw4.
17 Naomi Klein, *This Changes Everything: Capitalism vs the Climate*, Penguin, New York, 2015, p.21.
18 Pope Francis, 'Address to Participants in the World

Meeting of Popular Movements', Old Synod Hall, Vatican City, October 28, 2014, https://np4sd.org/nominees/pope-francis/.

19 Helen Mayer Harrison and Newton Harrison, *The Time of the Force Majeure*, Prestel, New York, 2016, p.430.

20 Agnes Denes, 'A Wheatfield – A Confrontation: Battery Park Landfill, Downtown Manhattan', Agnes Denes personal website, text originally written in 1982, http://www.agnesdenesstudio.com/works7.html.

21 Agnes Denes, 'Tree Mountain', *Critical Inquiry*, vol.16, no.4, summer, 1990, p.931, https://feministartpractices.files.wordpress.com/2014/07/denes_dream.pdf

22 Etty Yaniv, 'All the Way to Hell: In Dialogue with Eliza Evans', *Art Spiel*, November 5, 2020, https://artspiel.org/all-the-way-to-hell/.

23 Newton Harrison, quoted in Sue Spaid, *Ecovention*, greenmuseum.org, ecoartspace and the Contemporary Arts Center, Cincinnati, OH, 2002, p.21.

24 Monika Fabijanska, *ecofeminism(s)*, exh.cat., Thomas Erben Gallery, New York City, June–July 2020, https://www.monikafabijanska.com/ecofeminisms.

25 Helène Aylon, 'The S. A C. /SAC VOYAGE OF THE EARTH AMBULANCE', *Women Eco Artists Dialog*, no.5 (Atomic Legacy), 2012, https://directory.weadartists.org/the-earth-ambulance.

26 Lucy R. Lippard, 'The Garbage Girls', *Z Magazine*, December 1991, reprinted in Jeffrey Kastner and Brian Wallis, *Land and Environmental Art*, Phaidon, New York, 1998, p.261.

27 Barbara Matilksy, *Fragile Ecologies: Contemporary Artists' Interpretations and Solutions*, exh.cat., Queens Museum of Art, New York, September 15–November 29, 1992, Rizzoli with Queens Museum of New York, 1992.

28 ibid., p.46.

29 T.J. Demos, 'The Politics of Sustainability: Contemporary Art and Ecology', in *Radical Nature: Art and Architecture for a Changing Planet 1969–2009*, Barbican Art Gallery, London, 2009, p.20.

30 Matilsky, op.cit., p.3.

31 Heresies Collective, 'Earthkeeping/Earthshaking', in 'Feminism and Ecology' (ed. Lyn Blumenthal, Janet Culbertson, Shirley Fuerst, Sandy Gellis, Phyllis Janto, Sarah Jenkins, Ellen Lanyon, Lucy R. Lippard, Jane Logemann, Ana Mendieta, Sabra Moore, Linda Peer and Merle Temkin), special issue, *HERESIES*, vol.4, no.13, 1981, http://heresiesfilmproject.org/wp-content/uploads/2011/10/heresies13.pdf.

32 Holland Cotter, 'A Whitney Biennial of Shadow and Light', *New York Times*, March 31, 2022.

33 Donna Haraway, *Staying with the Trouble: Making Kin in the Chthulucene*, Duke University Press, Durham, NC, 2016, p.117.

34 Bonnie Ora Sherk, 'Interviewed by Nick Kaye', SiteWorks: San Francisco performance 1969–85, University of Exeter, Exeter, Devon, and Falmouth, Cornwall, UK, February 6, 2015, http://siteworks.exeter.ac.uk/interviews/bonnieorasherk.

35 'Lynne Hull', directory entry in WEAD/ Women's Eco Artists Dialog, 2022, https://directory.weadartists.org/artist/hulll.

36 Haraway, op.cit., pp 14–15.

37 Beatriz Da Costa, 'Beatriz da Costa Blog and Project Hub' (2006–8), https://nideffer.net/shaniweb/pigeonblog.php.

38 Caroline Jones, 'Symbiontics: A Polemic for Our Time' in, *Symbionts: Contemporary Artists and the Biosphere* (Caroline Jones, Natalie Bell and Selby Nimrod, eds.), exh.cat., Massachusetts Institute of Technology, October 21, 2022–February 26, 2023, MIT Press, Cambridge, 2022, p.14.

39 Robert Smithson, 'Frederick Law Olmsted and the Dialectical Landscape', *Artforum*, vol.11, no.6, February 1973, p.62.

40 Harrison and Harrison, op.cit., p.321.

41 James Lovelock, 'Beware: Gaia May Destroy Humans before We Destroy the Earth', *Guardian*, November 2, 2021, https://www.theguardian.com/commentisfree/2021/nov/02/beware-gaia-theory-climate-crisis-earth?utm_term=f53c29c2dfe67de1752fa0b4567f297e&utm_campaign=GuardianTodayUS&utm_source=esp&utm_medium=Email&CMP=GTUS_email.

Epilogue

1 Cotter, Holland, 'The Art of Feminism as It First Took Shape', *New York Times*, March 9, 2007, https://www.nytimes.com/2007/03/09/arts/design/09wack.html.

FURTHER READING

Performance Art and Action

Biesenbach, Klaus, ed., *Marina Abramović: The Artist is Present*, Museum of Modern Art, New York, 2010

Carr, C., *On Edge: Performance at the End of the Twentieth Century*, Wesleyan University Press, Middleton, CT, 2008

Cassel Oliver, Valerie, ed., *Radical Presence: Black Performance in Contemporary Art*, Contemporary Arts Museum Houston, 2013

Giannachi, Gabriella, and Jonah Westerman, *Histories of Performance Documentation: Museum, Artistic, and Scholarly Practices*, Routledge, London, 2018

Goldberg, RoseLee, *Performance Art: From Futurism to the Present*, Thames & Hudson, London, 2011

Goldberg, RoseLee, *Performance Now: Live Art for the 21st Century*, Thames & Hudson, London, 2018

Jones, Amelia, *Body Art/Performing the Subject*, University of Minnesota Press, Minneapolis, 1998

Phelan, Peggy, *Live Art in LA: Performance in Southern California, 1970–1983*, Routledge, London, 2012

Princenthal, Nancy, *Unspeakable Acts: Women, Art, and Sexual Violence*, Thames & Hudson, London, 2019

Wood, Catherine, *Performance in Contemporary Art*, Tate Publishing, London, 2018

Handmade: Art, Craft and Feminism

Adamson, Glenn, *Thinking Through Craft*, Bloomsbury Visual Arts, London, 2018

Bryan-Wilson, Julia, *Fray: Art + Textile Politics*, University of Chicago Press, Chicago, 2017

Black, Anthea, and Nicole Burisch, *The New Politics of the Handmade: Craft, Art and Design*, Bloomsbury Visual Arts, London, 2021

Constantine, Mildred, and Laurel Reuter, *Whole Cloth*, Monacelli Press, New York, 1997

Harrod, Tanya, ed., *Craft: Documents of Contemporary Art*, Whitechapel Gallery, London, 2018

Jacob, Mary Jane, *Dewey for Artists*, University of Chicago Press, Chicago, 2018

Parker, Roszika, *The Subversive Stitch: Embroidery and the Making of the Feminine*, The Women's Press, London, 1984

Sennett, Richard, *The Craftsman*, Yale University Press, New Haven, 2008

Shales, Ezra, *The Shape of Craft*, Reaktion Books, London, 2017

Sorkin, Jenni, *Live Form: Women, Ceramics, and Community*, University of Chicago Press, Chicago, 2018

Beyond Tragic and Timeless: Women, Abstraction and Feminism

Bashkoff, Tracey, ed., *Hilma af Klint: Paintings for the Future*, Solomon R. Guggenheim Museum, New York, 2018

Besant, Annie, and Charles W. Leadbetter, *Thought-Forms*, reprint of 1905 copy, Sacred Bones Books, Brooklyn, NY, 2020

Butler, Cornelia, and Gabrielle Mark, exh.cat., *WACK! Art and the Feminist Revolution*, Museum of Contemporary Art, Los Angeles, and MIT Press, Cambridge, MA, 2007

Macel, Christine, with Karolina Ziębińska-Lewandowska, eds., exh.cat., *Women in Abstraction*, Centre Pompidou, Musée National d'Art Moderne, Paris, 2021

Meyer, James, *Minimalism: Art and Polemics in the Sixties*, Yale University Press, New Haven, 2001

Nickas, Bob, *Painting Abstraction: New Elements in Abstract Painting*, Phaidon, London, 2009

Katy Siegel, ed., *'The Heroine Paint' After Frankenthaler*, Gagosian Gallery, New York, 2015

Sillman, Amy, *Faux Pas. Selected Writings and Drawings*, After 8 Books, Paris, 2020

Voss, Julie, *Hilma af Klint: A Biography*, University of Chicago Press, Chicago, 2022

Tuchman, Maurice, *The Spiritual in Art: Abstract Painting 1890–1985*, exh.cat., Los Angeles County Museum of Art, and Abbeville Press, New York, 1986

Challenging Dominionism: How Women Rewrote the Role of Humans in Nature

Haraway, Donna, *Staying with the Trouble: Making Kin in the Chthulucene*, Duke University Press, Durham, NC, 2016

Harrison, Helen Mayer, and Newton Harrison, *The Time of the Force Majeure*, Prestel, New York, 2016

Heresies Collective Inc., 'Earthkeeping/Earthshaking: Feminism and Ecology', *HERESIES* no.13, vol.4, no.1, 1981

Jones, Caroline, Natalie Bell, and Seilby Nimrod, eds., *Symbionts: Contemporary Artists and the Biosphere*, MIT Press, Cambridge, MA, 2022

Latour, Bruno, and Catherine Porter, trans., *Facing Gaia: Eight Lectures on the New Climatic Regime*, Polity, Cambridge, 2017

Lovelock, James, *The Ages of Gaia*, W.W. Norton, New York, 1988

Matilksy, Barbara, *Fragile Ecologies: Contemporary Artists' Interpretations and Solutions*, Rizzoli with Queens Museum of New York, New York, 1992

Merchant, Carolyn, *The Death of Nature: Women, Ecology, and the Scientific Revolution*, Harper, San Francisco, 1980

Phillips, Patricia C., Tom Finkelpearl, Larissa Harris, Lucy Lippard and Laura Raicovich, *Mierle Laderman Ukeles: Maintenance Art*, Prestel, New York, 2016

Tsing, Anna Lowenhaupt, *The Mushroom at the End of the World: On the Possibility of Life in Capitalist Ruins*, Princeton University Press, Princeton, NJ, 2021

ACKNOWLEDGMENTS

Our first thanks go to all the extraordinary artists discussed in this book, many of whom have helped us with practical matters and all of whom have inspired us by their work. *Mothers of Invention* is a tribute to their creativity and their courage. We are also immensely grateful to Lucy Clark, our sage editor at Lund Humphries, who has been wonderfully supportive from the start, and to the rest of the terrific editorial team: Rebeccah Williams, Lucie Worboys and Ellen Hurst. For their unflagging encouragement and forbearance, we would each like to thank our partners in life: Larry Litt, David Dorsky, Joseph LeDoux and Mike Stanley. Lastly, we'd like to make a four-way statement of gratitude to our little writing collective. Our nearly 20 years of collaboration have been enormously important to us all. We continue to learn from each other, easily the most pleasurable education any of us has had.

IMAGE CREDITS

© Courtesy of the Marina Abramovic Archives/ ARS, New York 2023, Photo: Donatelli Sbarra: fig.1; © Carolee Schneemann Foundation / Artists Rights Society (ARS), New York/DACS, London, Courtesy the Carolee Schneemann Foundation, Galerie Lelong & Co., Hales Gallery, and P•P•O•W, New York, Photo: Anthony McCall: fig.2; Photo: Minoru Niizuma: fig, 3; Photo: Maria Karras: fig.4; Courtesy Alexander Gray Associates, New York, © 2023 Lorraine O'Grady/ Artists Rights Society (ARS), New York: fig.5; © Cindy Sherman, Courtesy the artist and Hauser & Wirth: fig.6; © Guerrilla Girls, Courtesy guerrillagirls.com: fig.7; © Courtesy of the Marina Abramovic Archives/ ARS, New York 2023: fig.8; Courtesy of the artist and Petzel, New York: fig.9; Courtesy the artist and Tilton Gallery, New York: fig.10; Photograph by David Attie, courtesy of Eli Attie: fig.11; Photograph eeva-inkeri, Courtesy of the artist: fig.12; © Sheila Hicks, Courtesy of Sikkema Jenkins & Co., New York: fig.13; © 2024 Faith Ringgold / Artists Rights Society (ARS), New York, Courtesy ACA Galleries, New York: fig.14; Photograph by Ken Eck, ©J. Scott/Licensed by Goya Contemporary Gallery and the Artist Legacy Project, Baltimore: fig.15; Courtesy Alexander Gray Associates, New York, ©2023 Harmony Hammond/ licensed by VAGA art Artist Rights Society (ARS), New York: fig.16; Photograph by Alan Weiner, Courtesy of the artist: fig.17; Photograph by Andy Romer, Courtesy of the artist: fig.18; Photograph by Thibault Jeansen, Courtesy of Ann Hamilton Studio: cover, fig.19; Photograph by Kevin McConnell, Courtesy of the artist: fig.20; Photo: Eric Boman. Originally published in *Vogue*, 1990, Courtesy of the artist and the photographer: fig.21; Hilma af Klint Foundation, Stockholm, Sweden: fig.22; Artwork © 2024 Helen Frankenthaler Foundation Inc. / Artists Rights Society (ARS), New York, Helen Frankenthaler Foundation, New York, on extended loan to the National Gallery of Art, Washington, D.C., Photograph courtesy National Gallery of Art, Washington, D.C: fig.23; Courtesy of Michael Rosenfeld Gallery LLC /Artist Rights Society (ARS), New York: fig.24; Estate of Anne Truitt, All rights reserved 2023 / Bridgeman Images: fig.25; © Mary Heilmann, Courtesy of the artist, 303 Gallery, New York, and Hauser & Wirth, New York, Photo credit: Stephen White: fig.26; The Albright-Knox Museum, Buffalo, New York, Courtesy of the artist: fig.27; © Amy Sillman, Courtesy the artist, Capitain Petzel, Berlin and Gladstone Gallery, New York, Photo credit: Gunter Lepkowski: fig.28; Courtesy of the artist and Marianne Boesky Gallery, New York and Aspen, Colorado, © Suzanne McClelland, Photo credit: Lance Brewer: fig.29; Courtesy the artist, Wizard, Milan, Miles McEnery Gallery, New York, Photo credit: Antonio Maniscalo: fig.30; © Mierle Laderman Ukeles, Courtesy the artist and Ronald Feldman Gallery, New York: fig.31; Courtesy of the Harrison Studio and Ronald Feldman Gallery: fig.32; Copyright Agnes Denes, Courtesy Leslie Tonkonow Artworks + Projects: fig.33; Photo by Robin Scully, 2016: fig.34; Courtesy of the artist, Image: Benoît Mangin: fig.35; © LaToya Ruby Frazier, Courtesy of the artist and Gladstone Gallery: fig.36; Courtesy of the artist, Photo: Benjamin Tankersley: fig.37; Courtesy of the artist, Photo by Subhram Reddy: fig.38; Photo courtesy of the artist: fig.39; Image courtesy of The Living / David Benjamin, Photo by David Benjamin: fig.40

INDEX

Note: italic page numbers indicate figures; page numbers followed by n refer to notes.